The U.S. Navy and the Origins of the
Military-Industrial Complex, 1847–1883

The U.S. Navy and the Origins of the Military-Industrial Complex, 1847–1883

Kurt Hackemer

Naval Institute Press
Annapolis, Maryland

Naval Institute Press
291 Wood Road
Annapolis, MD 21402

Library of Congress Cataloging-in-Publication Data
Hackemer, Kurt.
    The U.S. Navy and the origins of the military-industrial complex, 1847–1883 /
Kurt Hackemer.
        p.   cm.
    Includes index.
    ISBN 1-55750-333-8 (alk. paper)
    1. United States. Navy—History—19th century. 2. Military-industrial complex—
United States—History—19th century.
    VA56 .H27 2001
    338.4'7359'0097309034—dc21   00-053281

Printed in the United States of America on acid-free paper ∞
08 07 06 05 04 03 02 01   9 8 7 6 5 4 3 2
First printing

FOR SUSAN

Contents

Acknowledgments

This book could not have been written without the generous help and support of a number of individuals and institutions. I apologize in advance for any inadvertent omission.

R. J. Q. Adams, James Burk, and Betty Miller Unterberger read and commented on early drafts of some of the chapters. William H. Roberts proved a useful sounding board on a number of occasions. The staff of the *Naval War College Review* made a number of important suggestions when editing an article manuscript that summarized my ideas midway in the process, as did B. Franklin Cooling and an anonymous reviewer who evaluated the completed manuscript for the Naval Institute Press. James C. Bradford brought his considerable knowledge of American naval history to bear at several stages of the project, improving it each time. Joseph G. Dawson's steady hand (and honest editing pen) provided continual guidance in every sense of the word. Any errors that remain are mine alone.

This project owes much to the dedicated archivists I worked with over the course of my research who helped track down obscure references and who pointed me to materials I might otherwise have overlooked. In Washington, D.C., Barry Zerby proved invaluable during my visits to the National Archives. In Boston, Stanley Tozeski went well beyond the call of duty during my stay at the National Archives New England Region branch. The staffs of the Library of Congress Manuscript Division, the Navy Department Library at the Naval Historical Center, the New York Historical Society, the New York State Library, and the Philadelphia Maritime Museum were similarly helpful. A special thanks to Alice Hanes of the Portsmouth Naval Shipyard Museum, who gladly photocopied and sent material about the *Merrimack* I could not find anywhere else. When all else failed, the interlibrary loan staffs at Texas A&M University and the University of South Dakota always managed to handle my requests, no matter how arcane.

Travel and research expenses were generously defrayed by grants from the College of Liberal Arts and the Office of Graduate Studies at Texas

A&M University, and a Vice Admiral Edwin B. Hooper Research Grant from the Naval Historical Center.

Some of the most important lessons I learned about becoming a historian were driven home far beyond the walls of the seminar room. I was fortunate to explore my craft with a collegial and inquisitive group of friends who enjoyed debating, at the drop of a hat, the intricacies of history and the profession. First at the Tomato Seminar and then later as residents and transients of Bob's Country Bunker, we had a lot of fun trying to put it all together. While I still have much to learn, that group made me a much better practitioner than I would otherwise have been, and for that I thank them all.

Finally, my wife Susan made it possible for me to have the time and space to carry on and complete this project, no easy matter when our first child entered the picture late in the process. To her, I lovingly dedicate the final result.

The U.S. Navy and the Origins of the
Military-Industrial Complex, 1847–1883

Introduction

Seated before an investigative committee in the House of Representatives, Charles M. Schwab found himself in an embarrassing predicament. He had come to Washington in this hot July of 1894 to defend himself and his employer, Carnegie Steel Company, from charges of fraud. Basing its case on evidence offered by Carnegie employees, the government alleged that the company had manipulated tests performed on armor plates manufactured for the Navy to hide imperfections and flaws that otherwise would have prevented entire lots of plates from being accepted for use by government inspectors. Responding to a charge by committee chairman Amos Cummings of New York that Carnegie employees "seem to have been somewhat animated by the desire to cheat the Government inspectors in every manner possible," Schwab acknowledged some irregularities but denied any widespread conspiracy to defraud the government. Instead, he blamed overzealous government inspectors for the company's woes, telling Cummings, "If you knew these Government people you would understand our position much better." Of course, because Schwab had been removed from his position as head of the Armor Plate Department of Carnegie Steel at the insistence of the Navy's Ordnance Bureau, his assessment of government workers had probably been colored by recent events.

After spending most of the summer of 1894 interviewing Schwab, countless other Carnegie employees, and the government inspectors and officials assigned to oversee the production of armor plate, Cummings's committee concluded that "the frauds . . . found are worthy to be called crimes" threatening "the dearest interests of the nation." This pronouncement called into question not only the current contract with Carnegie Steel but also the government's relationship with all of the nation's steel manufacturers. At a time when many Americans viewed these conglomerates with some trepidation, close ties had been forged between these corporate giants and the Navy. The Navy, engaged in the systematic modernization of its fleet, provided generous subsidies that allowed the steel companies to upgrade their physical plant in return for a commitment to the production of armor plate. This relationship, labeled by one historian as "the formative years of America's military-industrial complex," now came in for sharp criticism.[1]

Although congressmen blustered and postured over the issue and even agitated for the funding of a federal armor factory, nothing came of it. Despite some obvious flaws in the system, the government gained more from the relationship than it lost. The furor over the armor contracts eventually passed, and the relationship between the military and American business grew stronger over time, expanding beyond the Navy and big steel to include the rest of the military and significant sectors of industry. Still, Americans were never completely comfortable with the idea, as the uproar over the interwar Nye committee hearings attests. It fell to a former military officer and sitting president of the United States, Dwight D. Eisenhower, to coin a term describing the relationship: the military-industrial complex. Offering the benefit of his counsel to the nation in his 1961 farewell address, he warned that the military-industrial complex might someday "endanger our liberties or democratic processes." Whether it has or not remains a matter of perspective and conjecture, but the institution has clearly assumed a prominent position in American society, and, as such, deserves closer study.[2]

Defining the origins of ideas or concepts accepted as common knowledge presents a special challenge to the historian. While those ideas undoubtedly belong in the language, and certainly in the popular consciousness, their origins are less obvious, having somehow materialized in the distant past. Such is the case of the military-industrial complex. The idea has been around for quite some time, even before President Eisenhower popularized it in 1961. In its current, well-developed form, the military-industrial complex has been an integral part of American culture since the dawn of the cold war. Historians have since begun exploring the phenomenon, looking first to the great wars of the twentieth century and then further back to the later decades of the nineteenth century for causality. Here they have settled upon the United States Navy, particularly the construction of the new steel

Navy in the 1880s and the service's reliance on private contractors, as the precursor of the modern military-industrial complex.[3]

Drawing on a definition of the military-industrial complex first put forward by Samuel Huntington, Gary Weir has made a case in recent years for a subset he describes as the naval-industrial relationship. He defines the term as a "partnership between industry and the Navy [that] emerged as a network of independent relationships developing simultaneously." In its earliest form, it represented ongoing pragmatic attempts by the Navy to develop, build, and deploy technologically sophisticated warships. Weir's approach is useful in that it asks the historian to step back from the otherwise monolithic concept of the military-industrial complex and incorporate historical context into the story, considering both the technology and the circumstances of the day. However, Weir, like most who explore this issue, draws the line at the new steel Navy when he talks about a relationship that "had prevailed in surface ship construction as early as the 1880s."[4]

Although the still-unfolding story of the new steel Navy represents an important milestone in the search for the origins of the military-industrial complex, it does not signal the end of the quest. Instead, it suggests that it might be time to approach the problem from a slightly different perspective. Current scholarship focuses on the integration of steel technology into the Navy's shipbuilding practices during the 1880s. Yet the historical record suggests that conditions for the origins of the military-industrial complex existed decades earlier. William McNeill, for example, argues that the rapid industrialization of the first half of the nineteenth century triggered a fundamental change in military technology. Such technology, which was specialized not only in use but also in manufacture, had long been the purview of governments. However, as western Europe and the United States began industrializing on a significant scale, private enterprises began refining existing military technologies, often developed initially under official auspices, and introducing sophisticated variations that rivaled or surpassed the original versions.

This private experimentation was not confined to any single technology, and in fact soon reversed the traditional order of things, with private enterprise taking the lead in some areas. For example, the creation of steamship lines and railroads spurred development of steam power plant technology and improved metalworking skills. Firearms manufacturers, particularly in the United States, began resolving the problem of interchangeable parts on a large scale while lowering production costs using new machinery and techniques. In doing so, they not only made mass production a reality but also made it possible for semiskilled workers to handle much of the manufacturing process. The clock-making and sewing machine industries systematized machine-made mass production even further. All of these technical advances had military application and could not be ignored. And indeed, they were not. Countries such as France, which bitterly resented British military might, saw the new technology as an equalizing force and began transferring ideas and methods from the civilian sector to military production. The result, McNeill suggests, was that by the mid-1850s military leaders were exposed "to the acute discomfort of having to face the possibility of war under conditions and with weapons of which they had no direct experience."[5]

Transferring ideas and methods from the civilian sector to the military sector brought two often disparate entities together. The military, with its passion for order and control (both necessary qualities for waging war), often encountered more freewheeling institutions that placed a premium on experimentation and less rigid forms of organization. Resolving these differences in a constructive manner meant defining what the developing relationships would look like. That was not an easy transition, particularly in more democratic societies in which order could not simply be decreed. There, the process involved substantial trial and error, with some early attempts bordering on the embarrassing.

Despite the inherent difficulties, the transition was made, more successfully in countries in which strategic necessity required it. Nowhere was this more true than in western Europe, where a new naval arms race, driven by rapid technological change, was taking place between France and Great Britain. Even when allied during the Crimean War, these traditional adversaries kept as close a watch on each other as they did on their Russian foe. Necessity dictated closer ties between government and industry, and that is exactly what happened. For example, one British company received a government contract for eighty sets of marine engines with a delivery deadline of three months. The contractor, Messrs. Penn of Greenwich, made the deadline and fulfilled the terms of the contract, demonstrating the potential of government-industrial cooperation. That level of cooperation is more impressive when one considers the Royal Navy's skepticism of new technology in the preceding decades. Still, the moment demanded cooperation.[6]

The kind of relationship that became so important to the Royal Navy's survival barely existed, if at all, in the antebellum United States for several reasons. First, the strategic impetus was not there. Despite the war scares that periodically surfaced, the United States had no military rival in the Western Hemisphere whose presence might drive technical change. Therefore, there was no perceived need to integrate American industry into military planning and procurement. Even had there been such a perceived need, integration would have had to overcome the inherent bias Americans had toward a free-market economy. Integration implies some level of government interference in the market, an unacceptable notion to many at the time. Second, the American industrial base was not yet well developed enough to support a naval-industrial relationship based on cutting-edge technology. That is not to say that the United States lacked shipbuilding capacity. Indeed, the number of large ships built in American yards steadily increased from 1847 to 1857. However, they were the wrong kinds of ships, at least in terms of innovative hull design and steam technology. Americans built wooden sailing ships based on traditional designs and skills, whereas their foreign competitors developed iron-hulled vessels and more efficient steam power plants. Moreover, most of those wooden ships were built at small yards that rarely accumulated enough capital to experiment with new trends, so when the U.S. Navy turned to private industry, its options were limited.[7]

Still, it is important to note that the Navy did have some options available. Given the context of the times, this study argues that the search for the origins of the naval-industrial relationship in the United States should look beyond the technology of steel warship construction to the Navy's efforts to integrate other new technologies into the fleet several decades earlier. As the Navy struggled in turn with steam engines in the 1850s, ironclad vessels in the 1860s, and steel warships in the 1880s, it found that each technology exceeded the capabilities of its physical plant. In each case, therefore, it turned to private contractors out of necessity. Although the technologies changed over time, the procedures for dealing with contractors and the relationships that developed between the Navy and private firms show remarkable continuity and a clear evolutionary path. From this perspective, it appears that the historical antecedents of the military-industrial complex lie much further in the past than once thought, taking shape before the Civil War.

This book starts with the United States Navy's ill-fated encounters with steam technology in the 1840s and 1850s. Beginning with the construction of the *Merrimack*-class frigates in 1854 and continuing with the subsequent sloop-building programs in the late 1850s, I discuss the origins and implementation of formalized contract and trial procedures. I then move to the spring of 1861, when the mechanisms so carefully formulated by the politics of peace were challenged by the expediencies of war. Overwhelmed in terms of both technology and sheer numbers of ships and power plants required, the Navy fell back on the recently formulated contract procedures. Examining an evolving series of wartime ironclad, traditional hull, and machinery contracts allows conclusions to be drawn about the impact and efficiency of the prewar contract mechanism. Although they failed in many respects and created enormous controversy, these contracts played an important role in giving the Union the tools it needed to fight the war. Finally, using hull and engine contracts signed after the war, I link the antebellum procedures and lessons learned during the war with the new steel Navy, demonstrating the Navy's evolving relationship with private industry from the 1850s to the 1880s.

Each of these cases illustrates the Navy's response to the introduction of new technology. In some ways, the *Merrimack*-class frigates, laid down in 1854, represented a benchmark in the Navy's management of new technology. Because of the scarcity of funds, the antebellum Navy relied on private contractors for the majority of its steam power plants. It lacked enough specialized shops to manufacture more than a few engines from the ground up, although it slowly installed machinery to do its own repairs at the various Navy yards. During the late 1840s and early 1850s, a series of failed engine designs publicly embarrassed the Navy and brought about changes in the way the service dealt with contractors. Privately purchased steam engines became subject to performance guarantees, with substantial financial penalties for those that failed. Unlike earlier contracts, a percentage of the total contract price was withheld pending successful trials at sea. These frigates were the first newly constructed vessels with such guarantees written into their contracts.

The *Merrimack*'s engines are often portrayed as notorious failures and were the primary cause of the frigate's massive refitting that led to its capture at the Gosport Navy Yard in the spring of 1861.[8] However, those engines, like the power plants erected on the entire class, successfully met the Navy's requirements during their first six months of service, vindicating the stricter contract guarantees implemented by Secretary of the Navy James C. Dobbin. Designed to compensate for the loss of direct administrative oversight brought about by the necessity of using private contractors, these formal procedures worked well in a peacetime setting. They restored the Navy's control over all aspects of the shipbuilding process, at the same time allowing it to take advantage of technical advances pioneered by the civilian sector. The procedures codified by the 1854 engine contracts became standard practice in the latter half of the decade as the Navy adjusted to its new relationship with private industry, as clearly seen in the 1857 and 1858 sloop-building programs. The Navy used the 1857 program to expand the contract procedures to include the hull of the *Brooklyn*, which, although no one knew it at the time, provided important experience for the coming conflict.

When war came in 1861, the Navy relied upon the successful practices of the previous decade as a matter of course and applied the same kind of guarantees to a new technology: ironclad warships. Unfortunately, the service's wartime experience with what was thought to be an efficient protective mechanism for dealing with untried technology proved less than satisfactory. The prewar procedures had been designed for monitoring one component of a larger project. The Navy, pushed to its administrative limits by the magnitude of the conflict, tried to use those procedures to oversee construction of entire warships. This put far more reliance on this mechanism than was ever intended by its creators, as became painfully evident during the construction of the first ironclads. This phenomenon was not limited to naval contracts. As one observer has noted, "The Civil War . . . tested the contracting process—and it barely passed."[9]

The pressures of war made the problem even worse when the same system was applied to large numbers of contracts, whether for power plants or entire classes of warships, both traditional and nontraditional. Based on the Navy's experience with early wartime construction, it modified its contracts and introduced preprinted forms that incorporated many of the lessons learned thus far. The new contracts spelled out requirements and procedures in more detail, with the intent of protecting both the Navy and private industry. They were used for the majority of the hulls and power plants built over the course of the war and served their purpose well, at least when applied to traditional hulls and standardized power plants. However, when it came to ironclads, the Navy often placed additional burdens on the contract procedure by insisting on substantial design modifications during construction. Here, as William Roberts convincingly demonstrates, the system failed most notably because it was asked to provide a level of control clearly beyond its capabilities.[10]

Those capabilities, designed to manage the limited introduction of new technology in the forgiving time frame of peacetime construction, collapsed when applied to much larger and more sophisticated building programs operating under the time constraints, design modifications, inflationary pressures, and lack of contractor experience that characterized the wartime years. The primary oversight mechanism, the threatened withholding of contract funds for delays or poor workmanship, was not originally designed as a substitute for departmental oversight and therefore fell victim to the seemingly random conditions of war. Despite these shortcomings, the contract process led to increased contact with a larger number of companies, and the Navy became accustomed to dealing with many of the country's larger industrial establishments. Although these experiences were not always viewed as successes, they conditioned the Navy to accept closer interaction with American industry in the future. Those companies in turn grew more familiar with the often arcane intricacies of government contracts and procedures.

The postwar era witnessed continued contact between the Navy and many of these private firms. Even though the Navy faced shrinking budgets, it still required these companies' expertise and facilities. Not surprisingly, the Navy looked back to its earlier experience when awarding new contracts. These contracts, typified by the 1871 agreement between the Navy and John Roach for new engines for the *Tennessee*, borrowed much of their language and organization from the preprinted wartime contracts. There were minor differences, but those were often modifications based on past practice. The essential clauses remained, in some cases harkening back to the original 1854 frigate contracts. Therefore, when it came time to build the new steel Navy in the early 1880s, the traditional point of departure for earlier discussions of the military-industrial complex, the Navy knew which contractors it wanted to deal with and how the agreements for the construction of the *Atlanta, Boston, Chicago,* and *Dolphin* would be drawn up. The groundwork had been laid over the preceding three decades, making the special relationship that developed between the Gilded Age steel industry and the government possible.

What emerges in the end is a more sophisticated understanding of the Navy's contract process. Generally ignored in the historical literature, it tends to be oversimplified when discussed at all. As a public agency, the Navy regularly contracted for a variety of goods, ranging from ledger books to complete warships. That is the context in which contract discussions usually appear, with appropriate references to the congressional investigations that periodically examined fraud and waste. Isolating the introduction of new technology in the context of shipbuilding leads to a very different and more detailed understanding of the contract process. Rather than a haphazard process marred by corruption, it was evolutionary, with specific goals at different points in time. Fraud rarely entered the picture; in fact, the Navy was exonerated of such charges on more than one occasion. Problems that did occur were caused by other factors, most notably the urgent need for warships during the Civil War and political interference in the postwar world. Even so, those problems were rarely critical and generally led to improvements in the process as a whole. Viewed in proper context, the introduction of new technology into the fleet can be explained in a much more orderly and rational fashion.[11]

1   The Navy Confronts
New Technology, 1847–1854

Naval construction from the beginnings of the Republic until the Civil War proceeded in fits and starts, responding to the whims and desires of the various administrations holding the reins of power. Americans engaged in a running debate over the size, composition, and mission of their Navy, rarely reaching consensus but usually maintaining at least the minimum strength of the nation's maritime defenses. K. Jack Bauer suggests that the various building programs that came into being from 1794 until 1860 "resulted from no set policy but from a disorganized attempt to make the Navy strong enough, or weak but of sufficient strength to carry out the duties assigned it by each administration."[1] Although Bauer seemingly states the obvious, he nonetheless reflects a simple truth that governs the relationship of the American military to the political structure: the military exists to serve the needs of the country, not to dominate its institutions.

Americans were never more aware of this simple truth than in the first fifty years of the young nation's life. They understood the gravity of their position as the first great republican democracy and jealously guarded the ideals of the Revolution. Opinions about how those ideals should be put into practice, however, varied greatly from group to group and created bitter divisions within the political structure. As the traditional enemy of republican values, the military (especially the regular Army) became the focal point of many legislative battles, particularly in the years before the War of 1812, when the Democratic Republicans and the Federalists vied for control of the nation's destiny. Each sought to mold and contain it in their own image.

Neither completely succeeded nor failed, and their perspectives and ideological slants provided the basis of debate through the 1850s.[2]

Although ideology remained a significant factor in discussions of military policy in general and naval policy in particular, more pragmatic sectional concerns became increasingly important with the passage of time. During the 1820s, 1830s, and 1840s the commercial shipping interests of the Northeast became frequent supporters of naval expansion, or at least maintenance at existing levels. A strong, capable Navy meant more protection for the American merchant vessels that sailed around the globe. Southerners living in coastal commercial centers often supported naval bills, but those residing farther inland took the same point of view as westerners, who saw little reason for pouring federal dollars into the naval establishment; their agricultural economies would benefit more from internal improvements such as canals, railways, and road networks. As a result, naval expansion occurred sporadically when it happened at all. Too often the Navy was forced to improvise with monies channeled from funds not explicitly appropriated for new construction.[3]

Things began changing in the late 1840s and early 1850s. Naval expansion became more acceptable to a broader spectrum of the country's populace and led directly to the authorization of six steam frigates in 1854, five shallow-draft screw sloops of war in March 1857, seven additional screw sloops in early 1858, and another seven steamers in 1859.[4] Why the sudden shift toward a strong Navy? The answer rests somewhere in that morass of pragmatism and idealism loosely described as Manifest Destiny. Frederick Merk defines the general goal of Manifest Destiny of the late 1840s as "a free, confederated, self-governed republic on a continental scale" based on republican tenets. In accomplishing its purpose, this philosophy taught that it was "the duty of the United States to regenerate backward peoples of the continent" and make them acceptable citizens of the world community.[5] Of course, Manifest Destiny meant different things to different people. Two important variations of this theme played a significant role in the naval expansion of the 1850s: southern desires to increase the slaveholding territory of the United States and the ardent nationalism of "Young America."

The legislative battles of the late 1840s and early 1850s over the admission of new states to the Union made it painfully clear to some southerners that the balance of free and slave states could not be maintained indefinitely.

Although the Compromise of 1850 effectively nullified the Wilmot Proviso, many doubted whether the territory recently acquired as a result of the Mexican War could profitably support slavery. The bloodshed that followed the passage of the Kansas-Nebraska Act in 1854 reinforced doubts about the efficacy of further expansion of slavery in territory already held by the United States. Still committed to the peculiar institution, a number of southerners turned their attention even farther south, to the agriculturally promising lands of Central and South America and the islands of the Caribbean. Descriptive accounts of the region suggesting its potential filled the popular press, fueled by reports of Navy surveying expeditions only recently returned from the Amazon River basin.[6]

C. Stanley Urban suggests that a combination of the ideal of progress and frustration over the Wilmot Proviso and the Compromise of 1850 caused southerners to consider seriously the merits of expanding beyond the current boundaries of the United States. They thought the South "the most progressive section in the world's most progressive country" whose "prosperity was due to the institution of slavery." In their opinion, the Caribbean represented a vastly underutilized resource whose productivity had declined precipitously ever since the Wars of Liberation had released the enslaved Africans from bondage. By taking over the region and expanding into Central and South America, prosperity would return to an obviously fertile area, the inhabitants would be civilized, and the balance of free to slave states in the U.S. Senate could be restored by annexation. The great riches of the region might even offset the wealth of the North and make the South a legitimate economic power.[7]

The most adventuresome, such as William Walker, took matters into their own hands and organized filibustering expeditions, and it is these swashbucklers whom historians tend to remember. The filibusters enjoyed considerable popular support and had little difficulty selling bonds to underwrite their next adventures or finding businessmen to provide the necessary financial backing. When reined in or brought to trial by American authorities, filibusters often found themselves released by sympathetic juries and then made the object of admiration at local festivities across the South. Still, they rarely succeeded, and then only for brief periods of time. Other southerners, more conservative in their approach, saw opportunity in the rising tide of nationalistic fervor sweeping across the nation as the election of 1852 drew near and sought to harness its energy for their own purposes. This shift toward a political solution signaled a temporary halt to filibustering. The halt was short lived, however, and filibustering activities slowly resumed in the spring of 1854 as southerners grew disillusioned with what they saw as the inactivity of President Franklin Pierce.[8]

The nationalist fervor whose energy southerners hoped to tap labeled itself Young America. Although it contained a large southern and western contingent, Young America enjoyed widespread national appeal. Operating from within the Democratic party as a faction of younger members, it embraced the ideas of Manifest Destiny, motivated by a sense of mission that assumed all things American were clearly superior to the well-worn and often despotic ideas of Europe.[9] These lines, published in the *Democratic Review* in the summer of 1852, typify the rhetoric with which the Young Americans surrounded themselves:

> There! *there* is Young America, its grandeur and its truth—
> Its noble heart o'er gushing with ne'er dying blood of youth,
> Its iron hand outstretched to strike the tyrant wheresoe'er
> His jeweled brow, or lying lip, or acrid eye doth rear.
> There! there is Young America in youthful thought sublime,
> Its starry beacon flung out as a hope to every clime,
> E'en as the starry flag of God, the world's dark chaos o'er,
> Invites each man that will be saved to an immortal shore![10]

Needless to say, enough idealism existed within this movement to make party regulars, and some foreign governments, nervous.

Motivated by the crushing of the European revolutions of 1848 and convinced that the United States must act in support of republicanism, the youthful members of the Democratic party made Young America an issue in the 1852 presidential election. The Young Americans wanted Stephen A. Douglas on the Democratic ticket, but party politics gave them Franklin Pierce. Although disappointed, they thought that Pierce might advance their program and so they campaigned vigorously on his behalf. The party platform contained several planks inspired by Young America advocating a more activist United States. For one thing, they wanted a more dynamic foreign policy openly sympathetic to the European republicans. Of course, they also intended for the United States to reap the benefits of increased international participation.[11]

Franklin Pierce, recognizing the importance of the Young Americans to both the Democratic party and the country at large, made a special effort to assuage their worries and capture their support after his election. He began his inaugural address with a brief survey of the nation's history, taking special note of America's role as the international repository of liberty and republican values. This, he said, gave the United States special responsibilities, a mandate to serve as an example to the rest of the world. Building on this idea, Pierce declared that

> the policy of my Administration will not be controlled by any timid forebodings of evil from expansion. Indeed, it is not to be disguised that our attitude as a nation and our position on the globe render the acquisition of certain possessions not within our jurisdiction eminently important for our protection, if not in the future essential for the preservation of the rights of commerce and the peace of the world.[12]

This must have warmed the hearts of the Young Americans, for now they had a president who, although not their first choice for the office, seemed supportive of their goals. Pierce followed his rhetoric with action, sometimes to the embarrassment of the nation and the detriment of national unity, as was the case with the Ostend Manifesto. To the Young Americans and southern expansionists paying close attention to the new president's inaugural address in March 1853, however, the future looked promising.

For all their bluster and bravado about America's role in the world, the Young Americans knew that rhetoric meant little unless the nation could project force when necessary. The most obvious means of projecting such force was the Navy, whose expansion and reform became an urgent priority for these political upstarts. In their minds, expansion presented little problem for a country with the resources of the United States. The future belonged to steam warships, and although Europe's leading navies possessed far greater numbers of naval steamers than the United States, a concerted building effort utilizing the nation's industrial might would quickly outstrip even England, whose Navy provided the measure against which all others were judged. The Young Americans based their predictions on the industrial capacity of the nation, which lay beyond the control of the government. They wanted expansion to be a collective effort that would take advantage of the engineering expertise found in the country's private shipyards. In this sense, they showed some foresight; most of the steam warships built in the decades that followed relied on private contractors for key components of their construction.[13]

Still, it would take more than new construction to forge an instrument capable of "[fulfilling] that lofty mission to which we are solemnly called by the condition and opinion of the Continent of Europe, and by the concurrent voice of all civilized mankind."[14] The Navy's officer corps was old and inefficient. The absence of any retirement system meant that officers stayed in the service as long as possible, which, in conjunction with repeated cuts in the size of the Navy, made promotions few and far between. The Young Americans knew what was wrong and explained it with language they regularly employed when describing hidebound members of their own party: "Thirty years of Fogy night-mare rule have ruined its esprit de corps, blighted its energies, stifled progress, suppressed every stimulus to honest emulation, destroyed all hope of advancement to talent, energy, or character, and done their best to bring every body and every thing connected with the navy to the dreary level of Fogy dullness, sloth and mediocrity." They had a solution, albeit controversial, for this problem, too: forced retirement of older officers. Only by rebuilding the Navy and replacing old "fogies" with younger, more active, leaders could they get the kind of institution they thought the country needed. After Pierce's election, they began calling in their political debts, played up nationalist sentiment, and started pushing for just such a program.[15]

Maxwell Woodhull gave voice to the Young Americans' concerns about the Navy just as the first steps were being taken to rectify the situation. Writing as the first proposal for building six steam frigates started working its way through Congress, he denounced the deplorable condition of America's maritime defenses. As England and France began mobilizing for the Crimean War, Woodhull alleged that they proclaimed "they will act in concert also in such interference as they may deem it prudent to make in the affairs of the Western hemisphere." The Young Americans knew exactly what Woodhull meant: the European powers could just as easily impose their will in the Caribbean as in the Crimea. In one sense, Woodhull's fears proved accurate; witness the joint invasion of Mexico by England, France, and Spain after the start of the American Civil War. Still, he exaggerated the extent of the problem.[16]

Woodhull thought that the construction of six steam frigates would be an adequate start, but by no means a complete solution given the magnitude (at least in his eyes) of the problem facing the United States. Like many of his contemporaries, he thought the vessels already in service, especially the sloops and frigates, were among the finest in the world. The problem was quantity, not quality. This pundit found it difficult to understand why the "large surplus" in the Treasury was not earmarked for naval expansion, "several millions of which could not better be disposed of than in the building and completion of something more than *six steam frigates.*" The country possessed the requisite "skill, science, the material, and the means . . . to make the Navy of the United States all that our greatness as a nation, our commerce, and our honor demand." All it required was the foresight to do so. Looking back to the events leading up to the War of 1812 in light of the developing situation in the Crimea, Woodhull argued that "neutrals not prepared to resist or resent insult cannot hope to be respected." In taking appropriate action, the United States could avoid international embarrassment and take its rightful place among the leading nations of the world.[17]

Enthusiasm for naval expansion extended well beyond the idealism of the political sphere. Younger naval officers supported it for a variety of reasons, not the least of which was ambition. Some hoped to tap the political energy of the Young Americans for expansion, always a priority within the Navy. Still, these men were professionals and advocated expansion for professional reasons. They knew that the United States would find itself in an embarrassing position if involved in a conflict with a major European power. The Mexican War and a brief war scare over settlement of the Oregon boundary reinforced latent opinions and encouraged many navalists, officer and civilian alike, to express their views publicly. Almost to a man they pleaded for a stronger Navy but, interestingly enough, did so using the same ideas about the inherent superiority of the United States as the Young Americans. In effect, their professionalism lent legitimacy to an otherwise political cause. One might disagree with the Young Americans about the extent of "fogyism" and its impact on the Navy. After all, it might be perceived as little more than an excuse to politicize the military establishment. However, the opinions of respected naval officers making their points on the basis of facts, figures, and the current state of technology appeared to be above the political fray, although many sympathized with the Young Americans.[18]

Cdr. Samuel Francis Du Pont entered the debate with his *Report on the*

National Defences, written at the request of the Navy Department and published in 1852. Taking heed of budding nationalist sentiment, he noted that "these United States have hitherto been advancing the general cause of human liberty, by an active and progressive peace." However, he thought that events in Europe and the Caribbean indicated "that we may, at no distant day, be forced, in our own defence, to aid this cause of freedom by an active war." Du Pont made the case for expansion by comparing the current status of the British and French navies with that of the United States. Britain clearly dominated, as had been the case for decades. As of April 1850, the Royal Navy contained more than 150 war steamers of all types. Although some were obsolete, new steamers joined the fleet every year. In addition, preparations in Britain were well under way for the rapid conversion of merchant steamers into war vessels if necessary. Likewise, the French navy, although well below the strength of the Royal Navy, still presented a formidable challenge to a lesser power like the United States. It carried seventy steamers of various classes on the Navy's rolls. The United States, by comparison, could send only six steamers to sea. Individually, these vessels equaled or outclassed most ships in the British and French navies, but Du Pont worried that they could be overwhelmed in battle by greater numbers.[19]

Despite the great disparity in naval strength, Du Pont approached the idea of expansion with cautious optimism. Like the Young Americans, he expressed great confidence in the nation's inventive nature and productive capacity. Looking back to American victories in the War of 1812, he asked whether the country could "once more render obsolete one-half or two-thirds of the English and French navies, and compel these powers to remodel their steam as well as their sailing ships." He thought it could, pointing out that other officers familiar with the technology of heavy ordnance believed that the upper limit of the armament that could be carried by a warship had not yet been reached. The closer the United States could come to that theoretical limit, the fewer vessels it would take to approach parity with the British and French navies. Du Pont proposed that the Navy build several ships capable of carrying larger cannon similar to those being developed by Cdr. John A. Dahlgren at the Washington Navy Yard. These ships should be fast sailers but also should be equipped with a steam power plant below decks and a propeller, rather than paddle wheels, for propulsion. In short, he wanted a larger and more powerful version of the USS *Princeton,* a vessel built for the Navy in the early 1840s whose career had been tarnished by the explosion of a heavy deck gun amid a group of dignitaries visiting the ship in early 1844.[20]

Charles B. Stuart, engineer in chief of the United States Navy, echoed Du Pont's conclusions the following year in his book *The Naval and Mail Steamers of the United States*. Like Du Pont, Stuart acknowledged the disparity in numbers between several European navies and the U.S. Navy. Unlike Du Pont, however, the engineer in chief challenged the notion that domestic industry could be counted upon to make good the difference in time of war. The sheer size of the American merchant marine, second largest in the world at the time, and the extreme length of coastline that needed to be defended required an operational Navy of sufficient size to defend American interests. Domestic industry promised great potential, but that potential needed tapping now, before the United States found itself embroiled in war. Stuart suggested that the "nucleus of the finest naval force which the world has yet to see" already existed in the American steam Navy, whose steamers currently rivaled anything afloat in Europe. The Navy only required immediate "encouragement and development."[21]

An official investigation conducted by the Navy Department at about the same time as Stuart was drawing his optimistic conclusions helps place those assertions in a more realistic perspective and foreshadows some of the problems encountered by the Navy before the Civil War. Secretary of the Navy James C. Dobbin created a Board of Engineers in 1851 at the request of Thomas S. Bocock, chairman of the Committee on Naval Affairs in the House of Representatives, to report on recent problems with three of the Navy's steamers, the *Allegheny, Princeton,* and *San Jacinto.* The Virginia Democrat later sponsored a bill in the House authorizing construction of the *Merrimack*-class frigates, underscoring the potential impact of this report in shaping opinions. The internal report took the Navy to task for poor planning, shoddy engineering, and extravagant expense of public funds in the construction and maintenance of these three vessels. Three ships might not sound like a serious matter, but given the modest size of the U.S. Navy, they represented a significant portion of America's fighting strength.

The Navy completed the *Allegheny* in 1847 as an experimental vessel mounting the Hunter wheel, an internal horizontal paddle wheel that proved a remarkable failure. It was rebuilt in 1851–52 as a conventional screw steamer and rejoined the fleet, but it never performed satisfactorily, with one journal reporting her "completely disabled . . . in her first engagement with the enemy (wind and tide and fair weather)." Repairs made during active service and the alterations made in 1851–52 added more than $150,000 of work to a vessel that originally cost $242,596.

The *Princeton* was a rebuilt version of the vessel originally designed by John Ericsson. Constructed at the Boston Navy Yard, it faced delay after delay as the engine builders and the Navy argued about the installation of the machinery. Part of the problem stemmed from the secretary of the Navy at the time, William A. Graham, who never fully understood the implications of steam warships and exercised insufficient leadership when it was sorely needed. When finally launched in November 1852, the steam plant proved such a disappointment that the ship was taken back to port and "put in the hands of the doctors; but this time a change has been made in the practice, and there is some hope for the better, although but little can be expected where the patient has suffered so badly from malpractice." The *Princeton* retired soon after from active service and ended its career as a receiving ship.

The construction of the *San Jacinto,* launched at New York in April 1850, ruined several naval careers. The Navy's conscious effort to avoid royalty payments on existing patents saddled the vessel with flawed engines, an off-center shaft, and an obsolete propeller. The nation's engineering establishment almost universally damned the *San Jacinto*'s machinery before it ever built up a head of steam. Unfortunately, the ship lived up to their low expectations. When Secretary Dobbin ordered new engines from a different builder and demanded guarantees for their performance, one leading technical journal observed that "in departing from the usage of the Department, the Secretary has made a bold stand for the right," hardly a ringing endorsement of the Navy's past practices.[22]

Secretary Dobbin charged the Board of Engineers "to institute searching investigation, not only as to the causes of those repeated disasters [with the ships' steam machinery], but as to the officers or individuals who are responsible." Dobbin understood the critical nature of the investigation. Congressional inquiries focused national attention on the issue. The result, claimed Dobbin, was that "the service suffers in reputation; money is expended liberally, producing results only requiring further outlay; the interests of the government are subjected to inconvenience, and perhaps hazard." The board conducted its investigation, poring over letters and plans, and produced both a list of flaws similar to those described above and the scapegoats required by Secretary Dobbin. In the case of the *San Jacinto,* the board chastised a former engineer in chief, Charles H. Haswell, who may not have drawn up the engine plans but who certainly approved them. As for the *Allegheny* and the *Princeton,* the board squarely placed the blame on another former engineer in chief, Charles B. Stuart, the same man who expressed such optimism in *The Naval and Mail Steamers of the United States.* Stuart had championed Lamb and Summer boilers, used in commercial vessels in England. The boilers failed in both ships. Stuart had also pushed for the conversion of the *Allegheny* into a screw steamer.[23]

Not everyone agreed with the Board of Engineers' lambasting of Stuart; it smacked of departmental infighting and personal animosity. Still, the board's report made an important point. Building a credible steam fleet would require more effort than the Young Americans and other navalists thought. Steam technology existed in a constant state of flux. A quick glance through any of the technical journals of the day, such as the *Journal of the Franklin Institute* or *Scientific American,* reveals a constant stream of articles on discoveries and patents concerned with steam machinery. Even the professional engineers of the Navy Department found it difficult to keep up with each new advance and preferred making recommendations about equipment only after careful study and comparison. No universally acknowledged design for steam power plants yet existed, and each ship's engine was a unique piece of machinery attuned to the peculiarities of design of that particular vessel. A team of engineers might agree on the basic components, but each vessel had its own idiosyncrasies. Such an approach almost guaranteed mistakes and miscalculations. It also offered the potential of vast rewards to those who succeeded, further spurring experimentation and innovation.

Secretary Dobbin had to deal with more than just Representative Bocock's query about the failure of the steamers and their machinery. George Houston, chairman of the House Committee on Ways and Means, had similar questions about the Navy's budget at about the same time. In looking over the budget for the coming year, Houston was struck by the large sums requested for "increase, repairs, &c." by the secretary and asked for an explanation. He received his answer the same day as Bocock. Actually, Dobbin had a straightforward answer, telling the chairman, "All our ships are *old,* and consequently require heavy and increasing repairs to keep them in a serviceable condition." New ships cost less to maintain but eventually became old ships. Even mundane expenditures for rigging, sails, and masts rapidly added up after a few years. The introduction of steam into the fleet compounded the problem. The secretary estimated that maintenance of a given engine would double its cost in ten to twelve years. The immense weight of steam engines also weakened hulls more quickly. Still, he admitted that "the great expenditures upon the steamers *Allegheny, Saranac, San Jacinto,* and *Princeton,* much exceed the usual estimated wear and tear, and a portion of them could not be foreseen at all."[24]

Although the optimistic assessments of the Young Americans and the navalists seemed in direct conflict with the report of the Board of Engineers and Dobbin's report to Houston about the quality and potential of American industry and the Navy, they led policy makers to the same conclusion: the Navy must expand to make up for its deficiencies. In fact, Secretary Dobbin spent the months preceding the release of those reports contemplating an increase in the Navy's ships. No individual or single group dominated naval policy during the 1850s. Dobbin, nominally in charge of the Navy Department, had to muster support among his bureau chiefs, powerful committee members in the House and Senate, and the president. Any of these could conceivably bring expansion to a halt, either formally or informally, if they disagreed with Dobbin's plans. Dobbin knew he must tread carefully.[25]

Appointed because of his role in getting Pierce elected, Dobbin had no practical experience in naval affairs. Still, he tackled the duties of his office with sincerity and dedication; as a widower who avoided the Washington social scene when possible, Dobbin devoted most of his time to naval matters. This single-minded devotion paid off as the Navy converted from sail to steam and entered one of its greatest periods of expansion, a period the officers of the 1870s would remember fondly. However, in the fall of 1853, still learning his job, Dobbin retained the caution of the uninformed and turned to his bureau chiefs for advice about the future of the Navy, as tradition dictated.[26]

The reports of two of the bureau chiefs, Joseph Smith of the Bureau of Yards and Docks and Samuel Hartt of the Bureau of Construction, Equipment and Repairs, provided the basis for the program Dobbin submitted to Congress in December 1853. Smith, whose bureau encompassed all that occurred in the various Navy yards, believed that the Navy's future rested in steam engines and urged Dobbin to take the necessary steps that would allow the Navy to manufacture and assemble its own engines instead of relying on outside contractors. Smith thought that "the mistakes which have been made in, and the inefficiency of some of our steam-vessels, make the necessity of such improvements very evident." He proposed erecting permanent facilities at the yards in Boston, New York, and Norfolk, the Navy's primary shipbuilding establishments. Shops and equipment at the six remaining Navy yards would follow as funds became available in later years.[27]

Samuel Hartt, whose bureau actually constructed and maintained the Navy's ships, recommended a new building program that would take advantage of recent technological advances and allow the United States to narrow the gap with the European powers. Any serious effort to join the first rank of naval powers would "require the building of more *new* ships, embracing the improvements of the age and profiting by the knowledge of past experience, rather than continuing to make extensive repairs on *old* ones—the expense of which often amounts to nearly the cost of the new." Hartt suggested building "six first-class steam propellers" as the first step. He estimated a total cost of $4,630,626, of which $1,389,186 could be defrayed by materials already on hand, leaving $3,241,240 to be covered by appropriation. Of that appropriation, he reckoned that $1,080,000 would be required for the coming fiscal year, the remainder coming in subsequent years.[28]

Dobbin made these recommendations the centerpiece of his annual report. Issued on 5 December 1853, it called for fundamental changes in the organization, regulation, and composition of the Navy. His views on all three aspects echoed the calls for reform sounded by both the Young Americans and the navalists of the preceding decade, but he presented them without the vitriol usually associated with such appeals. Dobbin submitted a realistic program that, although controversial in some respects, would prove politically acceptable to enough senators and representatives to receive the required support. Not all of his proposals immediately passed or were successfully implemented, but Dobbin's report provided the concrete foundation on which the naval expansion of the rest of the decade would build.

Reforming the Navy's organization and regulations proved more than the current political climate could support, so Dobbin devoted his energies to expansion of the fleet. Drawing on Hartt's report, the secretary painted a bleak portrait of the Navy's current condition. Technically, the Navy register carried about seventy vessels, embracing all from the ships-of-the-line to the smallest brig, schooner, and store-ship. Of these many ships-of-the-line, frigates, steamers, and sloops-of-war are not only unfit for service, but . . . are not worth repairing. There are not now in the navy forty vessels which could be brought into service in ninety days, if needed. There is no steamer in the Pacific or African squadron, but one of two guns in the Brazil squadron, and we have no steamer of more than ten guns.

In short, the Navy could not hope to contend with America's European rivals, no matter how industrious the country might be or how much undeveloped potential its manufacturers possessed. The geography of the United States only made matters worse; with two thousand miles of Atlantic coastline and several hundred miles of Pacific coastline, all "studded with magnificent cities and thriving towns," the nation was susceptible to seaborne aggression. Add to that the impressive tonnage of the vulnerable American merchant marine, and the country's shortage of adequate naval protection verged on the embarrassing.[29]

Making an argument that could have come right out of Woodhull's booklet, Dobbin argued that "[securing] respect to a neutral flag requires a naval force, organized and ready to vindicate it from insult and aggression." Showing his political maturity and grasp of the realities of Washington, he proposed that the Navy begin acquiring and stockpiling the necessary materials at the Navy yards for a larger Navy. Construction would proceed as resources allowed. Still, the nation had to start somewhere, and Dobbin knew where: with the immediate construction of six steam-propeller warships, just as Hartt suggested. These frigates would mount fifty guns each, making them the equals of any steam warship afloat. Given the combination of materials on hand and materials readily available from suppliers, Dobbin thought that these ships could be built and launched within twenty months of their authorization. He also proposed using this expansion to make the Navy more self-sufficient in terms of machinery. Dobbin hoped to avoid the problems outlined in the Board of Engineers' report by having Congress authorize a corresponding increase in the machine shops at the Navy yards. Unfortunately, this request, although approved, would prove less successful than the secretary hoped because the new machine shops would not be ready in time for use in building the steam frigates.[30]

Dobbin received important support for his program from President

Pierce just as he released his report. In his first annual message to the Congress, the president declared himself "fully satisfied that the Navy of the United States is not in a condition of strength and efficiency commensurate with the magnitude of our commercial and other interests." He went on to "commend to your especial attention the suggestions on this subject made by the Secretary of the Navy." The confiscation of the packet vessel *Black Warrior*'s cargo in Havana by Spanish authorities in February 1854 reinforced the urgency of Dobbin's request. That seizure, justified by the *Black Warrior*'s violation of customs regulations rarely enforced in the past, sparked vociferous debate in Congress and demands that ranged from financial indemnification to the American seizure of Cuba. While the State Department cajoled and threatened, the Navy did nothing, convincing both southern expansionists and Young Americans of its impotence. This incident had an immediate impact. The Senate passed a bill calling for the construction of six steam frigates without debate, but the House proved more difficult. The old Jacksonian holdovers, led by Thomas Hart Benton of Missouri, vigorously challenged the bill after its first reading on 21 February 1854. Their efforts proved fruitless, however, as the bill's primary supporters, Thomas Bocock and Caleb Lyon, pushed it through. The bill passed by the comfortable margin of 112 to 43.[31]

The final bill, dated 6 April 1854, appropriated $3 million for the construction of six steam frigates and the alteration and completion of two frigates already on the stocks, the *Santee* and the *Sabine*. Specifically, the bill authorized Secretary Dobbin

> to cause to be constructed for the United States Navy, at as early day as practicable, consistently with a due regard for economy and efficiency Six first class Steam Frigates to be provided with screw propellers and properly armed and equipped for service; said vessels and machinery to be built by contract or in the Government Navy Yards as the Secretary of the Navy may think most advisable for the public interest.[32]

Any doubts about congressional support for naval expansion were put to rest less than six weeks later, when the Senate Committee on Naval Affairs released its own report on the subject. Although decrying past waste in the Navy's administration of government funds, the committee agreed that "in reviewing the condition of our own naval establishment, we cannot but express the confident opinion that, with unequaled mechanical skill, abundant material and resources, we have within ourselves the means of excelling all nations in naval power." Clearly, the Navy now had its mandate.[33]

Dobbin got the design process started almost immediately, assembling a board consisting of three bureau chiefs, Commo. Charles Morris of the Bureau of Ordnance and Hydrography, Commo. Joseph Smith of the Bureau of Construction and Repair, and John Lenthall of the Bureau of Construction and Repair, along with Daniel Martin, the Navy's engineer in chief, "for the purpose of consultation." In his letter of appointment, dated 17 April 1854, Dobbin informed his new board that the steam frigates would be built in the Navy yards. Lenthall, one of the most prolific ship designers of the nineteenth century, whose "high reputation" Dobbin admired greatly, would actually draw up the plans. Actively engaged in naval construction since 1828 and mentored by Samuel Humphreys, he possessed a breadth of knowledge far beyond that of most of his contemporaries and is considered by some to be "the most eminent shipbuilder of the corps of naval constructors during the first years of the steam navy."[34]

Taking the congressional mandate for "economy and efficiency" to heart, Secretary Dobbin reminded Lenthall of earlier plans to use structural frames already stored at the various Navy yards. Gathered for the *Congress*-class frigates authorized in 1839, they provided the basic framework around which Lenthall would design the new vessels. In an additional concession to economy, the spars of the new vessels had to "be the same as those of the present Frigates of the first class." Because these frigates would also be steamers, they required extra room for machinery and coal. Lenthall eventually lengthened the frigates to almost 260 feet, about 80 feet longer than the frames at hand. The difference in length was made up from extra timbers already stockpiled at the Navy yards. A screw propeller, the accepted naval standard, would provide motive power.[35]

These budgetary considerations placed a tremendous burden on Lenthall. Instead of designing a first-class vessel from the keel up, he was forced to make do with materials already on hand, even though they originally had not been procured for the type of construction mandated by Congress. Lenthall faced one more problem: Dobbin had promised Congress that the frigates would be built in twenty months, quite a feat for a nation that often allowed vessels to sit building in the stocks for several years at a time. The secretary wanted these frigates "built with despatch" and wasted no time with preliminary details. Following normal practice, the department decided that the frigates' hulls would be built at the various Navy yards. However, inadequate facilities throughout the Navy meant that the various power plants would be built by independent contractors, a process discussed later. Lenthall responded well to the added pressure and quickly generated the necessary hull plans. By 11 July 1854, the first of the six keels, belonging to the *Merrimack,* had been laid in Shiphouse 2 at Charlestown, signaling the start of construction.[36]

Actually, designing the six frigates proved less problematic than it appears. During the early 1850s, the Navy investigated the possibility of replacing the seventy-four-gun *Franklin* with a frigate of the same name incorporating many of the features later found on the *Merrimack*-class frigates, including Dahlgren shell guns, steam propulsion, and an auxiliary screw that could be hoisted out of the way when necessary. Technically, a board of engineers and constructors recommended the new vessel, but the task of preparing the ship's plans squarely rested with John Lenthall. These plans, completed in February 1854, bear more than a passing similarity to five of the frigates designed by Lenthall just a few months later and probably served as his inspiration. Although each frigate differed slightly from the others, they all showed the *Franklin*'s influence.[37]

The sixth frigate, later named the *Niagara,* differed radically from the other five and should not be considered a ship of the same class. Designed by George Steers, its lines resembled those of a clipper ship more than a standard naval vessel of the time. Unlike the five frigates, it carried the main battery on the spar deck and, in its original configuration, was not pierced for broadside gun ports on the gun deck. The vessel sacrificed throw weight for speed by design. Donald Canney suggests that the Navy used the *Niagara* as an experimental vessel to see how much speed could be coaxed out of a well-armed warship. Unlike the rest of the authorized warships, it "was a deliberate exercise by the navy to determine the compatibility of extreme clipper lines and naval purposes." The Navy never took full advantage of the *Niagara*'s capabilities, however, and it received more criticism during its career than it deserved. Canney argues that the ship served as a useful prototype of a vessel with "sharp lines, long hull, and relatively few large guns." Nevertheless, its uncommon heritage makes this ship peripheral to the larger story.[38]

Modern critics have claimed that "lacking foresight," the government "accepted a naval building program that would become obsolete during the

Civil War." This simplistic analysis, drawn with the advantage of historical hindsight, assumes a prescience not found in any Navy of the world at the time. Naval contemporaries almost universally praised the five frigates for their sailing qualities after their launchings; Frank Bennett declared them "objects of admiration and envy to the naval architects of Europe." Not only did Lenthall design functional warships, but those warships proved the equal of anything afloat until the launching of the ironclads *Warrior* and *Gloire* by Britain and France at the end of the decade. That the ships were authorized, planned, and placed under construction in such a short period of time is a testament to the Pierce administration's political skills and the potential power of groups like the Young Americans.[39]

The six steam frigates approved in April 1854 did not come into being as the result of any long-term naval policy, echoing K. Jack Bauer's conclusion about this period in general. Nor were they designed from the keel up as steam vessels of war. These vessels were politically expedient. Their construction satisfied eastern merchants with significant stakes in overseas commerce, southern expansionists who thought the United States needed a stronger Navy to extend the nation's slaveholding territories, young nationalists from all regions who believed in some form of Manifest Destiny, and navalists concerned about potential problems with Europe. Of course, notable pockets of opposition raised their voices, like westerners and the old Jacksonians, but they proved incapable of successfully resisting those forces advocating a stronger Navy.

Despite the apparent political success in authorizing the six steam frigates, the Navy still faced serious obstacles. Not only would the ships have to be built around the previously stocked frames, never intended for ships of this size, but the Navy Department had to overcome its own recent history of technological failures and mismanaged contracts for steam machinery. The Navy anticipated complications and delays, and eventually got the first of the six frigates, the *Merrimack,* launched relatively close to the projected date, but the extent of those difficulties surprised even professional officers and constructors. Closer examination of how the secretary, his bureau chiefs, and their subordinates dealt with these potential problems offers a useful point of departure for considering the origins of the military-industrial complex.

2

The *Merrimack*-Class Frigates

Learning to Manage New Technology, 1854–1856

Authorizing the frigates was only the beginning of a process fraught with twists and turns. Construction of these ships was certainly a major project, but the effort had far greater implications for the Navy's future than merely adding six warships to the fleet. In some ways, the future of the fleet depended on the Navy's ability to successfully administer this building program and demonstrate to Congress that a service whose reputation had taken a beating in recent years could be trusted with public funds. As a result, the political pressure exerted by a restive Congress and passed down through the secretary of the Navy made its presence felt throughout the construction process. The Navy's task was complicated by the fact that building the frigates would be a dual enterprise between the service and a number of private companies. Making this program work meant dealing with American industry on a larger scale than ever before.

In many ways, the Navy's organization made the task that much more difficult. The bureau system, introduced in 1842, resulted in no single entity below the secretary of the Navy assuming complete authority for the erection or repair of any given warship. Each bureau took care of its own responsibilities, which meant that a Navy yard commandant, charged with administering his command, dealt with five sets of instructions during the course of construction, all emanating from Washington and all demanding equal attention. Still, there were circumstances that helped mitigate this problem, and the Navy managed to make things work. Outside contractors would deal with only two of the five bureaus. The Navy yards, responsible for building the frigates' hulls, were working within the service, so no matter how inefficient the process might seem, there was still a chain of command, tortuous though it might be, for resolving difficulties and providing direction.[1]

Two bureau chiefs, Joseph Smith, chief of the Bureau of Yards and Docks, and John Lenthall, chief of the Bureau of Construction, Equipment and Repair, were heavily involved in overseeing the building of the six steam frigates. Smith, who became the longest serving bureau chief in the Navy's history and who would play a pivotal role in overseeing the construction of the Union's first ironclads during the Civil War, earned a deserved reputation for fiscal austerity during his tenure at Yards and Docks. The *Merrimack's* construction typified Smith's approach. The commodore personally directed the preparation of the estimates submitted to Congress for the physical improvements made at the Boston Navy Yard for the frigate's construction. He also inspected the results of the expenditures himself, making a formal visit to the Navy yard on 13 September.[2] John Lenthall shared Smith's sense of financial responsibility, telling the commandant of the Boston Navy Yard to "please have an account kept of the cost of all kinds, separate from any other work. All expenses . . . must be charged to the ship and *not to general service.*" He emphasized this point more than once during the summer of 1854 to all of the Navy yard commandants and kept himself apprised of the various costs accrued by the Navy as construction got under way.[3]

Why did these two bureau chiefs take such a deep interest in the accounts of the *Merrimack* and its sister ships? Part of the answer comes from the personal integrity of the two men involved. The naval establishment held Lenthall in the highest regard; he had labored in its service since 1835. Although he had only been chief of the Bureau of Construction and Repair since 18 November 1853, his zeal for duty had long been evident. Smith enjoyed a similar reputation. He spent much of his career making sure that the government got the most for its money. But the real reason went beyond the personalities of these two men, although personality played an important role. The Navy saw the frigates' authorization as the first step in the comprehensive rebuilding of the nation's fleet. Secretary Dobbin would begin lobbying Congress for funds for seven sloops of war in December 1854. The lobbying effort might go more smoothly if the Navy could convince the legislators that the government's money was being wisely spent. If the authorization process proceeded along the same lines as that of the frigates during the winter of 1853 and spring of 1854, reports submitted by the bureau chiefs would play an important role in convincing the Congress not only of the need for the new vessels but also of the Navy's ability to handle public funds. The bureau chiefs would be all the more credible if they could point to current evidence of fiscal responsibility, which made their stewardship of the frigates' construction even more important.[4]

Building the hulls was relatively easy, although the Navy had to deal with some interesting design issues. The biggest problem was modifying stocked structural timbers originally cut for an entirely different class of ships to fit the Navy's new needs. Still, the constructors at the various Navy yards proved up to the task and the Navy made steady progress on the frigates through the summer and fall of 1854. The thorny issue for this class of warships was the construction of the steam power plants. Secretary Dobbin would have preferred that the Navy itself build the engines and declared himself embarrassed "on account of the Governments being so entirely dependent upon private establishments" for their construction. Although he had secured funding for the construction and expansion of machine shops suited for building engines at the Norfolk, Boston, and New York Navy Yards, those facilities would not be ready for some time. The only naval facility capable of manufacturing marine engines was the Washington Navy Yard, and then only in limited quantities. The secretary, therefore, found himself with no alternative but to turn to the network of private companies along the east coast that had supplied some the Navy's mechanical needs in the past.[5]

Dobbin placed an advertisement for steam machinery in the *National Daily Intelligencer* at the beginning of July. The advertisement merely reprinted a departmental circular dated 1 July that informed potential contractors that they had until 1 August to submit proposals for the steam machinery of one or more of the frigates. Briefly, the announcement explained that "each offer must be for a specific sum, and include all patent fees for any arrangement that may be proposed, and must state the period within which the work can be completed." Each bidder could arrange the machinery as it pleased, the only stipulation being that it fit within the allotted space and "obtain the greatest speed and power, with the most economical consumption of fuel."[6]

The secretary used the advertising of these substantial contracts to make recent changes in contract guarantees a matter of policy. Machinery

The U.S. Navy and the Origins of the Military-Industrial Complex

contracts awarded to private engine builders in the 1830s and 1840s had been relatively unsophisticated, and they had favored the contractor. In the case of the *Missouri* and *Mississippi*, for example, the Navy issued the contract, assigned an engineer to supervise construction, inspected the finished product, took possession, and paid the contractor in full. Possession terminated the engine builder's responsibility, much to the Navy's chagrin in some cases. In 1853, it will be recalled, Dobbin began addressing the problem of substandard power plants by attaching a performance guarantee to a contract for a new set of engines for the *San Jacinto*. He expanded on this precedent in advertising for the new frigates' steam engines, making clear the following terms of payment:

> When one-third of the work provided for by the contract shall have been completed to the satisfaction of the Department, there shall be a payment of one-fifth of the whole amount of the contract; when two-thirds of the work shall, in like manner, be completed, there shall be a further payment of one-fifth; when the ship shall have made a trial trip, satisfactory to the Department, of not less than one week at sea, there shall be a further payment of one-fifth; and when the ship shall have been in the possession of the Department, and performed satisfactorily for six months, the remaining sum shall be paid; the repairs necessary during this period, from defective workmanship and material, being at the expense of the contractor.

As if that were not enough, Dobbin required that bidders awarded contracts by the Navy post a secured bond equal in value to three-fourths of the amount of the contract. If a bidder could not meet the terms of the contract, it forfeited the bond.[7]

Clearly, the Navy's relationship with private contractors was slowly changing. As building programs went from the occasional steamship, often experimental, to entire classes of warships, procedures became more formalized and contractors became more accountable for their craftsmanship. The uncertainty of experimentation still exerted some influence, but the sheer size of the building programs and their funding, coupled with the notable failures of the preceding decade, led to closer supervision of contracts by the Navy. Of course, mistakes were still made, but by 1854 the Navy had recognized the scope of the problem and had taken realistic steps to correct it. The success of the contract guarantees in the construction of the steam frigates would set an important precedent and become standard policy for later warships.

By the end of August several bids and their accompanying plans had been received at the Navy Department and awaited the secretary's decision. Dobbin, ever the competent administrator, delegated responsibility to a board of engineers. The board, created on 6 September, consisted of Bureau Chief John Lenthall, Engineer in Chief Daniel B. Martin, and Chief Engineers William W. W. Wood, Henry Hunt, William H. Everett, and Charles W. Copeland. Dobbin selected these men because of his "confidence in [their] judgement skill, practical acquaintance with steam machinery and disposition to act in this matter for the public good." The secretary charged the board with a twofold task. He not only expected an opinion about the relative merits of each design but also wanted a verdict on the terms proposed by each manufacturer. Design and price would receive equal consideration.[8]

For all the caution that surrounded the advertising and issuing of the engine contracts, the importance and urgency that attended the original authorization of the frigates permeated the deliberations over the machinery. Even though the 6 April bill momentarily satisfied the appetites of the navalists and the Young Americans, Dobbin and the rest of the Pierce administration understood the temporary nature of the lull. Another *Black Warrior* incident could trigger a similar wave of pro-Navy sentiment that might prove awkward for the government. Likewise, another major shipbuilding blunder might cost the Pierce administration dearly at the polls. Dobbin warned the new board that "a failure in the machinery for these new steamers will be a National Calamity and attended with a National embarrassment and inconvenience." He expected them to balance speed with judicious thought and asked for "the earliest action compatible with thorough and deliberate investigation." The message was simple: the secretary would not tolerate mistakes on his watch.[9]

The board quickly settled to its task and submitted its first report two weeks after its creation. The report contained recommendations for four of the six vessels, the ships slated for construction at Boston, Philadelphia, and Norfolk. By this time the Navy had decided to construct one engine itself, for the frigate building at the Washington Navy Yard. The sixth warship, earmarked for construction at New York, was the future *Niagara,* which shared little in common with the other five frigates. For the purposes of this book, it is considered a unique ship type beyond the scope of this discussion.

Lenthall and the engineers recommended three different engine designs as suitable for the four ships: horizontal trunk engines, horizontal steeple engines, and John Ericsson's horizontal engine with vibrating shaft. Trunk and steeple engines differed in the mechanisms used to transfer power from the piston to the shaft. The Ericsson engine, similar in design to the engine first used on the *Princeton* more than a decade earlier, actually consisted of two smaller engines with semicylinders operating on the shaft at the same time from two directions. All three engine types addressed one of the major concerns of the day: protecting the machinery from hostile gunfire. The horizontal orientation of each accepted design placed the machinery below the water line, decreasing the chances of a disabling enemy shot finding the power plant. Strategically placed coal bunkers provided additional protection, creating a shot-absorbing barrier between the hull and the machinery.

As for the boilers, the board agreed that all of the vessels would use a well-received design patented by Daniel B. Martin, one of its members. Martin's boiler, which used a series of two-inch copper tubes to carry water past the fires, offered a number of advantages over the conventional fire-tube system, where the tubes carried the hot air through the water. Steam could be gotten up much quicker, the boiler took up less space, and it burned less fuel. More important, the Martin boiler was safer. In case of an explosion, the boiler contained the scalding water instead of spreading it. Last but not least, this design could be built either horizontally or vertically. The board accepted both variations and left the final decision up to the builders, on whose shoulders fell responsibility for fitting the power plant into the allotted space.[10]

In a shorter second report submitted to Dobbin two days after the first, Lenthall's board recommended that the "Government would be well served by distributing the Engines and Machinery for the Steamers to several establishments giving the Machinery of but one ship to each." In doing so, the Navy would realize two important benefits. First, the individual engine builders would be engaged in an informal competition. Because the five hulls shared the same basic design, the company whose engine performed best might gain the upper hand when it came time to award future contracts. Second, the perceived necessity of building and launching these vessels as quickly as possible would be met if each builder were only responsible for one engine. Designing and manufacturing this kind of machinery remained something of an art because of the constant refinements in the technology. Whether or not the Navy wanted to admit the inexact nature of engine construction, its more enlightened engineers understood the delicate nature of the building process. The contracting of a second engine to even the most respected builder might lead to lengthy delays for one or more of the frigates.[11]

Despite the board's recommendations, one company, Anderson and Dulaney of Richmond, Virginia, was awarded contracts for the engines of two of the *Merrimack*'s sister ships, the *Roanoke* and the *Colorado*. These ships, both under construction at the Norfolk Navy Yard, suffered from the very delays feared by the board. Whereas the *Merrimack* set out on its maiden voyage in February 1856, the *Roanoke* did not put out until March 1857 and the *Colorado* until August of that year. Although the government took no action against the builders and found itself quite pleased with the workmanship of these engines, it seems that building two power plants at the same time taxed the resources of Anderson and Dulaney, proving the board's point.[12]

By the beginning of October, the board advised Secretary Dobbin which companies it believed should receive contracts for the machinery of the five frigates. It recommended that the West Point Foundry of Cold Spring, New York, build the machinery for the frigate under construction at the Boston Navy Yard, that the New York firm of Pease and Murphy construct the power plant for the frigate building at the New York Navy Yard, that Merrick and Sons of Philadelphia manufacture the machinery for the vessel under way at the Philadelphia Navy Yard, and that the Richmond firm of Anderson and Dulaney build two engines for the frigates taking shape at the Norfolk Navy Yard.[13]

The Navy's contract with the West Point Foundry for the *Merrimack*'s engines illustrates the new relationship between the government and contractors. The only deadline imposed was that the machinery "be completed and properly erected on board the ship, ready for operation and trial by steam within Four months from the date at which said ship shall be launched and ready for the reception thereof." This gave some protection to the contractor and made the Navy responsible for getting the project under way. The contract also restated the terms advertised by the Navy during the summer

The U.S. Navy and the Origins of the Military-Industrial Complex

of 1854 and added specific details. The contractor would be paid in install-ments as the work progressed, the final payment coming after the vessel had been in service for six months. Given the Navy's past experience with engine contractors and power plants, the six-month waiting period seemed important because

> in the event of a failure from improper design, malconstruction, defec-tive materials or workmanship of the said Engines, Propeller, Boilers &c. to work successfully at sea for at least six months, and to the satis-faction of the Navy Department, or in the event of a failure from the causes before named at any time within six months of the said Engines, Propeller, Boilers &c. to work successfully at sea; then it is hereby agreed and understood that the Navy Department is authorized to have all repairs, alterations and modifications made so as to secure the success-ful operation of the aforesaid machinery at sea, which repairs, alterations and modifications shall be made at the expense of the said Robert P. Parrott, and the sum or sums paid therefore shall be deducted from the last payment aforesaid.

These conditions may have sounded more stringent than normal to the com-panies involved, but the Navy was intent on getting its money's worth out of these ships. It also could not afford another public relations setback.[14]

Different construction sites for the hulls and the engines made the exchange of ideas and information essential. As the contractors began craft-ing the power plants in the fall of 1854, the Navy made special efforts to maintain open lines of communication between the Navy yards and the various firms. In the case of the *Merrimack,* one of Dobbin's first acts after signing the contract with Robert Parrott was to inform Commo. Francis Hoyt Gregory, commandant of the Boston Navy Yard, that "you will be pleased to furnish him with all information connected with the ship, that he may desire." More than just information exchanged hands. The Navy yards and contractors also sent emissaries back and forth when the situation required. For example, Gregory ordered Benjamin F. Delano, the naval con-structor overseeing the erecting of the hull, to Cold Spring in the middle of December "for the purpose of consulting with the contractors for the steam engine and apparatus for the Frigate Merrimac . . . to obtain the nec-essary information for your guidance on the subject." Likewise, Chief Engi-neer William H. Shock, assigned to the West Point Foundry by the Navy to oversee construction of the engines, made at least one trip to Boston to examine the hull.[15]

Interaction between the Navy and the contractors also occurred on a higher level, with Washington getting directly involved. Engineer in Chief Daniel Martin thought it necessary to dispatch assistant engineers to all of the contractors "to assist in copying the Drawings and such other duties as may be assigned." Their presence served as yet another reminder to the different firms that the Navy took this matter very seriously. Martin himself got personally involved several times. He made an undetermined number of whirlwind tours up and down the eastern seaboard inspecting the progress made at the various businesses involved in building the engines and forging the shafts for the new frigates.[16]

In the case of the *Merrimack,* the extra attention seemed to work. On 17 January 1855, Robert Parrott confidently sent a telegram to Secretary Dobbin announcing, "I can be ready to put [the engines] in if the Ship is launched and in readiness to receive them, on the 1st day of June next." This was fully four months earlier than his contract specified. As it turned out, Parrott would not make the promised deadline, but he would come very close. The Navy was obviously pleased with his progress, because it consistently transferred money to Parrott's account all through the winter and spring of 1855. It will be recalled that the Navy's advertisement for engines in the summer of 1854 specified a series of payments to contractors, an attempt to prevent the kind of quality problems that had plagued the Navy during the previous decade. Each installment was directly linked to the contractor's progress, which was certified by the superintending engineer. Parrott received his first installment of $34,400 on 17 February 1855. The second installment followed two months later, on 16 April. Clearly, the Navy was satisfied with the pace and quality of construction up to this point.[17]

The Navy launched the *Merrimack* on 14 June 1855, making it the first ship of its class in the water. In strategic terms, the early launching, made possible in part by Parrott's ability to deliver key components well ahead of schedule, meant little. After all, this was a country at peace, not war. In terms of political impact, however, it was very important, as an early launch date might enhance the Navy's stature in Congress. Preliminary planning for the next naval authorization bill, which included a request for seven lighter-draft steam sloops, was already under way. The rapid progress on the *Merrimack* would reflect well on the service's abilities.[18]

The launching's public relations impact was equally important, because it affected political perception. The *Boston Daily Advertiser* gave the highlights: "Greeted by the cheers of a vast concourse of people and a salute of twenty-one guns, the *Merrimac* was launched. As she passed into the water the ancient ceremony of christening was performed by Miss Mary E. Simmons, who broke a bottle of water from the Merrimac River over the bow." The *Boston Daily Evening Transcript* estimated the crowd on hand at approximately one hundred thousand. Included in the crowd was a group described by Gregory as "most of the eminent shipbuilders of this section of the country." In his report to Secretary Dobbin, he noted that those shipbuilders "with one voice pronounced the ship as being the most splendid and finished specimen of Naval Architecture ever produced anywhere." A local weekly magazine described the vessel as "light and graceful as a swan," and exulted that "we shall, at last, have something like a steam navy." No congressman considering a naval appropriations bill would ignore an event that attracted one hundred thousand onlookers and prominent professionals, especially in New England, as that region's representatives would provide crucial swing votes when the Navy's next steam warships were authorized two years later.[19]

Robert Parrott's failure to meet his self-imposed 1 June delivery date should not have surprised the Navy Department. In the first place, his contract did not require delivery until 1 October, four months later. Second, the Navy's experiences with contractors during the preceding decade prepared it for the incidental delays associated with the application of new technology. After consulting with Parrott, William Shock, the Navy engineer supervising the project, reported that the boilers and heavy machinery would not arrive in Boston until after the launching of the *Merrimack*. Even so, he expected that it would be a matter of weeks, not months, before all of the components arrived at the Navy yard, which was still well ahead of schedule.[20]

Parrott and the artisans of the West Point Foundry labored through the month of June and into July, crafting the various components and preparing them for shipment to Boston. By the middle of July, they had shipped the majority of the machinery to Boston. The remaining components arrived in Boston during the early days of August and found their way on board the vessel by the middle of the month. With the exception of a few minor pieces undergoing fabrication back in Cold Spring and some chain work soon due from the Washington Navy Yard, the majority of the steam apparatus was ready for installation. The commandant reported that "the Contractors seem to be taking all the necessary measures towards an early completion of this work" and pronounced himself satisfied with Parrott's progress.[21]

Still ahead of schedule, Parrott's men pressed on. At this point, the inherent difficulty of working with new technology came into play. The contracts for the steam frigates called for the machinery to be "completed and erected on board ready for trial by steam within Four months from and after the time said ship shall have been launched and prepared for the reception of said machinery, even should the same take place before the time above mentioned." The "time above mentioned" was 1 October. Because Parrott had the machinery on board by 16 August, technically he should have fulfilled the terms of the contract by the middle of December. By early October, Commandant Gregory reported that "the Contractors have now got the Merrimacs [sic] shafting, and the principle parts of the Engines in place, and are proceeding in a satisfactory manner towards the completion of their work."[22]

That sounds optimistic, but one wonders if Gregory knew much more about the power plant's progress than what he was told, and then, if he understood what he was hearing. The Merrimack's engines, never intended as anything more than auxiliaries, were beneath the province of most officers, except for those who voluntarily lowered their social status by service in the Corps of Engineers. The path to advancement passed through the quarterdeck, not in the hold with its greasy machinery and choking coal dust. Officers at sea scrupulously avoided a ship's machinery compartments. Chances are, officers on land observing the Merrimack's progress did the same. Many of them accepted steam machinery as a necessary evil, but one better dealt with by social inferiors or civilians. Parrott's men, supervised by Chief Engineer Shock, worked on, probably content in their relative isolation.[23]

However, installation of the power plant proved much more difficult and time-consuming than either Parrott or the Navy had anticipated. The original 1 July 1854 advertisement calling for machinery proposals did not give a time frame for construction and erection, requiring instead that "each offer . . . must state the period within which the work can be completed." The documentary record does not identify the source of the four-month installation period, but obviously both the Navy and Parrott thought it was realistic when the contract was signed. In their defense, neither party had much practical experience in marine engine construction. Both the Navy and its contractors would become more adept in the future at the process of marrying a power plant made by one party to a hull built by another, but the situation in the fall of 1855 was a learning experience for everyone involved.[24]

As fall came to a close and New England prepared for what would be one of the area's bitterest winters, pressure mounted to complete the *Merrimack* and prepare it for sea. Delays or not, Secretary Dobbin wanted the frigate available for a cruise down the Atlantic coast and into the Gulf of Mexico. The twenty months' construction time that Dobbin had promised Congress would be all that was required for the new frigates was nearly up. Delays were nothing new to both the Navy and Washington politicians, but Dobbin's ambitious rebuilding program demanded results if it was to continue. John Lenthall's Bureau of Construction, Equipment, and Repair alone had seen its budget more than double between 1854 and 1855, from $2 million to well over $4 million. Continued support on this scale required evidence of progress. Of the five frigates now building at the various Navy yards, the *Merrimack* was the closest to completion. Therefore, the department made this vessel the focus of its efforts.[25]

However, as the new year approached, it became clear to those at Boston that the trial trip would not happen anytime soon. At the end of December, the Navy yard's new commandant, Silas Stringham, regretfully informed Lenthall and Dobbin in separate letters that "it will take some three weeks additional time to complete the Engines, and the remaining work to be done by the Carpenters after the completion of the Engines will consume two weeks more time." Two key problems had surfaced. First, an expected shipment of copper piping for the boilers arrived in Boston behind schedule, further delaying Parrott's crew. Second, the Navy's carpenters found themselves compensating for minor design flaws at the last minute. Compartments that had been overlooked in the initial plans, like a mess area for the assistant engineers and officers, were designed and built on the spot by the naval constructor and his laborers. The shipwrights found that they had less room than they thought for stowing the ship's boats because of the extra space required for the telescoping funnel's hoisting gear. This did not reflect badly on the *Merrimack*'s design but pointed out the ancillary problems associated with the introduction of evolving technology. Again, the process of integrating naval construction with work contracted out to private parties needed further refinement.[26]

Parrott's crews finished their work on 26 January 1856. The Navy continued working on the hull for another three weeks, mounting the ordnance and loading stores on board for a trial trip. After additional delay resulting in the assignment of a new commanding officer for the frigate, the *Merrimack* officially entered service on 20 February. Some last-minute adjustments to the engines delayed the trial trip for a few days as the mechanics from the West Point Foundry scurried around in the bowels of the vessel. They completed their work by the afternoon of the twenty-fourth and spent the remainder of the day running the engines and testing the propeller hoisting mechanism. By the wee hours of the following morning, they declared themselves satisfied and turned the ship over to its captain, who wasted no time and cast off that afternoon. Commodore Stringham reported back to Washington later that day that "from all I have seen . . . of the Merrimac I am fully convinced of her superior qualities and believe her a credit to the service and the nation whose flag she bears."[27]

The first published reports that appeared about the *Merrimack*'s performance on the trial trip echoed Stringham's confidence. The *Journal of the Franklin Institute* claimed that the frigate made nine and a half knots exiting Boston Harbor with a slack tide and a speed of seven and a half knots against the wind. Even more incredible to those contemporaries with some expertise in the area, the journal gave the slippage of the shaft at 10 percent in one case and at 28 percent in another. Both figures seemed remarkably low and suggested a very efficient power plant. Because "this trip was for the particular purpose of testing her machinery, and was of limited duration, no opportunity occurred for obtaining the best speed under canvass and steam." However, the journal confidently reported that "her officers have no doubt of her ability to make 15 knots," another stunning claim given the technology of the day and the relative weakness of the engines compared to those carried by commercial steamers. A correspondent to the *U.S. Nautical Magazine and Naval Journal* echoed this optimistic assessment, telling its readers that the ship's trial trip "resulted to the entire satisfaction of all concerned, her machinery having been kept in constant operation for seven consecutive days." The Navy agreed that all went well during the trials, and on 6 March 1856 Dobbin authorized the third payment of $34,400 to Robert Parrott, as called for in the original engine contract. The final payment, 40 percent of the contract price, would come after the engines performed successfully for an additional six months.[28]

Early reports of the *Merrimack*'s speed and efficiency would not stand the test of time and probably had more to do with publicity than function. Whether these reports were intentionally exaggerated remains a matter of conjecture. Donald Canney's assessment of the frigate's steam log from the time of its initial voyage until the end of its active U.S. service in the fall of 1860 reveals much lower figures. On the trial trip, the best speed achieved under steam was only 6.1 knots. This figure increased to 10.5 knots with the addition of the sails. Over the rest of the *Merrimack*'s service life, average speed under steam alone was 5.2 knots, with a reported maximum of 8.8 knots. Mean speed with sails was 7.6 knots. The screw slipped as much as 73 percent, but averaged about 38 percent, a much lower figure but still substantially higher than the figures reported on the trial trip.[29]

Some contemporaries recognized and reported these problems. Benjamin Franklin Isherwood, one of the most talented engineers in the old steam Navy, examined the logs and machinery of the steam frigates in some detail. In the case of the *Merrimack,* he found that the propeller, an English design patented by Robert Griffiths, caused some of the excess slippage but compensated for that slippage with its lower resistance to the water in which it worked. More important, he criticized the frigates for being underpowered. Although he understood that the Navy never intended the power plants to be the frigates' primary source of propulsion, he thought that the service put the wrong engines aboard these ships. They performed reasonably well in smooth water and calm air. However, when "the vessel was brought head to wind, or encountered a rough head sea, its resistance increased enormously and, the slip of the screw rising in proportion, the speed fell to mere steerage way, while the consumption of fuel continued nearly the same." For a vessel of this type to be truly effective, Isherwood thought that it should be able to make at least ten knots under steam "uninfluenced by wind or current" and that the slippage of the screw should not exceed 10 percent. The *Merrimack* met none of these conditions.[30]

Isherwood was not alone in his criticism of the underpowered frigates. The editors of the *U.S. Nautical Magazine and Naval Journal* shared his sentiments. They ridiculed their own correspondent who suggested that the *Merrimack* placed the Navy on new ground, opining that this new ground was "so far inland as to be high and dry ashore." They thought the whole concept of auxiliary engines flawed to begin with and wanted the government to build full-powered steamships. The editors made an interesting point. The British government had subsidized the construction of a number of mail steamers for the Cunard line, reserving the right to impress these vessels as armed naval auxiliaries in time of war. Any of these ships would easily outrun the new frigates. Instead of blaming the secretary of the Navy for the underpowered frigates, the editors blamed the department's engineers, claiming they should have known better and should bear the brunt of the responsibility for mechanical failures and shortcomings. Finally, they faulted the *Merrimack*'s overall design, suggesting that it was top heavy because the Navy insisted on incorporating the old *Congress*-class frames, never intended to support a hull of that breadth or carrying that much weight. The unflattering analysis, although somewhat exaggerated, would be borne out by practical experience.[31]

Frank Bennett's description of the *Merrimack* as "the most beautiful of all the ships of her class" says much about its lines but little about its utility as a steam frigate. In some ways, the vessel proved a remarkable failure. After the trial trip, the *Merrimack* steamed to its new home port, Norfolk, and made ready for its maiden journey, a trip to Havana. Four days into the voyage, the propeller malfunctioned, and the frigate glided into the Cuban harbor under sail alone. It left Cuba and headed for Key West. Yet even sail power could not get the ship there. The rudder came unhung and the pride of the Navy suffered the ignominy of being dragged into port there by four boats. As the ship was now thoroughly disabled, the Navy had it towed by the *Susquehanna* back to Boston, where it underwent a minor refit. The Navy yard mechanics found that the frigate suffered from a technical problem experienced by other ships in the U.S. Navy as well as the Royal Navy. The bushings and bearings of the propeller shaft had been made of brass, following common practice. However, the excessive wear caused by contact with brass components of the shaft itself caused unforeseen leakage. Replacing the brass bearings with pieces made of lignum vitae solved the problem, and the *Merrimack* made ready for its European debut in the fall of 1856.[32]

These early mechanical problems directly affected the payments received by Robert Parrott. About 40 percent of the contract price, or $68,864, remained unpaid when the vessel embarked on its trial trip. According to the terms of the contract, the final payment should have come about six months after the trial trip, in September 1856. Between March and November 1856, the Navy disbursed money to Parrott on four different occasions. He received $20,000 on 19 March, $19,000 on 15 May, $14,400 on 22 August, and $33,464 on 15 November. Only the third payment of $14,400 can be directly linked to the power plant. The fourth payment was probably for the engines as well; the odd dollar amount corresponds to the odd dollar amount of the entire contract. Those two payments still leave $21,000 unaccounted for. One of the two remaining payments may have been for the engines, even though the timing was wrong, while the other was for the frigate's ordnance, which Parrott was also under contract to build. Or, in a worse-case scenario, both remaining payments were for ordnance. In any case, he was clearly penalized for the ship's mechanical shortcomings.[33]

The subcontracting of power plants to private establishments proved to be a good deal for the Navy in both cost and efficiency. The only Navy yard capable of building the required steam machinery, the Washington Navy Yard, constructed the *Minnesota*'s engines for a total cost of $170,445. The remaining power plants, manufactured by private firms, cost an average of $169,647, essentially the same. Although all of the engines "require some repairs within three years," the secretary of the Navy noted in 1860 that "the duration of the machinery built at private establishments has been the same as that built at the Washington yard." Granted, these engines were far from perfect, but it seems that the mechanical problems and difficulties with contractors experienced by the Navy during the late 1840s and early 1850s had been at least partially alleviated by the rigid controls and requirements enforced by Secretary Dobbin during the frigates' construction. The Navy thought so; the performance guarantees became standard policy for subsequent engine contracts. How these same controls would respond under the pressure of wartime conditions remained to be seen.[34]

The *Merrimack*'s arrival in Britain came at an opportune time for the Royal Navy, whose ranking officers had kept themselves informed of its progress during construction. Although they considered the frigate underpowered and muttered amongst themselves that "the Americans indeed have never yet built a paddle-wheel or screw-frigate which has realized the expectations of its builders," they respected its imposing armament and tonnage. Some popular journals condemned the frigate's Dahlgren shell guns as being of "inferior calibres," but the professionals knew better, and they used the *Merrimack* and its battery for their own purposes in persuading Parliament to authorize two new classes of steam frigates for the Royal

Navy. The *London Times* added fuel to the fire, castigating the Navy's surveyors general for possessing "the imitative talent of a Chinaman" and wondering how the Royal Navy would respond to this latest threat to naval supremacy. After visiting England, the *Merrimack* stopped at naval stations along the Atlantic and Mediterranean coasts, including Brest, Lisbon, and Toulon, before returning home in the spring of 1857. By this time, the engines and boilers badly needed repair, and the Navy briefly decommissioned the vessel while its engineers conducted an overhaul that eventually cost almost forty thousand dollars.

The *Merrimack* returned to active duty in September 1857 as flagship of the Pacific Station, where it served until early 1860, when it docked at the Norfolk Navy Yard, again requiring an extensive overhaul of the power plant. The outbreak of civil war and the ship's subsequent conversion into an ironclad brought an abrupt end to its career as a U.S. naval vessel, and it entered into a second, more famous, career as the CSS *Virginia*. The *Virginia* would spark a naval revolution in the United States as the Union Navy found itself forced to deal with this new technology. Ultimately, the Navy would decide that the only antidote to the formidable casemated ironclad ram taking shape at the captured Norfolk Navy Yard was the same kind of technology, backed by the might of northern industry. Once again, the Navy would be called upon to build a specific kind of ship for a particular situation. Until then, however, it would continue refining the contract process and its relationship with private industry, forging a partnership that would prove most useful in time of war.[35]

3 Expanding the Fleet

The Shallow-Draft Sloops, 1857–1860

The *Merrimack*-class frigates signaled the beginning of a new era of expansion for the United States Navy. Driven by sporadic war scares with Great Britain and supported by southerners convinced that slavery needed more territory to survive, the fleet evolved into one more suited for operations in shallower coastal waters. Ironically, most of the vessels authorized and built in the latter half of the 1850s would be used to great effect during the Civil War against the same southern ports they were designed to protect. As the fleet physically evolved, so too did the contract procedures that oversaw its construction, further defining the relationship between the Navy and private industry. Most important, that relationship began to broaden. For the first time since its purchase of the *Demologos* in 1814, the Navy let out the contract for a wooden steamship's hull to the private sector. In doing so, it would draw heavily upon the language and conditions of the steam machinery contracts that had seemed to work so well for the *Merrimack* class.

The authorization of those six frigates barely began to address the underlying motives behind their construction. The expansionist fervor that provided the base of support for the 1854 authorization had not diminished; indeed, if anything it remained unsatisfied. The relative ease with which the United States defeated Mexico in the 1846–48 war led many Americans, especially southerners, to cast a longing eye even farther south. They considered the relatively undeveloped economies of Central and South America rich potential markets, if not possible future additions to the United States.

Among the most prolific and persistent advocates of market expansion and possible annexation was Matthew Fontaine Maury, a lieutenant in the

United States Navy. His writings appeared in a number of southern newspapers and journals, pointing out the obvious benefits of developing inter-American commerce.[1] An article reprinted in the influential *Commercial Review* (later renamed *De Bow's Review*) envisioned a bright future for the Gulf of Mexico and the Caribbean Sea. Maury, who recognized the potential impact of an isthmian canal far earlier than most contemporaries, foresaw a time when such a canal would place

> this country . . . midway between Europe and Asia; this sea becomes the center of the world and the focus of the world's commerce. This is a highway that will give vent to commerce, scope to energy, and range to enterprise, which, in a few years hence, will make gay with steam and canvas, parts of the ocean that are now unfrequented and almost unknown. Old channels of trade will be broken up and new ones opened.[2]

Of course, echoing the ethnocentrism of the day, Maury expected that the United States would be "the standard-bearer in this great work."[3] These kinds of ideas were not confined to a small elite group, nor just to southerners. By the early 1850s, they had entered the common discourse of American political life. More important, the ideas moved out of the realm of conjecture as politicians and other interested parties began formulating pragmatic solutions to make them a reality.

The key obstacle preventing the United States from exercising greater influence in the Gulf and Caribbean was its inability to project power, a mission traditionally reserved for the Navy. Commentators such as Cdr. Samuel Francis Du Pont marveled at the "extraordinary expansion" of the nation's commerce since the end of the Mexican War but warned it "should lead all reflecting minds to consider how great would be the revulsion in our prosperity, if, through any untoward event, we should lose the means of protecting this commerce."[4] Traditionally, the United States had relied on the goodwill of the English and French navies in assisting American merchantmen, but rising tensions in the Caribbean basin suggested that such goodwill could not be counted on in the future.

Authorization of the six steam frigates in 1854 was the first step in augmenting the fleet, but few who studied the problem saw the frigates as the final solution. In his 1853 annual report requesting approval for the six frigates, Secretary of the Navy James Dobbin acknowledged the scale and scope of America's "new empire [which] has, as by magic, sprung into existence." He argued that rapid commercial growth now required "a naval force, organized and ready to vindicate it from insult and aggression."[5] The steam frigates were only the first step in what Dobbin saw as a limited but steady expansion, a point he made abundantly clear the following year. His 1854 annual report appealed to the nation's broader economic interests, concluding that a Navy strong enough to protect the American coast generated an intangible but nonetheless important dividend: peace. Although Dobbin did not present a specific building program for Congress' consideration, he made his willingness to "co-operate with the legislative department of government in practically carrying out these views" perfectly clear.[6]

President Franklin Pierce echoed Dobbin's concern in his second annual message to Congress, delivered on 4 December 1854. The president reiterated his support for the six frigates then building but urged Congress to keep the larger picture in mind. American commerce had grown so quickly and now ranged so far around the globe that the Navy could not hope to provide adequate protection. From Pierce's perspective, the problem was only going to get worse as the United States began developing its newly acquired Pacific coastline. Monitoring and policing this territory would require even more warships. Implicit in this message was the idea that the Navy should focus future building programs on vessels better suited for that kind of mission. The frigates, though important in the larger scheme of national defense, were simply not suited for commerce protection.[7]

Congress took immediate action, although it is not clear whether that action was motivated by President Pierce's message or by other forces. In any case, Representative Thomas Bocock, the chairman of the House Committee on Naval Affairs who had been instrumental in pushing through the appropriation for the *Merrimack* class, sent a letter to Secretary Dobbin on 15 December 1854 requesting clarification of the Navy's needs. He specifically asked about the number of ships the Navy wanted, their size and armament, and for an explanation justifying their authorization.

Dobbin's response was concise, to the point, and very specific. Drawing on information provided by his bureau chiefs, who probably could not believe their recent spate of good luck, he forwarded a detailed proposal to Bocock on 23 December, barely one week after receiving the initial request. In it, he stressed the benefits of a balanced fleet, noting that despite the "formidable character" of the *Merrimack*-class frigates, they could not enter many of the nation's major ports. What the Navy needed, Dobbin suggested, were "well-armed vessels of lighter draught" better suited for coastal operations. He recommended building seven heavily armed steam sloops. Appealing as he had one year earlier to congressional budget concerns, the secretary stressed economy in his request. He pointed out that the Navy already had seven well-seasoned frames on hand that could be used for vessels of that class. The end result, he noted, was that "their cost will be about one-half of the same number of steam frigates."[8]

Despite Dobbin's best efforts, Congress declined to authorize the necessary funds. Undeterred, the secretary pushed the idea again in his 1855 annual report. This time, he was more blunt about it, deeming it his "duty to candidly express the opinion that our Navy is not only too diminutive to be expected to contend fairly with that of other respectable nations, is insufficient to give adequate protection to our commerce, but is unquestionably *too feeble to command the waters of our own coast.*" This worried Dobbin because such a deficiency could not be quickly corrected in time of war. Unlike the Army, which the Mexican War had shown could be rapidly augmented with civilian manpower, the Navy required specialized equipment that took time to properly build. What if, Dobbin wondered, the United States found itself at war with a naval power like Great Britain or France? He feared the worst, predicting the destruction of American merchantmen and the plundering of American harbors. Given the potential financial loss of such a war, he considered the construction of additional warships a relative bargain if the ships could prevent enemy depredations.[9]

Congress was unmoved, again rejecting Dobbin's request. Battered but not beaten, Dobbin made one more plea in his final report as secretary of the Navy. His 1856 annual report found "no reason for withdrawing the recommendation heretofore made to build additional sloops-of-war." From his perspective, "the arguments and considerations for a steady and gradual enlargement of our navy have lost none of their force." He tried downplaying the idea of "increase" by pointing out that new warships would replace, not supplement, older vessels deemed unworthy of further repair. This was not idle speculation on the secretary's part. Earlier in the year he had received an assessment from John Lenthall, chief of the Bureau of Construction, Equipment, and Repair, detailing the Navy's physical condition, including the revelation that nine of the service's eighteen sloops "require costly repairs, but they cannot be abandoned until there are other ships to take their place." Still, Dobbin, who must have been frustrated by this point, and who knew that he would be replaced by the incoming James Buchanan administration, devoted far less space to his request in his annual report than in previous years. Ironically, this time a supporting bill working its way through Congress would succeed. On 3 March 1857, Dobbin's last day as secretary, Congress appropriated $1 million for five sloops.[10]

This authorization resulted not only from Dobbin's persistence, but also because of the perception that American national interests were being challenged in the Caribbean. The pronouncements of Matthew Maury and other southern expansionists reflected a more aggressive American foreign policy. Throughout the 1850s, the United States increasingly asserted itself in the region, especially when the Democrats returned to the White House in 1853. There were some very public disagreements, especially the *Black Warrior* incident, the Ostend Manifesto, and the sacking of Greytown, Nicaragua. Although these incidents resulted in a certain amount of chest-thumping by the respective parties involved, they were never serious enough to lead to war. They were, however, indicative of larger issues. There was an open question of which country or countries would control a future isthmian canal and, by implication, its associated trade routes. Although the Clayton-Bulwer Treaty of 1850 between the United States and Great Britain seemed to settle the issue by guaranteeing joint access to a canal and prohibiting the fortifying or colonizing of Central America, competition in the region was a fact of life for the rest of the decade. All of this was complicated by the increasing frequency of American-based filibustering expeditions and a steadily expanding British naval presence in the region that by 1857 was larger than the entire U.S. Navy. Dobbin had not been wrong; he had merely offered a solution before the problem was widely apparent.[11]

Despite the Navy's legislative triumph, incoming secretary Isaac Toucey was not able to push forward with construction for more than a year. The delay was not his fault; he and the Navy merely fell victim to circumstance. Six weeks after the appropriations bill passed, the Ohio Life Insurance and Trust Company suspended payment on its notes. To those who followed such matters, that bankruptcy reflected growing tension in the financial world, which became increasingly skeptical of the country's ability to sustain the rapid speculation and economic growth of the 1850s. In early fall, several other major eastern banks suspended payment on their notes. By the middle of October, the entire New York banking system had collapsed, triggering the national financial crisis known as the Panic of 1857. Local, state, and federal authorities did what they could to alleviate the crisis, but there were limits to what government could do. Ultimately, the federal government decided to continue ongoing building projects but postpone action on anything new. The five sloops unfortunately fell into the latter category.[12]

The legislation authorizing the five sloops gave Toucey the same latitude in building the warships that Dobbin had with the 1854 steam frigates. The bill allowed "said vessels and machinery to be built by contract or in the government navy yards as the Secretary of the Navy may think most advisable for the public interest." Toucey, like Dobbin before him, decided to use a combination of private contractors and Navy yards. Three of the five power plants would be built outright by private firms. The remaining two engines would be built in the Navy's own shops, but one of the two would have a civilian engineer on hand to try an experimental engine arrangement. Unlike Dobbin, Toucey did not restrict private involvement to the power plants, reserving one hull for a private contractor. Frank Bennett claims this was done "to incite a healthful rivalry between the naval constructors and civilian ship-builders." It is unclear whether Toucey's goals were quite that high-minded, but regardless, his decision marked an important turning point for the Navy. For this first time in over four decades, the Navy was not going to build a warship's hull in one of its own yards using its own laborers.[13]

As in the case of the 1854 frigates, construction of the new sloops would take place all along the Atlantic coast. Four of the hulls were assigned to the Navy yards at Boston, Philadelphia, Norfolk, and Pensacola. The fifth would ultimately be built in New York City by shipbuilder Jacob Westervelt. Power plant construction was more concentrated, in part because of the relative lack of facilities. The Navy would build two engines, one at the Washington Navy Yard and the other at the Gosport Navy Yard in Norfolk. The remaining three engines were contracted out to private companies.[14]

Despite the delays imposed by the Panic of 1857, the Navy did not sit idly by and wait for conditions to improve. Instead, it used the delay to discuss the hull and engine design of four of the five sloops, a luxury not available with the 1854 frigates. Two different boards were convened in the fall of 1857 and early 1858. The first, consisting of Joseph Smith (chief of the Bureau of Yards and Docks), John Lenthall (chief of the Bureau of Construction, Equipment, and Repair), Duncan Ingraham (chief of the Bureau of Ordnance and Hydrography), and Chief Engineer Samuel Archbold, considered hull designs for the four warships to be built at the different Navy yards. Their report, issued at the end of October, recommended that three sloops be built with a flush gun deck containing fourteen cannon and the slightly larger fourth with a covered gun deck carrying eighteen cannon. The fifth sloop's design had already been chosen by an earlier board charged with considering competitive bids received from civilian contractors.

The second board, comprising the Navy's chief engineers, met in early 1858 to consider power plant designs. The Navy had placed advertisements in Philadelphia and Boston newspapers in November 1857. Four firms responded to the Philadelphia ad, and thirteen submitted proposals for the sloop to be built in Boston. After carefully considering both the design and cost of the various proposals, the board awarded the Philadelphia contract to Reany, Neafie and Company and the Boston contract to the firm of Loring and Coney. Because it was connected directly to the larger contract for the fifth sloop, later named the *Brooklyn,* the New York machinery had been considered separately and was already contracted for by the time this board met. Ultimately, James Murphy and Company would build that power plant under subcontract to Jacob Westervelt.[15]

All of the contracts, whether for a power plant or hull, derived their basic structure from the 1854 frigate contracts. Although drawn up later than the *Brooklyn* agreement, the Navy's 19 April 1858 contract with Philadelphia engine builder Reany, Neafie and Company for the *Lancaster's* power plant will be considered first because it serves as a useful benchmark in assessing the lessons learned from building similar engines for the *Merrimack*-class frigates. In general, the basic language of the contract remained the same, with entire paragraphs lifted verbatim from the 1854 agreement. However, the Navy drew upon its past experience in two important ways.

First, the Navy took the opportunity to increase the level of detail when specifying the construction and installation of the engines. Both contracts allowed the engine builder to "arrange and proportion" the power plant "in such manner as he shall deem best adapted to secure the most successful results," as long as the basic specifications outlined by the Navy were followed. However, the *Lancaster* contract was much more specific about how and when the machinery would be integrated into the ship. For example, it mandated that "the Engines to be well secured to the ship by holding down bolts. Twelve of which are to pass through the floor timbers nearest the line of keel with heads let into the wood on washers." There were similarly detailed instructions regarding the placement of boilers and the timetable for fitting the propeller, part of the shaft, the hoisting gear, and a number of smaller items. Most important, it spelled out when the entire power plant had to be on board and functional relative to the Navy's progress on the rest of the ship. In other words, the Navy was not going to let the power plant dictate the pace of construction.[16]

The majority of these new stipulations can be traced back to the Navy's experience with building the frigates, especially the problems it encountered when synchronizing construction and launching of the hulls with construction and installation of the power plants. These kinds of issues were a natural byproduct of the service's efforts to deal with new technology. Decentralized construction of a warship's component parts, the Navy was learning, required improved management of the entire shipbuilding process.

The second important modification to the 1854 contracts was the insertion of new clauses to further protect both the Navy and its contractors from each other and from unforeseen problems. Commercial steam power plants were still a developing technology that made each engine a unique challenge to build. Even so, there were obvious areas where corners could be cut to reduce costs at the expense of quality. In time of war, the Navy would expect a lot from its engines and therefore wanted the best product possible from its contractors. Robert Parrott's 1854 contract tried to make that explicit, decreeing that "the workmanship thereon shall be of the best quality and description and shall be satisfactory to such superintending Engineer or Engineers as may be selected by the Navy Department to inspect the same."

Still, the performance of the various frigates' engines suggested several qualitative design deficiencies, as outlined by Chief Engineer Benjamin Franklin Isherwood in his authoritative *Experimental Researches in Steam Engineering.* He reported in great detail parts that repeatedly broke, deficient materials, and improper installation of the engines on board ship. Although Isherwood's magnum opus had yet to be published, some of the problems he outlined were well known to the Navy's engineering corps by 1858. To compensate, the Navy inserted a new clause in the sloop contracts that gave the superintending engineer "the authority to condemn any of the work in any stage of progress, either from improper design, improper or bad material or workmanship." Clearly, at least on paper, the Navy was going to hold its contractors to a higher standard than it had just four years earlier.[17]

At the same time, the Navy realized that the relationships it was building with these private firms would be ongoing. Therefore, it would not be in the Navy's best interest to unnecessarily alienate them. Instead, it became apparent that the contracts had to offer some degree of protection to these companies as well. Building once again on its practical experience with the frigates, the Navy made a key adjustment in its latest contract. One of the biggest problems facing any company awarded an engine contract was cash flow. Power plants were very expensive items. For example, the *Merrimack's* contracted engine price was $172,064, an enormous sum for the day. No engine manufacturer had that kind of capital on hand and therefore needed money from the government. On the other hand, the Navy was not about to advance money to a private firm, fearing potential loss. The solution used in the 1854 contract was a series of payments linked to steady progress on the power plant. When one-third of the work was completed and certified, the Navy paid the manufacturer 20 percent of the contract price. An additional 20 percent would be paid when two-thirds of the work was finished, and yet another 20 percent when the engine was completed and had successfully passed a one-week trial. The remaining 40 percent of the contract price would be paid only after the ship and its machinery underwent a six-month trial voyage.[18]

While a definite improvement over previous contracts, this system of graduated payments still put enormous financial pressure on the contractor. Even after the engine was fully built, which meant that all materials had been purchased and all salaries had been paid, he still had received only 60 percent of the contract cost. To survive in this environment, he needed deep pockets. Even so, staying financially solvent must have been interesting at times. This doubtlessly weighed on all of the contractors' minds. For example, during the construction of the *Merrimack*, Robert Parrott wrote a letter to the commandant of the Boston Navy Yard explaining the "exceeding importance to me to get the trial of the machinery of the Merrimac." He had finished building the engines but would not get his third installment from the Navy until that trial was conducted. At that point, he had paid all costs associated with construction while having received only 40 percent of the full contract price. Deep pockets or not, that created quite a burden.[19]

The Navy tried to remedy the problem in the new contract by changing the payment schedule. The first payment of 20 percent of the contract price would be made after one-quarter of the work was completed. Additional 20 percent payments would be made after one-half and three-quarters of the engine was built. A fourth payment of 20 percent would be made when the engine was fully operational and completed a one-week trial on board ship. The final payment, also 20 percent, would be paid after the machinery performed successfully on a six-month trial cruise of the new sloop. As with the earlier contract, progress during the various stages of construction was certified by a naval engineer assigned to the contractor's premises.

This arrangement potentially benefited all parties involved. The contractor's cash flow problem was alleviated in two important ways. First, he received payments much earlier than before. Smaller increments, one-fifth rather than one-third, put the money into his hands much faster, which made it easier to pay for materials and labor. Second, he was paid a higher percentage of the total contract price by the time the power plant was ready for its six-month trial—80 percent rather than the old contract's 60 percent, which again helped his cash flow. The government also gained from the new arrangement. More frequent payments meant even closer inspection by the on-site engineer, which hopefully translated into a higher quality finished product. Concerns that a contractor might default on an agreement after substantial funds had been paid out were alleviated by a new clause that gave the Navy a lien on the uncompleted machinery and all materials. The same clause also required the contractor to insure the power plant and boilers against fire. The final benefit was less tangible but certainly more important. In adjusting the payment schedule, the Navy clearly demonstrated its commitment to its developing relationship with civilian industry. No matter how much it would have liked to build all of its engines in its own Navy yards, that was almost impossible from a practical standpoint. These contract changes reflected a new reality that demanded closer cooperation between the Navy and American business in an era of increasing technical sophistication.[20]

Even before assessing power plant proposals for the sloops designated for construction in its own yards, the Navy forged ahead into new territory: the contracting of a complete ship. The process was essentially the same as that used for soliciting bids for power plants. The Navy placed public advertisements in leading newspapers requesting bids for a completed sloop,

The U.S. Navy and the Origins of the Military-Industrial Complex

fully equipped with the exception of its ordnance. Thirteen shipbuilders took up the challenge and sent detailed proposals to Washington for the Navy's consideration. Jacob Westervelt of New York won the competition and signed a contract with the Navy on 7 September 1857 for the *Brooklyn*.

Like the *Lancaster* engine contract, the *Brooklyn* agreement benefited from the Navy's experience with the *Merrimack*-class contracts, incorporating most of the same adjustments and refinements. It gave the superintending engineer the same expanded authority to reject materials or finished work for not meeting the Navy's standards. It also included a more flexible payment schedule designed to preserve the contractor's cash flow. Over the course of construction, Westervelt could expect to receive more than 60 percent of the *Brooklyn*'s contract price. Successful completion of the mandatory one-week postconstruction trial trip raised that number to more than 83 percent of the contract price, slightly higher than the percentage in the *Lancaster* engine contract at the same stage of the contract. As with the *Lancaster* engine contract, the remainder would be paid after the ship and machinery proved itself on an extended three-month trial cruise. Because the Navy was paying out greater sums earlier than it had in the 1854 engine contracts, it protected itself just like it did with the sloop engines, stipulating that the service had a lien on the *Brooklyn* until the vessel was formally delivered.

There was one noticeable difference between the *Lancaster* and *Brooklyn* contracts, but it was a difference of practicality, not philosophy. The *Brooklyn* contract did not contain the same detailed clauses specifying how the power plant would be mounted in the hull and at what point that would take place in the construction process, in part because such clauses were not necessary. Those clauses were an important part of the *Lancaster* contract because they helped smooth the integration of components (the hull and engines) from two different sources. The *Brooklyn* was constructed entirely by one builder, who could monitor and determine the flow of construction by himself. That is not to say that Jacob Westervelt operated in a vacuum. Like the engine contractors working on the other sloops' power plants, he worked from a detailed set of specifications attached to the contract. If the finished product did not meet those specifications, or if the hull or machinery failed in any way before or during the three-month trial, he was responsible for the cost of all necessary modifications and repairs. Westervelt also worked under specific time constraints. His agreement with the Navy required that the *Brooklyn* be "ready for operation within six-teen months from the date of this contract," although it did not make clear what penalties, if any, would be levied if he missed the deadline. In short, while the language differed slightly from the *Lancaster* contract, the intent remained the same. Although the Navy would not build the *Brooklyn*, it would exercise ultimate authority over its construction.[21]

Because the *Brooklyn* was the first warship in decades built entirely out-side the Navy yards, it was somewhat controversial. Some naval officers questioned whether a civilian-built vessel could really meet the Navy's stan-dards. On that count, the *Brooklyn* acquitted itself rather well. Of the five ships in its class, only one went longer before undergoing a major rebuild-ing. Even in the late 1880s, the secretary of the Navy reported a longer life expectancy for the *Brooklyn* than its sister ship, the *Hartford*. Even if it was not markedly better than the other ships in its class, it was certainly no worse from a construction perspective. From an economic perspective, however, the *Brooklyn* clearly outperformed the rest of its class. It was the least expensive of the five sloops to build, and by a significant margin. The *Brooklyn* cost $417,921. The next cheapest ship was the *Hartford*, constructed for an additional $83,000. The remaining sloops cost even more. Despite the concerns of contemporary officers and larger fears of corruption in naval contracts, the *Brooklyn* proved that the Navy could rely on the civilian sec-tor to handle at least some of its construction needs. Just as important, it also showed the Navy that it was possible to effectively manage a project of that scale without compromising on quality or speed of construction.[22]

The stabilization of the American economy and increasing tension between the United States and Great Britain in Latin America led to a fur-ther increase in the fleet in 1858. The five sloops authorized in 1857 were a necessary and positive step forward, but the fleet still suffered from glaring deficiencies in operational capabilities, which Secretary Toucey pointed out in his 1857 annual report. The immediate problem, he suggested, was the lack of "small steamers of light draught, which are very much wanted in the public service." The secretary presented the problem to Congress in terms of commerce protection, noting that no ship in the fleet could "pen-etrate the rivers of China" and that few could "enter most of the harbors south of Norfolk." Those harbors, he implied, were therefore vulnerable in time of war. He recommended building ten smaller sloops for $2.3 million, assigning at least one to each of the Navy's squadrons and three or four to both the Atlantic and Pacific coasts. Although not an insignificant sum, Toucey suggested that $2.3 million was relatively cheap given the proposed ships' utility in safeguarding American commerce at home and around the globe.[23]

What Toucey did not say, perhaps because of the potential political implications, was that vessels of this type would be admirably suited for service in the Caribbean. His omission certainly did not reflect a lack of interest in the region. Increasingly frequent diplomatic clashes with the British, coupled with southern interest in expanding American slavery, kept Latin America both in the news and on the minds of many Americans. As they had in the first half of the decade, the British maintained a friendly but firm relationship with the United States over the Caribbean. They openly increased their military presence in the area while continuing a dialogue with the United States over the future of the region, especially a potential isthmian canal. Nevertheless, by 1857 they concluded that a strong British presence counterbalancing the United States was not a top priority in British foreign policy and began reducing their presence in the region. That decision was not readily apparent in Washington, however, so the United States maintained a guardedly aggressive attitude toward the British in Central America.[24]

A driving force behind American mistrust of the British was the expansion of slavery. Even though the United States continued its own westward expansion, much of the newly settled territory was unsuitable for plantation agriculture, which threatened to disrupt the traditional balance between slave and free states. Southerners, worried about losing their voice in national politics, therefore looked south toward the Caribbean basin, where a history of fertile soil and slavery seemingly offered ideal prerequisites for annexation. One might easily dismiss these ideas as rabid sectionalism confined to filibusters such as William Walker, but that would overlook the powerful support expansionism received from prominent national politicians. While still minister to England, President James Buchanan had gained international notoriety in the fall of 1854 as principal author of the Ostend Manifesto, which advocated the acquisition of Cuba from Spain and implied that force be used if necessary. Secretary of the Navy Isaac Toucey, although from Connecticut, had gone on record as a member of the United States Senate during the debate over the Kansas-Nebraska bill as supporting the right of American citizens to take the institution of slavery with them wherever they settled. Although he used his authority as secretary to take active steps to suppress the African slave trade, he carefully distinguished between banning the importation of new slaves and allowing the expansion of slavery. Simply put, he did not oppose slavery on moral grounds. The principal legislators involved in pushing through the bill authorizing the sloops, Senator Stephen Mallory (chair of the Senate Committee on Naval Affairs) and Representative Thomas Bocock (chair of the House Naval Affairs Committee), were prominent southerners often associated with expansionism.[25]

Ultimately, both domestic and diplomatic concerns were powerful stimuli in pushing legislation authorizing the additional sloops through Congress. Southern legislators, convinced that shallow-draft sloops offered one possible means to a larger end, crafted an amendment to the 1858 naval appropriations bill for the ten ships requested in Toucey's annual report. They immediately encountered significant opposition from northern congressmen, who could see no benefit in further enlarging the Navy. The northerners probably had enough votes to block passage of the amendment, but fate intervened. The Royal Navy, which maintained its antislaver patrols in the eastern Caribbean, had been stopping more and more American ships in early 1858. What really bothered many Americans was that several of these ships obviously could not have been slavers, so they interpreted the searching of American ships as unwarranted British aggression. Southern navalists seized the opportunity to create a small war scare, and on 12 June 1858 the amendment passed.[26]

Southerners (and the Navy) did not get everything they had hoped for. The final bill authorized eight, not ten, warships, and only seven were the kind of sloop requested by Secretary Toucey. The eighth vessel was a lighter-draft side-wheel steamer explicitly designed for service in China. Still, the end result must have been heartening for advocates of shallow-draft warships capable of operating in coastal waters and harbors. Unlike the earlier sloops, whose draft ranged from sixteen to just over eighteen feet, the law stipulated that the new sloops could not exceed a fourteen-foot draft. Actually, as they were built, four would draw thirteen feet of water and the remaining three only ten feet of water, making them even more versatile than their creators intended. When they entered service, along with the 1854 frigates and 1857 sloops, the United States would possess a balanced, albeit obsolescent, fleet, calling into question recent claims that "naval progress between 1848 and 1860 was piecemeal and uneven." Given the context of the time, especially the economic turmoil, the Navy was doing well.[27]

The law included two other important mandates. First, it required the sloops to carry as heavy an armament as possible, making them more lethal than comparably sized ships in foreign navies. Second, the law decreed that these ships be supplied with "full steam power," making them the first vessels in American naval history to rely on steam for primary, not auxiliary, propulsion. Sails would now take on a secondary role. These last two requirements may have been the result of a report describing British gunboats submitted by John Dahlgren after a tour of British Navy yards to Secretary Toucey. Dahlgren's account, which Toucey included in his 1857 annual report, described even shallower-draft vessels capable of mounting heavy cannon and powered primarily by steam. Dahlgren noted at the time that "this is a class with which we are entirely unprovided," a powerful rejoinder to politicians already nervous about British intentions. The requirement for steam as the primary mode of propulsion certainly reflected some of the professional thinking of the day. For example, in assessing the six steam frigates during their construction, the editors of the *Monthly Nautical Magazine and Quarterly Review* opined that they "were old models, in the general principles, if not in the details." Setting themselves up as champions of progressive design and pointing out recent advances in merchant ship construction, the editors argued that the future belonged to ships relying on steam as the primary, rather than auxiliary, mode of propulsion.[28]

With passage of the appropriations bill on 12 June, the Navy Department sprang into action to take advantage of the windfall. On 26 July, it published an advertisement soliciting proposals for power plants. It called for proposals "for the complete construction of the steam machinery and appendages, and placing the same on board, for each of the screw sloops," outlined the terms contractors could expect in a final contract, and gave a 7 September deadline for submitting designs and cost estimates to the Navy Department. The advertisement also made certain performance and design objectives very clear, specifying minimum horsepower and shaft revolutions, maximum weight of the machinery and coal to power it, and how much space on each sloop would be allotted for the power plant.[29]

The department's advertisement stirred up significant activity among East Coast engine builders. Fourteen contractors submitted forty-seven proposals for the seven power plants. Pleased with the response, Secretary Toucey created a board of engineers on 20 September to examine the proposals and recommend which firms should receive contracts from the government. The board, consisting of Engineer in Chief Samuel Archbold and Chief Engineers W. W. W. Wood, Henry Hunt, and Daniel B. Martin, was required to "report to the department, individually, in writing, which [proposals], in your opinion, . . . should be adopted." The board met immediately and began considering designs and bids, trying to determine the best combination of the two. Four days later they reported back to Secretary Toucey, recommending contractors for six of the seven sloops. There was some confusion over the seventh sloop, one of two to be built at the Philadelphia Navy Yard. Apparently only one of the six bidders had access to the plans of the vessel and realized that it was supposed to have two propellers, not one. The board therefore suggested that all six bidders be given the opportunity to resubmit their proposals based on more complete information. Toucey agreed and informed the contractors of his decision on 2 October.[30]

The first contracts were signed at the end of October 1858. As one might expect, they reflected the Navy's latest experience with the contracting process. In general, the new contracts continued the evolution toward greater control over its contractors by the Navy. Two factors made this shift possible. First, as the Navy gained more experience with both the mechanics of steam engines and working with private companies, it had a better idea of what to expect and how much leeway to give a contractor. Second, the earlier sentiment within the Navy that the service should ultimately build all of its own engines was fading. Steam had become such an integral part of the fleet that the Navy's capacity to supply itself had not kept up with expansion, nor would its capacity to do so increase in the near future. Many officers who carefully considered the problem concluded that it was in the Navy's best interests, especially in time of war, to identify private companies capable of building power plants and develop relationships with them. It was such an important issue that by 1860 the Navy had surveyed the entire country from coast to coast and identified fifty-seven companies in thirty-one cities capable of building marine engines.[31]

The language of the new contracts borrowed heavily from the earlier sloop contracts. Parts of the 1854 frigate contracts that were used for the 1857 sloops showed up yet again. In addition, most of the enhancements

The U.S. Navy and the Origins of the Military-Industrial Complex

made to the 1857 sloop contracts were carried forward to the new contracts as well. For example, clauses dictating the integration of the power plant and boilers with the hull remained, as did the clauses linking progress on the engine to progress on the hull. Similarly, the enhanced powers of the superintending engineer to "condemn any of the work in any stage of progress, either from improper design, improper or bad material or workmanship" remained intact. But there were changes.

The older contracts, both for the 1854 frigates and the 1857 sloops, included mechanical specifications: the diameter and stroke of the engines' cylinders, the aggregate heating surface and grate surface of the boilers, the number and kind of boilers, and, for the 1857 sloops only, the maximum weight allowed for the machinery and boilers. The new sloop contracts went beyond mechanical specifications and included, for the first time, basic performance requirements. For example, the *Seminole*'s contract called for the engine to develop at least 750 horsepower at sea and to make at least eighty revolutions per minute. It then explained the conditions under which the engine would be measured, in this case "by the Indicator on the standard of 3000 pounds lifted one floor high per minute."

Surprisingly, there were also major changes in the payment schedule. For the earlier sloops, contractors had been paid every time they completed an additional quarter of the work. More important, they had been paid a higher percentage of the total contract price at every step of the process, so that when they finished building the power plant, only 20 percent was held in reserve pending a successful three-month trial of the machinery at sea. Ideally, this provided greater cash flow to the contractor throughout the construction process and limited delays caused by lack of funds. The Navy regressed in the 1858 contracts, applying a payment scheme that looked more like the 1854 frigate contracts than its immediate predecessor. The new contract paid one-third of the contract price when half of the work was completed, one-sixth of the contract price when the rest of the work was completed and the machinery delivered, and an additional one-sixth of the contract price when the machinery was installed and had passed a one-week trial. That left a final third of the contract price held as reserve during the three-month trial. These conditions were clearly stated in the advertisement calling for proposals from manufacturers, so there were no surprises, but the contractors must have wondered why they were being punished.

The contract closed with a strong new clause: "It is further agreed that if the weight and other conditions specified in this contract be not complied with the Navy Department to be at liberty to reject the whole machinery, the parties of the first part to be at the expense of taking it out of the Ship and to refund whatever amount of the contract price may have been paid." This dramatically expanded the power of the Navy Department in contractual relations and, in some ways, put contractors on notice. The Navy was going to hold them to the performance claims so casually bandied about in the various proposals soliciting contracts.[32]

The majority of the contract changes seem to have been aimed at one person, Edward N. Dickerson. Frank Bennett facetiously described him as a man "who made the engineering life of the Navy Department exceedingly interesting for a number of years and enriched the annals of scientific experiment not a little, by injecting an element of novelty and humor into otherwise dry and technical matters." Simply put, Dickerson proved to be a continual thorn in the side of the Navy Department. A New York City patent lawyer who had been exposed to steam technology in the course of his practice, Dickerson convinced himself that he possessed natural expertise in matters of steam engineering. As he pored over engineering texts and studied the theoretical physical properties of steam, he concluded that the Navy's engineers were designing and approving faulty power plants. Determined to correct the situation, he set out to persuade the naval establishment of the errors of its ways.[33]

The main point of contention between Dickerson and the Navy was over how much steam it took to most efficiently push a piston down the full length of its enclosing cylinder. As a result of his studies, which assumed that steam behaved the same in the real world as it did in the realm of theory, Dickerson championed the idea that it took relatively little steam to power a piston. If true, an engine based on this concept would be very efficient. The Navy's engineers argued that steam would not approximate its theoretical behavior in the real world because of the inherent mechanical limitations of the current technology.

Ordinarily, someone like Edward Dickerson would have been dismissed for the crank he was. However, he was a very influential crank, whose political connections and alliance with respected inventor Frederick Sickels were brought into play during the issuing of contracts for the 1857 sloops. The end result of his wrangling, which included a promise that engines built on his design would weigh far less than contemporary power plants, was the issuing of a contract on 3 April 1858. This five-thousand-dollar contract called for Dickerson and Sickels to superintend the construction of engines of their design on the sloop *Pensacola,* whose machinery would be built at the Washington Navy Yard. Secretary Toucey tried to prevent the contract from being issued, but Dickerson's political connections proved too strong. Those connections are evident in the terms of the contract. Unlike every other engine contractor at the time, Dickerson and Sickels would be paid in full when the machinery was completed and a one-week trial had been successfully concluded. Their final payment would not be subject to the now customary three-month sea trial.

The Navy's fears were well founded. Construction of the *Pensacola's* engines was not complete by the time of the Civil War. By comparison, the power plants for the other four sloops in its class were completed and installed no later than 1860. To make matters worse, the *Pensacola's* machinery, when finally finished, weighed more than twice as much, 540 tons versus 246.5 tons, as the *Lancaster's.* Late in 1861, Secretary of the Navy Gideon Welles took supervision of the engines' construction away from Dickerson and Sickels. When the ship was finally completed in early 1862 and sent on its sea trials, it proved to be slower than the other ships in its class while burning 25 percent more coal.[34]

The Dickerson fiasco surely galled the Navy Department. The incredible weight of the *Pensacola's* engines must have been immediately obvious to the engineers who looked at the plans, which were filed with the Bureau of Steam Engineering. Even as Dickerson and Sickels began constructing their monstrosities, the Navy did what it could to protect itself in the 1858 sloop contracts. Weight restrictions had been a part of the earlier contracts, but the new closing clause gave the Navy the authority to reject a finished power plant, force the contractor to return all funds, and pay the cost of removing the engines looks like it was written with Dickerson and Sickels in mind. They might even be blamed for the more stringent payment schedule. Even if the Navy could not reject a faulty power plant outright, the new schedule with the increased percentage of total contract price withheld gave the service more leverage in forcing a contractor to address flaws revealed by an extended trial trip.

Even as these contractual refinements were taking shape, the Navy found itself dragged into the messy world of partisan politics. A certain William Norris of Philadelphia submitted a bid for one of the 1858 sloops designated for construction at the Philadelphia Navy Yard. Five other firms also sent in proposals. However, this was the case where only one bidder, who happened to be Norris, understood that the sloop would have two propellers, not one. The Navy sent out corrected plans and allowed all six companies to resubmit proposals, which they did. Before that happened, two of the four members of the Board of Engineers condemned Norris's design as unsuitable. Norris found out about it and asked that a new board be appointed with his detractors removed. Secretary Toucey agreed and replaced the dissenting engineers. Even as he did so, Toucey received a letter from Norris touting the number of votes his firm delivered for the Democrats in the last election and pointing out that his competitors "were most violent working opponents against the present administration." Norris followed up this missive by forwarding letters from prominent Democratic politicians testifying as to his unimpeachable political character.

Only three bids were resubmitted. When the second Board of Engineers met, examined the three proposals, and reported back to Secretary Toucey, it reported that it was split, with two members recommending Norris's engines and two recommending a proposal from Reany, Neafie and Company. After consulting with additional engineers and some deliberation, Toucey awarded the contract to Reany, Neafie and Company. Norris was furious. He charged that the Navy's process of letting contracts was rife with corruption. His claims, which were made as others leveled similar charges against the Navy's purchasing practices, played a part in the appointment of a special congressional committee to investigate the Navy's contract and purchasing procedures a short time later.

From the very beginning of its dealings with private companies, the Navy had recognized that political interference would be detrimental to the contract process. For that reason, every contract issued in the 1850s contained a clause, mandated by law, similar to this one found in the 1858 sloop contracts:

> And the same parties of the first part do further engage and contract that no Member of Congress, Officer of the Navy, or any person holding office or appointment under the Navy Department shall be admitted to any share or part of this Contract or Agreement or to any benefit to arise therefrom; and it is hereby expressly provided and this contract is upon this express condition that is any such member of Congress,

Officer of the Navy or other person above named shall be admitted to any share or part of this contract or to any benefit to arise under it or in case the parties of the first part shall in any respect fail to perform this contract on their part the same may be at the option of the United States declared null and void without affecting their right to recover for defaults which may have occurred.

The Navy took this very seriously, for its continued expansion depended on maintaining support both across the political spectrum and from administration to administration. Even the secretaries, who were political appointees, recognized the importance of impartiality.

In the end, the Navy acquitted itself rather well in the congressional investigation. The majority report found "that politics had no effect whatever in determining this result" and that the various contracts "have been carefully, impartially, and stringently made, and with a view only to carry out, in letter and spirit, and at the lowest practicable cost, the provisions of law which directed the construction of these vessels." The minority report attacked both Secretary Toucey and President Buchanan, alleging that they "have set an example dangerous to the public safety." Significantly, however, the minority report did not take the Navy's engineers to task for partisanship. The only engineer singled out was Daniel Martin, whose patented boiler design showed up in several of the proposals. The minority censured him for sitting on a board by whose outcome he stood to profit. John Sherman of Ohio was one of the two minority members. In his memoirs, he claimed victory because Congress insisted on reforms in the Navy's purchasing practices during its next session. He chose to ignore alleged flaws in the contract process, perhaps because the partisanship claimed by Norris did not have an impact on the recommendations of the Navy's professional engineers. Based on the documentary record, it is safe to conclude that the Navy's contract procedures, at least in the case of power plants and hulls, worked.[35]

Despite the unwanted attention of a congressional investigation, the Navy successfully settled a number of issues with the 1857 and 1858 sloop contracts and, with the notable exception of the *Pensacola,* got the kind of warships it wanted with the performance characteristics it wanted. The 1857 *Hartford*-class sloops, for example, received praise from both within and without the Navy. Chief Engineer Benjamin Franklin Isherwood, the

Navy's resident expert who seldom minced words in analyzing the performance of steam power plants, declared after an exhaustive survey of the *Brooklyn's* steam logs that "the details [of the engines] . . . have worked well and given great satisfaction." Englishman Hans Busk's 1859 survey, *The Navies of the World*, refused to give too high of praise to the U.S. Navy but allowed that "unquestionably the most efficient class of sailing-vessels they now possess are those rated under the denomination of sloops of war." The 1858 sloops seem to have performed just as well. After a thorough analysis of the Navy's antebellum steamers, Donald Canney concluded that "in the sloops of war of 1858, the navy obtained the most versatile and reliable ships of the entire wooden steamer era, and among the longest lasting."[36]

As the decade drew to a close, the Navy could take pride in its developing relationship with private industry. It had defined a contract process that seemed to work well and was working more and more with an established group of contractors on the nation's eastern seaboard. Little did the Navy realize that its procedures would soon be put to the ultimate test: wartime production. War, by its very nature, puts undue stress on institutions designed to function most efficiently during peacetime, sometimes causing them to work against the very purpose for which they were created. The Navy and its administrative apparatus proved no exception, as quickly became apparent.

4

The Union and
Ironclad Warships, 1861

America's Civil War, contrary to popular belief, did not create a revolution in naval design. At best, the sectional conflict provided "a rich testing ground for the technology of modern war." European navies, especially those of Great Britain and France, took the lead during the preceding decade in exploring experimental technologies. These wary rivals supplied the needed financial backing and industrial support for the pioneering work in armor, ordnance, and ship design that so dramatically altered the composition of the world's navies by 1860. The 1850s witnessed the widespread introduction of the shell gun, rifled artillery, steam and screw propulsion, armored batteries, and iron-hulled vessels. Great Britain and France each embarked on ambitious building programs designed to replace their obsolescent wooden ships with vessels incorporating the latest in naval technology. The pivotal vessel for each was the French *Gloire,* launched in November 1859, and the British *Warrior,* launched in December 1860.[1]

The ongoing revolution in naval design had not gone unnoticed or unheeded in the United States. Secretary of the Navy Abel P. Upshur called for the construction of an iron-hulled vessel as early as 1841. At least three were built but proved unsatisfactory, and ships of this type soon fell into disfavor among American (and European) navalists. The threat of war with Great Britain in 1841–42 over the Maine–New Brunswick boundary prompted the issuing of a contract for the first American armored vessel to Robert L. Stevens. This armored steamer, unfinished at the outbreak of the Civil War in 1861, underwent fits and starts of construction throughout the 1840s and

1850s and was the only serious American attempt to build an armored warship during that time.[2]

Congress viewed the expanded British and French fleets with some trepidation throughout the 1850s, and these fears played an important role in the authorization and construction of the *Merrimack* and its sister ships, as well as the sloops built later in the decade. The Senate Committee on Naval Affairs, with the assistance of the secretary of the Navy, produced a report in January 1859 assessing the needs of the United States Navy against the capabilities of the Royal Navy, considered the potential opponent. This report, taking recent technological advances into consideration, came to a number of conclusions. It recognized that "within the last fifteen years the application of steam as a motive power to naval vessels; their improved armament of heavy guns, equally applicable to shot and shell; their increased size and improved models, have revolutionized the character of naval warfare, and diminished, in a remarkable manner, the inequality between frigates and forts." Acknowledging the inability to compete with the British in terms of quantity, the report suggested that "in construction and equipment we must keep fully up with the times," with each newly constructed vessel being an improvement on its predecessor, not only in the U.S. Navy but also in the Royal Navy. Although the American naval establishment was aware of British experiments with armor and included information about several ironclad batteries in an appendix to the report, the report itself focused on the more pressing problem of applying adequate steam propulsion to the fleet, a process that had begun in all earnestness with the authorization of the six steam frigates in 1854. Accordingly, the committee recommended the construction of ten wooden steam ships of war, not realizing that technology, in the form of the *Gloire* and *Warrior*, would make them, along with the rest of the steam fleet, second-class vessels before they were ever built.[3]

The crashing of Confederate shells into the masonry walls of Fort Sumter forced the Department of the Navy to rethink its strategic mission. The Confederate States, not Great Britain, would be the immediate foe. On 15 April 1861, President Abraham Lincoln issued a call for seventy-five thousand volunteers to put down the rebellion. Confederate president Jefferson Davis, responding two days later, authorized the issuance of letters of marque by the Confederate States of America. Lincoln countered with proclamations on the nineteenth and the twenty-seventh declaring a formal naval blockade of the Southern coast. The Union Navy, which boasted only forty-two commissioned vessels, thus became responsible for blockading 3,549 statute miles of coastline and more than 180 navigable harbors and inlets.[4]

Needless to say, ironclad construction was not a priority during the first months of the war. Secretary of the Navy Gideon Welles concerned himself with the most pressing problems first, which meant securing the defense of the nation's capital. Steamers had to be leased or purchased to transport troops. Lincoln's proclamations also meant that Welles had to oversee the improvisation of a blockading fleet. Any available vessel capable of mounting the necessary ordnance was quickly pressed into service and posted to Southern waters. Hundreds of new sailors had to be clothed, fed, and trained. In short, Welles faced a logistical nightmare that defied simple solutions. As in most wars, both sides predicted a speedy victory that would not justify the time and expense needed to design and build these unproven ironclad behemoths. John Lenthall, chief of the Bureau of Construction and Repair, emphasized this point to Welles when he suggested on 11 May that "the necessarily large size, the cost and the time required for building an iron cased steam vessel is such that it is not recommended to adopt any plan at present." It would take an extraordinary turn of events to modify the Navy's pragmatic decision. Such a turn was not long in coming.[5]

The Gosport Navy Yard, near Norfolk, became an important early casualty to Southern secession. Fearful of provoking secession in neutral Virginia, President Lincoln did not fill the patronage jobs in the Navy yard with Unionists when he assumed office. In an effort to pacify the already precarious situation, he kept the current staff, primarily Southern Democrats, in their positions. The president and the Navy Department had two causes of concern. First and foremost, the Gosport Navy Yard was the most important facility of its kind in the United States. Its dry dock, ship houses, foundries, machine shops, and boiler shops were among the most modern in the Navy. The loss of this capacity would hurt the Union war effort. Second, the USS *Merrimack* awaited engine repairs in the yard. Lengthy cruises had taken their toll on its underpowered machinery; the power plant would not withstand further sea duty. The frigate carried two 10-inch pivot Dahlgren guns, fourteen 8-inch carriage guns, and twenty-four 9-inch Dahlgren guns, making it one of the most formidable Union naval vessels afloat. If it fell into Confederate hands, the vessel would present an instant threat to the blockade.[6]

A Virginia convention passed an ordinance of secession on 17 April

1861. Even though the ordinance would not be ratified by voters until the twenty-third, the state militia immediately took steps to secure important Federal facilities, especially the Harper's Ferry armory and the Gosport Navy Yard. On 18 April, the Southern officers stationed at Norfolk resigned as a body. The Virginia state militia seized Fort Norfolk, the Navy's powder magazine, the next day. Up to five thousand militia were rumored to be in the vicinity, bent on confiscating valuable Federal assets for their cause. Commo. Charles S. McCauley, commandant of the Navy yard, moved about in a befuddled state doubtlessly exaggerated by his advanced age and proclivity for alcohol. Although the *Merrimack*'s engines had been repaired since the eighteenth, McCauley not only refused permission for the vessel to leave for a safer port but also prevented its broadside armament from being put on board ship.[7]

Secretary Welles, kept informed of the situation in Norfolk, "became satisfied that the large amount of public property there was in a precarious condition. As a preventative, or matter of caution, it seemed to me advisable that a military force should be placed there to protect the yard, and to serve as a rallying point for Union men in case of emergency." Despite the initial objections of Gen. Winfield Scott and members of the cabinet, Welles dispatched an expedition under the command of Commo. Hiram Paulding to relieve McCauley and prevent Federal supplies from falling into the hands of the insurrectionists. However, just a few hours before the expedition arrived in Norfolk McCauley panicked and ordered the yard's guns spiked and the *Merrimack* scuttled. By the time Paulding landed, the once proud vessel had taken on too much water to be salvaged quickly. Rumors of the rapidly concentrating militia continually filtered in, and on the evening of 20 April a nervous Commodore Paulding decided to destroy the yard's remaining facilities and evacuate its garrison to Washington. Powder trains were laid to many of the dockyard facilities and remaining ships, including the *Merrimack*. Amid some confusion the trains were lit and the last members of the relief expedition withdrew to their waiting vessels. The ensuing conflagration lit up the night sky as Paulding's force withdrew to Washington, satisfied they had achieved their objective of destroying any property that might be of use to the Confederates.[8]

Unbeknownst to the retreating Yankees, their efforts failed to have the desired effect. Despite the spectacular blaze and resounding explosions, many valuable facilities remained untouched or only partially damaged. The Con-

The U.S. Navy and the Origins of the Military-Industrial Complex

federacy inherited vast quantities of naval stores, machinery, and tools. The yard's graving dock, required for the maintenance of ships' hulls, survived intact. More important, Norfolk's forges and foundries, which would play such a crucial role in the coming months, entered Confederate service fully functional. Somehow the retreating Federals neglected to put them to the torch. Above all, the most impressive acquisition lay partially submerged on the bottom of the James River. McCauley's decision to scuttle the *Merrimack* inadvertently saved the most valuable part of the ship. Even though fire destroyed its upper works, the hull and machinery remained untouched and still usable. All the vessel required was the application of ingenuity and vision.[9]

Fortunately for the South, Confederate Secretary of the Navy Stephen R. Mallory recognized the importance of the emerging ironclad technology. As a member of the Senate Committee on Naval Affairs before the war, he had kept abreast of European developments, especially after the success of French ironclad batteries at Kinburn during the Crimean War. While still quartered in Montgomery, Alabama, he sent a letter, dated 10 May 1861, outlining his hopes for the new Navy to Charles M. Conrad, the chairman of the Committee on Naval Affairs. In it, Mallory noted,

> I regard the possession of an iron-armored ship as a matter of the first necessity. Such a vessel at this time could traverse the entire coast of the United States, prevent all blockades, and encounter, with a fair prospect of success, their entire Navy.
>
> If to cope with them upon the sea we follow their example and build wooden ships, we shall have to construct several at one time; for one or two ships would fall an easy prey to her comparatively numerous steam frigates. But inequality of numbers may be compensated by invulnerability; and thus not only does economy but naval success dictate the wisdom and expediency of fighting with iron against wood, without regard to first cost.

Mallory knew the South did not currently possess the industrial capacity to build such a vessel. He closed his letter to Conrad by assuring the chairman that "an agent of the department will leave for England in a day or two, charged with the duty of purchasing vessels, and by him the first steps in the matter may be taken."[10]

Not content to rely on efforts to obtain ironclads abroad, Mallory, having moved to Richmond with the rest of the government, broached the idea

The Union and Ironclad Warships

of a domestically built ironclad to Lt. John M. Brooke. Cognizant of the Confederacy's limited industrial capacity, Brooke came up with a simple casemate design in the middle of June. This design, modified after consultation with John L. Porter, a constructor at the Gosport Navy Yard, became the basic plan for many of the Confederate ironclads built during the course of the war. Informed by the Tredegar Iron Works in Richmond that engines for such a craft were beyond its capabilities, the designers searched for alternatives. Confederate chief engineer William P. Williamson suggested they try to salvage what they could from the *Merrimack,* which had been freed from its resting place on 30 May by the Baker Wrecking Company. Porter and Brooke agreed that their design could be modified to fit the *Merrimack's* hull and submitted a report to Mallory on 25 June recommending that course of action. Revised plans were presented to the secretary on 10 July, and on that same day he authorized the conversion of the hulk into an ironclad warship.[11]

Rumors of a Confederate ironclad made their way around Washington. Whether or not these rumors were true, they prompted not only speculation, but also action. As early as 24 June, Congress passed a joint resolution instructing Secretary Welles to investigate the possibility of completing the Stevens Battery. Welles duly appointed a board whose report, issued at the end of the year, recommended against any further expenditures by the government toward what seemed to be a financial sinkhole. The battery returned to its intermittent retirement after briefly raising its head, not appearing again until after the war.[12]

President Lincoln called Congress together for a special session that began on 4 July. At this time, Welles, drawing upon material gathered by Cdr. John A. Dahlgren, presented a report describing the current condition of the Union Navy and offering suggestions for its improvement. The secretary noted that "other governments, and particularly France and England, have made [ironclad steamers] a special object in connexion with naval improvements." He conceded that "the period is, perhaps, not one best adapted to heavy expenditures by way of experiment, and the time and attention of some of those who are most competent to investigate and form correct conclusions on this subject are otherwise employed." Nevertheless, he recommended "the appointment of a proper and competent board to inquire into and report in regard to a measure so important." The secretary's report closed by requesting permission to proceed with the construction of ironclad vessels if the board's investigation found them feasible.[13]

Welles knew it would take more than a report to get Congress to seriously consider this radical new technology. He called on the services of a young Connecticut businessman named Cornelius Bushnell whom he had known from his days as a Hartford newspaper editor. Bushnell possessed more experience and wisdom than his thirty-two years belied. He had gone to work on a small coastal vessel at age fifteen and earned his own command, a sixty-ton schooner, one year later. After five successful years at sea, he entered into the wholesale and retail grocery business with his brother, Nathan Townsend Bushnell. In 1858, he became interested in the foundering New Haven and New London Railroad, a local line on the verge of bankruptcy. He applied himself to the problem, connected the railroad to larger lines in the east, restored its financial integrity, and was rewarded for his efforts with the presidency of the line. During his years with the railroad, Bushnell learned how to grease the legislative wheels at both the state and national levels, essential skills for the task ahead. Welles provided him with a copy of the proposed bill, which Bushnell began lobbying for almost immediately.[14]

Bushnell focused his efforts on Sen. James W. Grimes of the Committee on Naval Affairs, who, with some encouragement, took up Welles's cause. Prompted by a Navy Department that not only heard rumors of Confederate ironclads with trepidation but also cast a wary eye toward European intervention, the senator from Iowa reminded his colleagues that "however valueless or valuable armored ships may be as cruisers, they certainly are destined to be valuable for the defense of harbors." Therefore, he introduced a bill on 19 July authorizing $1.5 million "to provide for the construction of one or more armored ships."[15]

The bill faced a bitter two-week struggle, during which time the Stevens lobby desperately tried to amend the act's wording so their pet project would receive $812,000 of the allocated amount. After several passionate floor debates, Grimes outmaneuvered the opposition and arranged for the appointment of a special "commission of experienced officers" to examine "the condition and probable value" of the unfinished battery and report back to the Congress the next session with its recommendations, after which separate funding would be considered once again. This effectively dealt the

Stevens Battery its final blow and preserved the intent of the original bill. Congress approved the act on 3 August 1861, authorizing Welles "to appoint a board of three skilful naval officers to investigate the plans and specifications that may be submitted for the construction or completing of iron or steel-clad steamships or steam batteries." The act also appropriated the requested $1.5 million for ironclad construction should the board's report be favorable, signifying the Union's continued interest in the developing race for naval supremacy of the eastern seaboard.[16]

Secretary Welles, having received the necessary authorization from Congress, initiated a series of actions designed to achieve timely results. Deciding that the already overworked government Navy yards would not be responsible for construction of the first ironclads, he turned to the private sector. On 7 August he published an advertisement soliciting

> offers from parties who are able to execute work of this kind, and who are engaged in it, of which they will furnish evidence with their offer, for the construction of one or more iron-clad steam vessels of war, either of iron or of wood and iron combined, for sea or river service, to be of not less than ten nor over sixteen feet draught of water; to carry an armament of from eighty to one hundred and twenty tons weight, with provisions and stores for from one hundred and sixty-five to three hundred persons, according to armament, for sixty days, with coal for eight days. The smaller draught of water, compatible with other requisites, will be preferred. The vessel to be rigged with two masts, with wire-rope standing rigging, to navigate at sea.
>
> A general description and drawings of the vessel, armor, and machinery, such as the work can be executed from, will be required.
>
> The offer must state the cost and the time for completing the whole, exclusive of armament and stores of all kinds, the rate of speed proposed, and must be accompanied by a guarantee for the proper execution of the contract, if awarded.
>
> Persons who intend to offer are requested to inform the department of their intention before the 15th August, instant, and to have their propositions presented within twenty-five days from this date.[17]

Having made his wishes known to Northern industry, Welles prepared his department for the task ahead.

The day after publishing this announcement, Welles appointed three naval officers members of a board to assess proposals received. The secretary originally approached John Lenthall, chief of the Bureau of Construction and Repair, to oversee the selection and construction process. Despite the rumors of Confederate ironclad construction, Lenthall, like most of the other bureau chiefs, remained skeptical of these experimental vessels. He exempted himself from the board by claiming that his bureau was already taxed to its limits. Welles then designated Commo. Joseph Smith, chief of the Bureau of Yards and Docks and a close personal friend, as senior officer of the board. To aid Smith, the secretary appointed two assistants: Commo. Hiram Paulding, the man who burned the Gosport Navy Yard, and Cdr. John Dahlgren. Dahlgren asked Welles to relieve him from duties with the board, probably because Dahlgren's work with ordnance already occupied most of his time. In his place, Welles appointed Cdr. Charles H. Davis. The board was ordered to "convene at the Navy Department as early as practicable, and . . . make a written report of the result of its investigations of the subject."[18]

The board met for the first time on 5 September and began working its way through the incoming proposals. On 16 September the naval officers submitted their "Report on Iron Clad Vessels" to Secretary Welles. Admitting at the outset that they had "no experience and but scanty knowledge in this branch of naval architecture," they considered it "very likely that some of our conclusions may prove erroneous." Smith had requested the services of Samuel H. Pook, a naval constructor, to act as a technical adviser on 2 September. However, neither Pook nor any other constructor was available at the time, forcing the officers to draw upon their own experience and the reports of others.[19]

Before making its final recommendations, the board briefly examined the current debate over armored warships. Two schools of thought dominated the discussion within naval circles. The first envisioned ironclads in a coastal and harbor defense role, usually in conjunction with shore-based fortifications. The board acknowledged the utility of such vessels, noting that "for river and harbor service we consider iron-clad vessels of light draught, or floating batteries thus shielded, as very important; and we feel at this moment the necessity of them on some of our rivers and inlets to enforce obedience to the laws." However, the board also recognized the limitations of these vessels, especially against fortified emplacements ashore.[20]

The second school, primarily composed of members of the British and French naval establishments, thought that ironclad steamers represented the future of oceangoing cruisers. The board was "skeptical as to their advantage and ultimate adoption." They listed a number of disadvantages inherent to ironclad construction, including "the enormous load of iron, as so much additional weight to the vessel; the great breadth of beam necessary to give her stability; the short supply of coal she will be able to stow in bunkers; the great power required to propel her; and the largely increased cost of construction." While acknowledging the primacy of ironclads in ship to ship combat, they pointed out that the greater speed of wooden cruisers allowed those vessels to pick and choose their fields of battle. Despite their disinclination toward ironclad cruisers, the board remained conscious of French and British efforts, noting "whilst other nations are endeavoring to perfect them, we must not remain idle."[21]

Smith, Paulding, and Davis grappled not only with what kinds of ironclads to build but also where to build them. Ordnance tests conducted in Europe and the United States indicated that these vessels required at least four and a half inches of iron plate to resist fire from standard naval armaments. Unfortunately, there were no mills in the United States capable of rolling plates of that thickness. Plates of four and a half inches could be hammered out, but rolled plates proved more resilient to shot and shell. English contractors possessed both the requisite rolling machinery and the shipbuilding expertise needed by the Union Navy. However, the board voiced two objections to signing contracts with the English. First, "a difficulty might arise with the British government in case we should undertake to construct ships-of-war in that country." Second, and perhaps more important, "we are of opinion that every people or nation who can maintain a navy should be capable of constructing it themselves."[22]

The naval board ultimately adopted a pragmatic construction strategy based on the requirements of the current conflict and the vessels of foreign navies. The board recognized that current demands required "vessels invulnerable to shot, of light draught of water, to penetrate our shoal harbors, rivers and bayous" and recommended "the construction of this class of vessels before going into a more perfect system of large iron-clad sea-going vessels of war." Although uncertain of the ability of such vessels to bear the necessary armor, the board bowed to necessity and advised that they be built. Meanwhile, they suggested that the United States carefully observe the progress of the British and the French in ironclad construction so that larger and more technologically advanced vessels could be built when circumstances permitted.[23]

Secretary Welles, reviewing the board's actions for Congress in December 1861, acknowledged the obstacles faced during the selection process. He noted that "the difficulty of combining the two qualities of light draught and iron armor, both of which are wanted for service on our coast, could not be entirely overcome; but the board, in this new branch of naval architecture, has, I think, displayed great practical wisdom." The vessels finally chosen reflected different schools of naval thought, producing a true light-draft ironclad, a prototype cruiser capable of dealing with the *Gloire* and the *Warrior*, and a hybrid gunboat that never quite found its own identity.[24]

In the eleven days between the board's first meeting and the issuing of the "Report on Iron Clad Vessels," seventeen proposals underwent the scrutiny of these officers. The board, which was skeptical to begin with, rejected the majority of the proposals. In several cases, the board doubted a design's technical merits. So, for example, John Nystrom's proposal was shelved because "the plan of (quadruple) guns is not known." Other proposals, such as those submitted by Whitney and Rowland and William Perine of New York City, and John Westwood of Cincinnati, were set aside because the board seriously doubted whether or not the finished vessels would float. Still others were not considered because the potential contractors did not submit preliminary sketches, models, dimensions, or prices. A proposal from William Kingsley of Washington, D.C., was rejected out of hand because he offered to build a rubber-clad warship. That was too much for a board still questioning the merits of ironclad vessels. As ridiculous and incomplete as some of these proposals look in hindsight, they reflected the aura of confusion surrounding ironclad construction at the time.

Five proposals emerged from the screening process with qualified recommendations. The board shelved two of them because of their estimated cost. The board was impressed by a proposal submitted by E. S. Renwick of New York, which seemed to meet all of their needs. His vessel was "of large capacity and powerful engines, with great speed, capable of carrying a heavy battery, and stated to be shot-proof and a good sea-boat." Unfortunately, this came at a high price. Renwick affixed a price of $1.5 million to his plan (equal to the entire amount allocated by Congress). Donald McKay of Boston, famous for designing clipper ships, submitted a plan that the board found generally acceptable, although they thought the ship might be a bit slower in speed than they would like. McKay thought it could be built for $1 million. The board rejected both as too expensive and recommended that the remaining three proposals be issued contracts.[25]

The first recommended proposal, submitted by John Ericsson of New York, was for "a floating battery . . . based upon a plan which will render the battery shot and shell proof." Although unconvinced of the vessel's seaworthiness, two of the three board members were so intrigued by the design that they authorized its construction. The result was the USS *Monitor*, which gave its name to a new type of ship. The second proposal, tendered by Merrick and Sons of Philadelphia, was considered "the most practical one for heavy armor" by the board. This belt and battery vessel, similar in armor and displacement to the *Gloire* and *Warrior*, had the highest price of the three accepted ships: $780,000. The traditional lines of the proposed vessel must have provided some comfort to the members of the board, on whose shoulders rested the fate of the Union Navy. Christened the USS *New Ironsides*, this ship participated in more engagements and fired more shots than any other Civil War ironclad.[26]

The final accepted proposal, proffered by C. S. Bushnell and Company of New Haven, Connecticut, called for an ironclad armored on the rail and plate principle. The board expressed caution over this design, fearing "that she will not float her armor and load sufficiently high, and have stability enough for a sea vessel." They nevertheless recommended that the ship be built, as long as it overcame these objections. Accordingly, on 27 September 1862, the United States, represented by Gideon Welles, entered into a contract with Cornelius S. Bushnell and Henry L. Bushnell for "an Iron-Clad vessel upon the principle of iron rails and iron plates . . . [to] be completed and delivered at the Navy Yard, New York in four months from the date of this contract ready for trial."[27]

It was one thing to award contracts for ironclads, quite another to build them. All three contractors faced interesting technical challenges in designing and manufacturing an effective system of iron cladding. They were handicapped by an iron industry that had long been developing but had not yet reached full maturity. The technology they needed, as had been the case with steam engines a decade before, was still in its infancy. Still, the American iron industry had come a long way. At the beginning of the nineteenth century, the majority of iron was manufactured using a two-step smelting

The U.S. Navy and the Origins of the Military-Industrial Complex

and refining process that depended on local supplies of ore and charcoal. The predominantly agricultural economy of the time dictated the type of items produced. Most ironworks catered to local needs, fabricating cast-iron utensils and their principle product, the bar iron used by blacksmiths. Because of the high start-up cost associated with such an enterprise, they were often owned by partnerships. Still, by 1860 ironworks "were in production for a time at least in every state east of the Mississippi, except for three in the Deep South, as well as in several states of the trans-Mississippi West."[28]

The introduction of rolling and puddling technology changed the character of the industry. Although traditional ironworks continued to manufacture their wares, the cutting edge of the industry moved to more urban facilities that utilized anthracite coal for production and the developing transportation infrastructure to distribute goods. First the rolling mills and then the blast furnaces gravitated toward the cities as the scale of many operations jumped dramatically. The expense of the new technology also facilitated this shift; more investors could be found in urban areas. The addition of these investors, many of them shrewd businessmen interested in securing sources of supply for their own ventures, helped foster modernization. Production figures reflected increasing technical sophistication. The scattered ironworks around the United States manufactured 113,000 tons of hammered and rolled iron goods in 1830. That figure increased to more than 500,000 tons just before the outbreak of hostilities in 1861.[29]

The emerging iron industry concentrated itself in western Pennsylvania, which had plentiful supplies of anthracite coal and access to the network of ore-carrying steamships and railroads that linked the recently developed Lake Superior ores to the hungry mills. Between 1830 and 1840, production in Pennsylvania quintupled. By 1847, it had more than doubled again. By 1860, Pennsylvania manufactured almost 60 percent of the iron ore produced in the United States, Ohio and New York also adding sizable quantities. Allegheny County, Pennsylvania, which made more iron than any other county in the United States in 1858, produced about 90,000 tons. New York churned out 74,645 tons from fifteen furnaces in 1860, mostly located in the southern highlands and the Lake Champlain region. Significantly, Rennselaer County, New York, where the iron for both the *Monitor* and the *Galena* was processed and refined, produced about 30,000 tons of iron in 1858, the second highest total in the country.[30]

The iron industry did not develop and mature in isolation. The ready availability of large quantities of iron meant that a number of related industries rose into prominence during this period. Like the iron industry, they tended to concentrate in the Middle Atlantic States around Pennsylvania. The key offshoot industry related to the construction of the three ironclads was steam technology. American industry expanded too fast to continue to rely on traditional sources of power, especially water. The introduction of efficient cost-effective steam engines released manufacturers from dependence on running water to power their enterprises and allowed them to expand to potentially lucrative areas that had been closed to them for logistical reasons.[31]

The original steam engine developed in England by James Watt at the close of the eighteenth century worked on the basis of low pressure, which limited the amount of work it could perform. The Watt engine "was a heavy and complicated mechanism, costly to build and difficult to maintain and keep in repair." An American engineer named Oliver Evans, who operated two production facilities in Philadelphia and Pittsburgh, tackled the problem after the turn of the century and created an engine capable of operation at much higher pressures, thereby increasing the amount of work an engine of a given size could perform. It was simpler to build than the Watt engine, easier to maintain, lighter, and cost less. As a result, it revolutionized American industry and transportation. The most powerful engines were placed on the steamboats that plied the Atlantic coast and the inland river system. By the time of the Civil War, more than thirty-five hundred steamboats had been built. Although their safety record was dubious at times, the sheer number of engines produced ensured a vibrant industry open to experimentation and continued improvement of design. That experimentation had an important side effect; iron rolling required equally powerful engines, which large foundries introduced into their establishments in the 1850s.[32]

Despite the steady progress in industrial capabilities that had been made in the iron industry before the Civil War, when the conflict began Northern industry could not produce iron plates as thick as those manufactured in Europe. From a practical standpoint, this troubled those contemplating American ironclads in the summer of 1861. British and French tests during the latter half of the 1850s concluded that only plates at least four and a half inches thick could resist the naval ordnance of the day. However, the manufacture of plates this thick was still a relatively complicated process

The U.S. Navy and the Origins of the Military-Industrial Complex

not yet achieved in the United States. *Scientific American* explained the process, "a matter of greater difficulty than those unacquainted with the work would imagine," to its readers in the spring of 1862: "A pile of four plates," each two and a half inches thick, "is heated in a special furnace . . . and is drawn out by a liberating chain . . . on to an iron carriage, which conveys the pile to the rolls. . . . As the plate passes through the rolls it is received on the other side upon a roller frame." This receiving frame was inclined, so that when the iron had gone through the rolls, the rolls could be reversed and the iron would go back through to the carriage. The carriage took the iron back to the furnace where the entire process was repeated "until the 10 inches thickness is reduced to 4½ inches." The rolled plate was lifted off the carriage by a crane onto a slab of cast iron, where an iron cylinder weighing nine tons was rolled over it "until the curvature which the plate has acquired in the rolling is entirely removed." Finally, the crane removed the plate and put it onto a planing machine "where the final operation of planing its sides and ends is completed."[33]

Neither the North nor the South, for that matter, possessed a rolling mill capable of producing four-and-a-half-inch plate in 1861. The armor schemes of both the *Galena* and the *Monitor*, which relied on laminating thinner sections of armor together, were designed to circumvent that technical problem while providing an equivalent amount of protection. Although the *New Ironsides* would be armored with four-and-a-half-inch plates, it would not be delivered to the Navy until September 1862, several months after the first two ironclads joined the fleet. The resulting interval gave industry time to convert its machinery to produce plates of the required thickness. However, given the uncertainties of wartime, the Navy demanded delivery of the new ironclads sooner rather than later, justifying the acceptance of laminated armor. Besides, not all contemporary experts agreed with the British and French about the superiority of thick plates over laminated armor. Laminated armor proved more resistant to the low velocity, heavy weight ordnance loads used by both the Union and the Confederate navies, while the thicker European plates were better suited against the higher velocity shells and shot used by the British and French navies. In any case, conventional wisdom had not yet decided which plating was clearly superior. The question was still open, not to be solved until the theories that were so passionately argued were put to the test of war.[34]

Despite its obvious shortcomings and the technical challenges looming on the horizon, by the beginning of the Civil War American industry showed great promise for the daunting task ahead. A recognizable industrial base was taking shape in the Northeast in the form of iron mills, machine shops, and other business endeavors. Although some aspects may not have been as refined as in Europe, especially with regard to specific products, the United States possessed a fluid and dynamic industrial base eager to accept the challenges of innovation required by the impending conflict. The peacetime pace of construction typified by even the relatively rapid building of the frigates and sloops of the 1850s would no longer suffice; the Navy needed serviceable warships as soon as possible. The nation's booming industrial sector presented a possible solution to the immediate problem. The Union recognized this, which made the marriage of convenience between the Navy and private industry plausible, if not inevitable.

James C. Dobbin of North Carolina, who served as secretary of the
Navy from 8 March 1853 to 6 March 1857.

U.S. Naval Historical Center

The frigate *Minnesota,* one of six frigates authorized in 1854.

U.S. Naval Historical Center

The sloop *Pensacola* in 1861, with its Dickerson-designed engines still not finished.

National Archives

The ironclad *Galena*, ill-fated competitor of *Monitor* and *New Ironsides*.
U.S. Naval Historical Center

Commo. Joseph Smith, longtime chief of the Bureau of Yards and Docks.

A ninety-day gunboat built early in the Civil War.
U.S. Naval Historical Center

A double-ended gunboat built during the Civil War.
U.S. Naval Historical Center

A *Canonicus*-class monitor, the high point of wartime monitor design.

U.S. Naval Historical Center

The light-draft monitor *Casco*, used here as a torpedo boat.

U.S. Naval Historical Center

The commerce destroyer *Tennessee*, whose engines were rebuilt after
the Civil War by John Roach.

U.S. Naval Historical Center

The cruiser *Chicago,* one of the Navy's first four steel warships.
U.S. Naval Historical Center

5   Confronting Reality

The Problems of Wartime Construction, 1861–1862

Building the *Monitor, New Ironsides,* and *Galena* provided valuable experience that would be applied to future naval contracts as the government groped its way through the murky waters of wartime procurement. Clearly, the timetables that had seemed acceptable during the building of antebellum warships no longer applied; ships now had to be constructed in months, not years. Transforming the specifications of the first ironclad contracts with the United States government into reality presented Northern industry with a tremendous challenge. Despite the occasional work on the Stevens Battery and the few iron-hulled vessels built during the previous twenty years, no discernible pool of shipwrights and contractors skilled in the art of ironclad construction existed in the Union. Fortunately for the North, its industrial base proved dynamic and responsive to wartime exigencies, adapting reasonably well to the task at hand. Even in the case of the *Galena,* whose construction history was easily the most troubled of the three vessels and which therefore will be explored in the most detail, industry ultimately fabricated a product that met the intent of the contract, if not most of the terms.

As required under the conditions of the advertisement published by the Navy Department on 7 August 1862, Cornelius Bushnell had informed the service of his intention to seek a contract before the fifteenth of that month. However, building an ironclad was an expensive proposition and a technical challenge. Bushnell, who became involved in a number of shipbuilding projects in the early years of the war, needed partners to help absorb the risk and provide additional expertise and access to materials. Barely one week after the Navy solicited offers and designs for ironclads,

Bushnell and his brother entered into a formal agreement with John F. Winslow and John A. Griswold of the Rensselaer Iron Works of Troy, New York. The partners resolved "to construct an iron clad steam vessel of war upon their own plan," sharing in the risks and rewards.[1]

The government's contract with the new partnership was an interesting variation on both its antebellum contracts with private firms and its first wartime contracts for more conventional warships, the so-called ninety-day gunboats, whose terms are explained in the next chapter. In many ways, the agreement with C. S. Bushnell and Company looked very familiar. Certain sections were taken directly from the sloop contracts of the late 1850s. First, it strictly defined the amount of time allotted for construction of the ironclad, "four months from the date of this contract ready for trial" in this case. Second, it also defined performance objectives, mandating a minimum speed in smooth water carrying a specified amount of coal. Third, attached to the contract were three sets of specifications, one for the hull, a second for the power plant, and the third for the armor. Attached specifications had been a part of all the Navy's contracts during the 1850s. Next, the contract gave the Navy a lien on the vessel in case Bushnell and Company defaulted. Finally, the agreement sported the standard prohibition against any "member of Congress, officer of the Navy, or any person holding any office or appointment under the Navy Department" from holding shares in the vessel or gaining any personal benefit from its construction. If such improprieties occurred, the government could unilaterally declare the agreement null and void.

Other parts of the contract looked familiar but were adjusted to compensate for the potential vagaries of ironclad construction. As it had in the past, the Navy would assign a superintendent to the project. While the superintendent had the traditional "right to reject any of the materials and work which shall not be of the best quality," the prewar clause allowing him to do the same because of "improper design" was removed, perhaps because the issue of proper versus improper design of ironclad armor was still so uncertain. In fact, as the construction process got under way, Commo. Joseph Smith expressly released Bushnell from design flaws in the armor, writing him that "if the armor of the vessel is destroyed, it is not your loss or your fault."[2]

The contract contained a payment schedule, but it too looked a little different. The sloop contracts had specified payment based on a percentage of work completed, with a portion of the total contract price reserved for payment after a successful trial. The ironclad contracts were different, pay-ing the contractors on the basis of bills approved by the superintendent. In the case of the *Galena,* as the contractors submitted bills for at least $20,000 approved by the superintendent, the Department of the Navy would reim-burse them for three-quarters of that sum. The remaining 25 percent was to be paid "after completion and delivery and satisfactory trial" for a total contract cost of $235,250. The trial itself was interesting. Unlike the earlier agreements, the *Galena* contract did not specify how much time the gov-ernment had to conduct its trial. Cornelius Bushnell must have picked up on this rather quickly and questioned the Navy Department, for barely three weeks after the contract was signed he received a letter informing him that the Navy would "require three months to test satisfactorily the quali-ties specified and warranted."[3]

A final clause, new to the Navy's dealings with private firms, reflected the uncertainties of ironclad shipbuilding. In an apparent effort to reconcile evolving technology with practical necessity, the final paragraph "stipulated that any immaterial improvements which the said parties may agree to, as the vessel progresses, may be made without prejudice to principal points in this contract." Such flexibility both created and solved many problems dur-ing the course of construction.[4]

The contracts for the first three ironclads, which shared similar language, were not, as one recent author contends, "remarkably mean-spirited." They reflected the Navy's past experience with private contracts and uncertain-ties about new technology. All three warships were built during a period of national crisis as peacetime institutions, including the Navy, frantically scrambled around, trying to bring some order to an inherently chaotic situ-ation. The *Galena's* construction history, illustrative of the problems facing all three of the first ironclads, demonstrates many of the problems faced by the Navy Department as it rushed to harness the industrial might of the Northeast for the war effort using procedures and guidelines determined by years of peacetime construction.[5]

The building of these armored vessels offers a useful counterpoint to the construction of the frigates and sloops in the 1850s. In each case, the Navy was trying to build a ship. As a bureaucratic institution, it relied on precedent and rules in accomplishing that task, but precedent and rules often fall by the wayside in times of national crisis, as they did when it came time to build the first ironclads. The shortage of time and the uncertainties of new technology would force the Navy to alter its procedures, demonstrating the weaknesses of what had seemed to be a very effective peacetime policy. The Navy ultimately moved toward a formalized contract mechanism that took the realities of wartime construction into consideration. But it would take time and a series of mistakes and misunderstandings before the Navy fully grasped the extent of the problem and what it would take to fix it.

On a more personal level, the interaction between the Navy Department and private contractors demonstrates the tensions that developed between businessmen motivated by financial gain and naval officers who wanted to quickly and efficiently introduce ironclads to the fleet. The expectations of all parties were artificially high at the start of construction, which meant each had to compromise over the course of the process and accept a more realistic relationship with the other. None of the first three ironclads demonstrated this better than the *Galena*.

By necessity, Bushnell's ironclad underwent design modifications, some of which met considerable resistance from the Navy Department for a number of reasons. Not surprisingly, construction of the inner hull proceeded almost without incident because this part of the ship used traditional construction techniques and experienced nothing more than modest delays. The experimental nature of the vessel allowed certain shortcuts to be taken, although not without some disagreement between the contracting parties. The primary points of contention that developed in the coming months focused around the implementation of the new ironclad technology. Throughout the process, the superintending naval officer, rigidly adhering to the guidelines set up during the 1850s, took great pains to ensure that the government received exactly what it was paying for and exercised adequate control over the project, at the same time urging the contractors to proceed as quickly as possible because of the pressing need to get ironclads into service.

Commo. Joseph Smith, chairman of the original ironclad board and a veteran bureau chief, oversaw the building of each of the three ironclads. Several years after the war, Gideon Welles reminisced that Smith, "in addition to great nautical and civil experience, possessed a singularly mechanical and practical mind."[6] The efforts of the following months severely tested both the patience and limits of Smith's "practical mind." He fought to protect the interests of the government from contractors whose devotion to the cause he must have doubted at times. Despite the seemingly rigid requirements appended to the contract, specific details remained open to negotiation during the construction process as either the government or the contractors changed their minds about how the vessel should be built. Some of those changes were motivated by efforts to cut costs or ease construction while others were necessary modifications unforeseen at the time of the contract.

In the case of the *Galena*, Smith at least enjoyed the luxury of dealing with a naval constructor with some experience building ironclads. Although the Bushnells provided financial backing, the *Galena*'s actual design sprang from the mind of Samuel H. Pook, a civilian employed by the Navy Department. The son of a naval constructor himself, he had almost twenty years of design experience when the war began. The potential of armored warships had occupied Pook's mind since the outbreak of hostilities. He spent the summer of 1861 in the West modifying the design of the first armored river gunboats, the "city class" vessels that played such a crucial role in campaigns in the Mississippi Valley. The exposed machinery and shallow draft of these river boats made the addition of armor plating a necessity, and Pook wrestled with the problems of weight, draft, and a means of securing armor to a vessel. Although he was unable to resolve all of these issues before being recalled to Washington in July, the experience gave him a solid grounding in the mechanics of ironclad design and construction.[7]

Still, building these ironclads was unlike any construction project the Navy had ever overseen. As if the technical challenges were not enough, the urgent need to get them into service as quickly as possible complicated matters even further. In the *Galena*'s case, although the hull would be built at the Maxon, Fish and Company shipyard in Mystic, Connecticut, the vessel would be finished elsewhere. The Navy Department's four-month completion deadline forced Bushnell to distribute the work among various subcontractors in the region. John Ericsson, a Bushnell acquaintance challenged with building the *Monitor,* faced similar difficulties. This was not surprising, for Bushnell and Ericsson shared a similar circle of friends and associates, many of whom became involved in the construction of both vessels, as investors, contractors, or both. For example, Bushnell became a principal investor in the *Monitor.* Two of the men who joined Bushnell in backing both Ericsson and his own ironclad, John A. Griswold and John F. Winslow, also supplied the armor for both ironclads. Cornelius Delamater built both power plants. From a purely financial perspective, this gave the contractors a certain amount of freedom in an otherwise uncertain construction process; it did not matter which ship succeeded, as long as one of them did.[8]

This decentralized construction process would magnify the difficulty of building these ironclads in the first place. The problems were more frequent and more severe in the case of the *Galena,* in part because its design was not nearly as well conceived or as successful as the *Monitor's.* John Ericsson, despite his faults (and they were legion), was a brilliant engineer. He was so confident of his design that he promised to deliver the finished warship to the Navy in one hundred days, sooner than the *Galena's* four-month deadline and far earlier than the nine months allotted to the much larger *New Ironsides.* Not only had he conceptualized this revolutionary ironclad, but he proved able to translate precisely his vision to paper. Ericsson drew up detailed blueprints for distribution to the various subcontractors. The plans were so complete and so exact that the finished components required relatively little modification when they were finally assembled. The *Galena* was another story. Because its plans were not nearly as well defined at the outset, it suffered from continual modification over the course of construction. The *New Ironsides,* which faced similar obstacles, was not affected nearly as much because the longer time frame of its construction made modifications along the way easier to incorporate. It was a much bigger ship than either the *Monitor* or *Galena,* but the Navy also expected its builders to take advantage of their extended time frame, mandating a five-hundred-dollar-per-day penalty for each day the contractor had the ironclad beyond its stipulated completion date. Neither the *Monitor* nor *Galena* contracts contained such a clause.[9]

Modification of the *Galena's* design began almost immediately. Because of a scarcity of available ordnance, the original hull plans did not include either the specifications for or the number of gun ports for the ship. After a series of sometimes brusque letters between Commodore Smith and Naval Constructor Pook, it was agreed that while the exact number and type of cannon would be determined at some point in the future, the hull would be pierced for seven gunports on each side.[10] At about the same time, Pook requested permission from Smith to dispense with the India rubber underlay beneath the armor and replace it with a layer of thin iron, but the commodore did not approve "as one of the strongest arguments used by the contractor for the iron of your vessel was that vulcanized rubber would be most effective in resisting shot." Still, Smith exercised some discretion, opting to wait for the results of experiments conducted by the contractor on the armor scheme before making up his mind. Just over a week later, he gave in and approved the change.[11]

By far the biggest change came when Griswold and Winslow proposed an alternative armor design in early November 1861. Rather than the plate and rail system described by the contract, they suggested an interlocking armor design three and one-eighth inches thick that was supposed to be stronger. This proposal created all kinds of confusion, requiring Smith to consult with Griswold, Pook, Bushnell, and engineer Daniel Martin (who was supervising the armor). Although Smith was initially skeptical, he decided he liked the new armor better than the original plan after meeting with Griswold. Still he remained cautious. Only after the technical advisers agreed that the armor would work and the contractors received assurances that they would not be held liable if the revised armor failed in combat were the changes ordered. Of course, the changes came at some expense, and the amount of ship's hull protected by armor was reduced. Ironically, the amount of armor would be restored in yet another design change four months later.[12]

As changes were made not only to the *Galena* but also to the *Monitor* and *New Ironsides,* Smith kept the financial interests of the United States in mind. Throughout his correspondence with the contractors, he emphasized three points time and time again: first, that any changes were subject to an adjustment of the total contract cost; second, that he would not allow the changes to delay delivery as called for by the respective contracts; and third, that the government would penalize the contractors for such delays. The irony of the third point was that neither the *Monitor* nor *Galena* contracts directly supported such penalties. Smith did not let that temper his rhetoric. For example, in the midst of the squabbling over the rubber sheathing, ports, and rudder, he wrote Bushnell that he feared "in your eagerness to build an armored vessel, you did not reflect sufficiently on the many obstacles to be encountered, and which we now have to overcome as best we can." Despite his doubts, which surfaced continually until the ship was successfully launched, he refused to let Bushnell use them as an excuse to gain extra time. In his zeal to protect the interests of the government, Smith seemed determined to hold Bushnell and Company to its obligations, no matter what difficulties arose. As construction continued and other problems materialized, he would become even more strident, threatening financial penalties and possible abandonment of the project.[13]

Fiscal responsibility was a recurring theme throughout the construction of all three ironclads. Smith's emphasis on financial matters should be considered from two different perspectives. First, he exhibited genuine concern that the government was getting what it paid for. His lengthy tenure at the Bureau of Yards and Docks probably had imparted a healthy mistrust of civilian businessmen like Cornelius Bushnell, who always seemed to be scrambling for extra profits. Second, threats to withhold payment for delays or unauthorized design changes gave the commodore some leverage. Building ironclads was a very different process than building antebellum warships, as Smith, who had experience with both, could readily attest. Because the prewar frigates and sloops had been built, with notable exceptions, at government Navy yards, the Navy exercised complete control over every aspect of their construction except the power plant. However, by turning over direct supervision of the ironclads to private contractors, the Navy lost some of its administrative control. Even though it assigned supervisors to oversee the *Monitor, Galena,* and *New Ironsides,* they carried only limited influence in the daily operations of any private shipyard. Tight control of the purse strings compensated for some of the loss of administrative control to which Smith and the Navy had become accustomed before the war.

No matter how much the commodore cajoled and threatened, which he did with increasing regularity, delays inevitably arose. Not surprisingly, the delays centered around the armor and engines, the technologies that led the Navy to outside contractors in the first place. According to the agreement with Bushnell and Company, the *Galena* should have been completed on 27 January 1862. Griswold and Winslow did not deliver the rest of the armor until ten days before the deadline, which meant there was no realistic chance of applying it to the hull in time. The engines also provided their share of problems at this late date. They were subcontracted to the Delamater Iron Works of New York City, the same firm responsible for building the *Monitor's* machinery. Six days before the deadline, Pook could only write that "most of the engine is here upon the wharf" at Mystic, although the boilers remained unfinished in New York at the Delamater Iron Works. The engine, however, could not be installed until the hull was ready. The carpenters did not have the interior prepared until almost a week after

The U.S. Navy and the Origins of the Military-Industrial Complex

delivery of the machinery and just days before the launching deadline. Only then could the machinery be placed aboard and assembled. The deadline came and went. Not until 8 February could the naval constructor report that installation of the major components had begun.[14]

Adding insult to injury, Pook asked for additional funds to be released to the Bushnells. Smith responded with the only recourse available to him. Having given up on remonstrances, the piqued administrator turned to the one tool of persuasion Bushnell and Company would have no trouble comprehending: money. With what must have been some degree of satisfaction, he replied to Pook that "the Department has decided to make no further payments to the contractors until the vessel shall have been completed and accepted." Smith later relented on part of his threat to cut off payments, releasing some funds for the armor. However, the government still withheld a substantial portion of the contract price, pending successful completion and testing of the vessel.[15]

As frustrating as the *Galena* was for Smith, it represented only a third of his ironclad problems. The *Monitor,* which was supposed to be completed on 12 January 1862, one hundred days after the signing of its contract, was not commissioned by the Navy until 25 February. The *New Ironsides,* even though it had nine months allotted for its construction, took ten months to complete and was not ready for commissioning until 21 August 1862. In both cases, Smith bullied and threatened and pleaded with the contractors to meet their obligations on time while holding to the terms and conditions of their respective contracts. The Navy's experience with the *Galena* was the rule, not the exception.[16]

Although such delays had been tolerated in the peacetime Navy, wartime urgency made them less than acceptable to those officers charged with the conduct of the war. The Navy desperately needed its ironclads; rumors of the refurbished *Merrimack*'s impending launching sent nervous shivers down the spines of officers in Washington and on the North Atlantic Blockading Squadron, responsible for closing off Chesapeake Bay. In late February, Adm. Louis M. Goldsborough, commanding the North Atlantic Blockading Squadron, wrote Assistant Secretary Gustavus Vasa Fox, "I hope the Dept. will be able to send the *Ericsson* [*Monitor*] soon to Hampton Roads to grapple with the *Merrimac* & lay her out as cold as a wedge. She, & another like her, would do the work well." Fortunately, the *Monitor* finished building just in time, more than a month before the *Galena* and well before the *New Ironsides*. On 6 March John Ericsson's "tin can on a shingle" steamed south to join the vulnerable wooden ships at Hampton Roads.[17]

The *Monitor* performed as advertised. The converted *Merrimack*, now renamed the *Virginia*, steamed out of Norfolk on 8 March and delivered a crippling blow to the wooden Union blockading vessels in Hampton Roads. It sank the *Cumberland*, blew up the *Congress* (killing Commodore Smith's son in the process), and damaged several other warships before retreating back to the protection of Confederate batteries at Sewell's Point. Its officers planned to bring the ironclad out the next day and finish the job. However, late that night, the *Monitor* arrived, leading to the epic battle of Hampton Roads the following morning. Although neither ship won, the *Monitor* prevented the *Virginia* from wreaking havoc on the Union fleet, breaking the blockade, and, in the minds of some government officials, threatening Washington itself. Although the menace was not removed, it was contained. Nevertheless, pressure on Smith to get the *Galena* ready for battle remained. A few days after the Battle of Hampton Roads, a nervous Goldsborough, concerned about the ability of the *Monitor* to withstand another foray by the *Virginia*, wrote Fox, "Would to God we had another iron clad vessel on hand! Cannot something more be done to hurry up the *Mystic*, or whatever her name may be?"[18]

Smith kept up pressure on the contractors until he had what he wanted: delivery of the *Galena* to the Navy on 15 April. Smith could only "rejoice to hear that the *Galena* is at last in our hands. I had begun to regard her as a myth." Delivery came at a critical time for the Union. Although the *Monitor* turned back the *Virginia* at the Battle of Hampton Roads in early March, the Confederate ironclad still lurked upriver, threatening to come down and complete the destruction of the wooden blockading squadron that denied vital supplies to the Confederacy. No one knew if the *Monitor* could repeat its earlier feat, and all officers concerned eagerly awaited the new ironclad. The Navy was not the only service anticipating the *Galena*'s arrival. Gen. George McClellan, engaged in his ponderous move up the Peninsula since early April, urgently requested support from the Navy in the form of the new ironclad technology. The general thought he needed an ironclad to reduce the Confederate strong point at Yorktown and ensure the success of his campaign. Although not fully cognizant of the shortcomings of such

The U.S. Navy and the Origins of the Military-Industrial Complex

craft, McClellan understood their psychological impact on both his forces and the forces of the enemy, and he wanted them in his arsenal.[19]

As the Navy rushed to prepare its newest ironclad for commissioning, General McClellan pressured the Navy for the promised ironclad. He informed Assistant Secretary Fox that he was "fast reaching a point where the success of my operations must to a certain extent depend upon the fact of her co-operation or the reverse." He hoped that the *Galena* would "shorten my work here very much." On 21 April, the Navy formally put the *Galena* into commission, the log noting "the mechanicks still at work on board." The following day, the ironclad left New York under tow of the steamer *Baltic* and headed for "Hampton Roads direct." It arrived two days later, where its new captain, Cdr. John Rodgers, assumed the helm. As it turned out, the *Galena* never faced the *Virginia*. As Union forces advanced up the Peninsula, it became impossible for Confederate forces to protect their iron-cased leviathan, and its crew destroyed the ship on 11 May 1862.[20]

Shortly after the *Galena*'s arrival at Fortress Monroe on 24 April, and while the officers at the scene assessed the ironclad's combat readiness, Commo. Joseph Smith began haggling with C. S. Bushnell and Company over the final payment for the vessel. Refusing to bow to pressure from the contractor, Smith, using the precedent codified by the frigate contracts in 1854, suspended further payments and waited for "the report of the test of the *Galena*," after which "the Bureau will present its claim for damage in not complying with your contract."[21]

Even as Smith excoriated the *Galena*'s partners and made his threats, Bushnell's battered ironclad limped down the James River from another test, this one against an entrenched enemy guarding the approaches to Richmond atop Drewry's Bluff. The Confederate gunners clearly got the best of the *Galena* in a prolonged engagement on 15 May, hitting the ship forty-three times. Some of the shots glanced off, but the number of penetrating hits was far greater. Thirty-seven of the forty-three shots inflicted some tangible damage to the vessel. Even some of the glancing shots broke the armor before bounding off. A brief list assessing the injury inflicted by each enemy shot was almost two pages long when printed up. No area of the ship escaped the Confederates' attention. The *Galena*'s executive officer catalogued broken armor, gaping holes in the deck, broken timbers, shattered planking, damaged bulkheads, and a number of shots still lodged in the hull. In short, the ironclad had suffered massive damage. All parts of the vessel were affected; it had not been forced to withdraw because of one or two lucky hits.[22]

Despite the heavy damage suffered at Drewry's Bluff and the urgent need for major repairs, the *Galena* remained on station. The Navy made what on-site repairs it could, but the vessel was never the same after the Battle of Drewry's Bluff. It spent the summer of 1862 supporting McClellan's laborious movement up and down the Peninsula, providing fire support, covering troop movements, and harassing the enemy whenever possible. The ship's log recorded several brushes with small Rebel detachments, especially cavalry sent to disrupt McClellan's communications. Although the *Galena* was battered, its psychological impact as an ironclad made it worth more than any other ship in the James River Flotilla. Blinded by the almost mystical term "ironclad," the Confederates could not accurately assess its capabilities, which made its presence important and justified the Navy's reluctance to send the ship to a proper Navy yard for repairs. In the end, this may have been the *Galena's* most significant contribution. It held the line while the Union built more *Monitor*-style ironclads, not due for delivery until the fall of 1862.[23]

Its military and psychological impact aside, the status of the final payment on the ironclad's contract remained in doubt during the early summer months. Less than one week after the *Galena's* return from Drewry's Bluff, Smith sent a note to John Rodgers, the ship's captain, asking him to conduct a series of trials "for twelve consecutive hours in smooth water" to determine whether or not the terms of the contract had been met. These conditions implied an ocean test, for which the *Galena* was clearly not suited at this time. Smith did not know the extent of the damage at the time of his request, but when he found out he assured its builder that he was "mortified" at the outcome of the duel with the Confederate batteries. Although uncertain about what course of action he would pursue in light of its combat failure, he opined to Bushnell that he was sure that the government would find "it necessary to withhold all further payments on account of that vessel." It seemed as though Commodore Smith had finally won.[24]

Unfortunately, Smith found himself in a race with time. In its zeal to use the new vessel in combat, the Navy ran afoul of the administrative apparatus originally created to protect it from unscrupulous contractors. Following antebellum precedent, the agreement with Bushnell and Company stipulated that the government had ninety days from time of delivery to conduct the trials set out in the contract. The *Galena* had been delivered to the government on 15 April. Ninety days gave the Navy until the middle of July to conduct its trials and determine whether or not the vessel was deficient. Smith was confident that the report "will no doubt be received, and acted upon before the ninety days provided for the trial of the vessel expires." Still, he wrote Goldsborough and asked him to push along the trials. He gave up on the idea of an ocean test, asking instead that the ironclad make a day's run down the James River.[25]

For a variety of reasons, Smith's request could not be accommodated by the officers in the combat zone. Rumors of another Confederate ironclad at Richmond had reached the Union Navy on the James River, and Commo. Charles Wilkes, commander of the James River Flotilla, was not about to let the *Galena* go. Even though damaged, it was still useful, if only for its ordnance. He would have allowed the ship to make a run down the river, but that was impossible "owing to shoal water and narrow passages." On 16 July, he promised to send it down to the bay "as soon as circumstances permit" for trials, but by this time it was too late. The deadline had passed, and it was Smith, ironically, who fell victim to the terms of the contract, terms that had seemed to work so well during the peacetime construction programs. Reluctantly, he informed Bushnell that "the time having expired within which tests of her performance should have been made, the Secretary of the Navy will not, under all the circumstances, enforce a claim for damage for non-compliance of contract in regard to time of completion." Given the tenor of his letters to Bushnell in the preceding eight months, this must have been particularly painful to write. Adding insult to injury, Smith found himself forced to relinquish the money that had been held back pending successful completion of trials. On 6 August 1862, C. S. Bushnell and Company received the final installment of $26,134.74, bring the total cost of the *Galena* to $235,280, only $30 over the initial contract price.[26]

As was the case with the rest of the *Galena*'s tortured construction history, the Navy's problems with the ironclad's trial trip were not unique. Despite its delays, the *Monitor* was finished early enough for the Navy to conduct a satisfactory trial, although it appears to have been abbreviated because of technical difficulties. However, the *New Ironsides,* which entered service late in the summer of 1862, never underwent a trial as called for by its contract. Apparently it was in part for the same reason as the *Galena*.

William Roberts reports that this new ironclad was considered so valuable in the fall of 1862 that "Rear Admiral S. P. Lee, Commander of the North Atlantic Blockading Squadron, was apprehensive of the *New Ironsides* leaving her Newport News station for any length of time." In this case, the lack of a trial was a moot point. The *New Ironsides* did not suffer from the same embarrassing design flaws as the *Galena* when tested in combat. Despite the fact that the antebellum trial clause also failed in this case, final payment to the contractor must have grated on Commodore Smith's nerves far less than in the case of the *Galena*.[27]

With the final payment made, the *Galena* ceased to be an issue of any importance within the Navy. After duty with the North Atlantic Blockading Squadron, the battered ironclad was ordered to Philadelphia for repairs. After seeing the results of its miserable performance against the concentrated artillery fire of the Confederate batteries at Drewry's Bluff and probably unwilling to get replacement armor rolled, the Navy Department authorized the removal of the armor on 13 May 1863 and refitted the ship as a wooden gunboat. It was recommissioned on 15 February 1864 and sent to join the West Gulf Blockading Squadron. On 5 August, the *Galena* participated in the Battle of Mobile Bay, lashed to the steam sloop *Oneida* for protection from the fire of shore batteries. After another refit from 23 November 1864 to 29 March 1865, it rejoined the fleet and served as a blockader until the fall of the Confederacy in April. The ship was decommissioned on 17 June 1865, condemned by survey in 1870, and broken up at the Norfolk Navy Yard in 1872.[28]

Despite the fact that the Navy received two functional and effective ironclads out of three ordered, it was clear that the prewar standards that were supposed to help manage the introduction of ironclad technology into the fleet had been overmatched by practical realities. In the case of power plants, the prewar administrative mechanism had given the Navy an effective measure of control over private contractors because that was what the mechanism had been designed for. Although a major component whose complexity rivaled that of the hull itself, the power plant was only one part among many. Other components under the direct control of the various bureaus, such as the hull, stores, or rigging, were supervised by different mechanisms, usually through the bureau chains of command. In peacetime, the Navy also had time on its side. Despite occasional political pressure, the secretary of the Navy could always stall for a few weeks with no adverse effects.

The war had changed everything. In applying to the construction of entire ships—let alone to state-of-the-art ironclads—an administrative device that had been designed, however successfully, for a particular component system, the Navy lost the kind of day-to-day control it had enjoyed in its own shipyards, pegging its hopes instead on a comprehensive examination of the finished product. The government assigned on-site inspectors to these projects, but they had limited power over the contractors. The sheer magnitude and speed of construction, as well as the technical challenges, overwhelmed the administrative mechanism. The pressures of war destroyed any remaining flexibility, because the Navy no longer had the luxury of extra time. The need to bring ironclad warships into combat was very real; excessive delays might prove disastrous for the Union. As a result, the pre-war contract mechanism hurt the Navy as much as it helped. However, valuable lessons had been learned, especially the need for greater oversight and more stringent contract requirements when working with private contractors. Those lessons would be applied even as the first ironclads were still under construction.

6 Refining the Naval-Industrial Relationship

The Civil War Years

Between 1862 and the end of the war, the United States Navy solidified its relationship with a host of private companies. As contract provisions became more standardized, so did expectations. The Civil War found the Navy working closely with dozens of shipbuilders and engine manufacturers, many for the first time. Although significant disagreements cropped up between the Navy and its private contractors, by the end of the war both sides had formed a series of relationships that owed more to familiarity than comfort. Those relationships, tortured though they seemed at times, would have important implications in the postwar world.

The first ironclad contracts played a significant role in determining the content of subsequent wartime agreements between the Navy and private industry, but they were not the government's first experience in this conflict with wartime building contracts. As it became clear that hostilities were imminent, Congress appropriated funds in February 1861 for seven additional sloops based on the most recent prewar design. Despite the fact that the first incarnation of the 1858 shallow-draft sloops had all entered service before the outbreak of war and that more were authorized and building, the Navy still faced a major problem. The sloops were good ships. In fact, they inspired the design of additional sloops authorized in the summer of 1861. However, they did not meet the Navy's most pressing need: the ability to conduct operations in the coastal waters and river basins of the South Atlantic and Gulf coasts.[1]

The sloops were shallow draft only relative to the larger warships of earlier antebellum building programs, drawing fourteen feet or more of water. The Navy Department recognized the problem almost immediately and began conceptualizing plans for shallower-draft gunboats in the weeks following the firing on Fort Sumter, before Congress authorized construction. The drafts quickly evolved into plans, and by the end of June 1861, still without formal congressional authorization, the Navy began letting contracts. These warships, the famous "ninety-day gunboats," would have an almost immediate role to play in the war, with four getting their first combat experience at Port Royal barely four months later. Another thirteen would be on active service by the end of the year. Altogether, twenty-three gunboats were built, a number that seems to have been determined by the slips available at the time in private shipyards. These ships were unremarkable from a design perspective, but their sheer number, far larger than any class of warship built possibly since Thomas Jefferson's harbor defense gunboats, required further modifications, albeit relatively minor, to the contract process.[2]

Building so many vessels of the same class at once introduced one change symbolic of the Navy's increasingly standardized procedures: preprinted contracts for both the hulls and machinery, with blank spaces left to fill in only the most basic variable data. The language and requirements reflected recent antebellum experience, using much of the same language found in the 1857 and 1858 sloop contracts. The standard clause prohibiting any "member of Congress, officer of the Navy, or any person holding an office or appointment under the Navy Department" from having an interest in the contract remained, as did the injunction releasing the government from any patent fees. The Navy also retained the right to assign an inspector to both the engines and hulls with the authority to reject poor materials or workmanship at any stage of construction. As in the peacetime contracts, the contractor operated on a timetable, with delivery mandated at a given time after the signing of the agreement. Until that delivery happened, the Navy retained the customary lien on the contracted item. Throughout the construction process, the contractors were paid according to progress made. In the case of the gunboats' power plant, the success or failure of the contract, and therefore the status of two payments, would be determined by a ninety-six-hour short trial and a four-month long trial, similar to the one-week short trial and three-month long trial used to assess the 1858 sloops. If any components failed for a specified period after the trial because of faulty workmanship or materials, then the contractor was liable for the cost of repairs.[3]

The pressing need for the ninety-day gunboats introduced two important new modifications to the contract process, one applying to power plants only and the other to both hull and machinery contracts. First, the Navy Department standardized more of the contract than ever before. It gave its engine contractors much less leeway in the design and manufacture of the power plants. Before the war, private firms were given general characteristics —diameter of cylinder, length of stroke, heating and grate surface of the boilers, and so on—and told to produce a finished product that met the Navy's needs. The new contracts contained the same general characteristics but required the builders to "conform in all respects" to the specifications and general drawings furnished by the Navy. The Navy needed reliable power plants capable of extended periods of operation without major repairs. It was not interested in arguing the merits of this or that design. Therefore, Benjamin Franklin Isherwood, perhaps the most brilliant engineer in the wartime Navy, was charged with developing a standard engine design. To account for any variation, the contract required the builders to furnish complete plans of the finished engines "embracing both general and working plans in sufficient detail . . . to enable the same to be again constructed." Although he admires the hull design of the gunboats, Donald Canney credits Isherwood's robust engine design, which powered at least nineteen of the twenty-three ships, as "the key to the vessels' success." In terms of operational longevity, the ninety-day gunboats certainly support Canney's contention. When the war ended, all twenty-three gunboats were still commissioned, with twenty-two of the twenty-three still fit for combat. The engines performed as expected, vindicating, at least in this case, the Navy's quest for standardization.[4]

The second modification introduced by these agreements reflected the urgencies of wartime construction. Not only did the Navy need ships, but it needed them as soon as possible. The leeway afforded to contractors in the 1850s simply did not exist, especially in the highly charged atmosphere of the war's first year, when every action reeked of consequence. The antebellum contracts all contained delivery deadlines. The deadlines were important more for political rather than strategic purposes, as became clear during the construction of the *Merrimack*-class frigates, but they were not critical enough to make those deadlines absolute. That was not the case in 1861, when operational planning depended on available resources. For example, Samuel Francis Du Pont, who commanded the joint expedition against Port Royal in the fall of 1861, was eagerly awaiting "the three or four gunboats which I earnestly trust will be finished in time." He considered them an important component in "a force calculated to stand the brunt of the first attack from the forts," for their shallow draft might be crucial in an area of operations known for its shoals and reefs. Because these ships (and others to follow) were so urgently needed, the Navy used the ninety-day gunboats to introduce penalties for delay into the contract process.[5]

Both the machinery and hull contracts for this class of gunboats dictated how many days a private firm had to complete its obligation, the hull contract also giving an exact completion date. The engine contracts carried a mandated penalty of two hundred dollars subtracted from the total purchase price for each day the contractor went past the deadline. The hull contracts seemed a bit more flexible, as they contained a blank to be filled in with an appropriate daily charge, but they were, in fact, more severe, with a unique clause that allowed the Navy to seize a hull that had fallen behind schedule and have it completed at the contractor's expense. Recognizing that the carrot is always more appealing than the stick, the Navy provided positive incentives as well. The total contract price was not preprinted on the contract; it would be filled in on a case by case basis. As it turned out, the hulls and power plants were contracted for at a variety of prices, with companies that guaranteed the earliest delivery dates rewarded with higher contract amounts. For the most part, the incentives worked, with the first gunboats reaching completion before or very close to the promised dates. The majority of the class followed suit, with only five of the twenty-three completed much later than anticipated. It also helped that the majority of the firms had dealt with the Navy before; they knew what to expect from the Navy and the Navy knew what to expect from them.[6]

Sensing that it had found a workable mechanism for facilitating the timely construction of traditional steam warships, the Navy began applying the terms of the ninety-day gunboat contracts to subsequent agreements. In the fall of 1861, as the details for the first ironclads were being hashed out, the Navy signed a second series of machinery contracts, this time for the seven *Ossipee*-class sloops authorized back in February. The hulls were built in the government's own yards, but the Navy's machine shops were so taxed with repair work that the power plants were contracted out to private firms. In an effort to save time, Secretary Welles insisted that wherever possible the Navy deal with the same firms that had built the power plants for the antebellum sloops. As with the gunboats, these engines would be built from the standardized specifications of an Isherwood design. The same thing happened with the seven *Sacramento*-class sloops authorized in the summer of 1861. The Navy devised a preprinted contract for all fourteen power plants, with blanks left for the name of the contractor, the Navy yard where each sloop was building, the delivery due date, and terms of payment.[7]

Much of the wording of the new contracts, with the exception of the technical requirements for the engines and the odd phrase here and there, was lifted verbatim from the ninety-day gunboat contracts. The now-standard familiar clauses were all there. The Navy's on-site inspector could still reject faulty materials and workmanship at any step of the process. The contract mandated a specific delivery date for the finished power plant, laid out a payment schedule, and required both short and long trials of the machinery. It also held contractors liable for repairs, gave the Navy a lien on the machinery, spelled out penalties for delays in completing the contract, and offered incentives for early fulfillment of the contract terms. However, in the few short months between these contracts and the agreements signed for the ninety-day gunboats, there had been two important modifications, driven both by concerns over the contract process and the differences between the sloops and the gunboats.

The first modification gave the Navy additional leverage when dealing with contractors. The agreement contained a clause that said that if the contractor did not complete the engines on time, the Navy could take over their construction and finish them at the contractor's expense. The idea was new only in the sense that it had not been applied to machinery contracts before. It had, however, been used in similar form in the gunboat hull contracts. The second modification was a concession to economic reality. The sloop engines were much bigger than those on the gunboats, and therefore more expensive. For example, the gunboat *Huron*'s power plant was contracted for $46,000 whereas the sloop *Juniata*'s machinery was contracted for $110,000. In the case of the *Huron*, the contractor received three payments: $23,000 when the machinery was ready for erection on the ship, $11,500 when it was erected and had completed its short trial, and an additional $11,500 after a successful long trial, with penalties or incentives compensated for. The same percentage breakdown—50 percent for the first payment and 25 percent for the next two payments—would have bankrupted all but the most solvent firms in the case of the sloops. Few companies could have afforded to tie up $55,000 in capital waiting for the first payment on one ship, especially if they had multiple contracts with the Navy. The Navy's solution was to pay the contractors earlier and more frequently, using five equal payments of $22,000 instead of three.[8]

The Navy made two more changes, one minor and one major, to its wartime contracts for non-ironclad vessels. These changes are readily apparent in the contracts for three classes of double-ended gunboats built over the course of the war. The double-ended gunboats were shallow-draft paddle-wheel steamers with rudders at each end of the ship. They were designed for riverine operations, where space was often so limited as to severely hamper maneuverability. The two rudders restored some maneuverability by allowing a gunboat to reverse direction without turning around. As with the ninety-day gunboats, the need for such vessels became readily apparent to the Navy in the first months of the war, which decided to build twelve of the ships, the *Octorara* class. As with the earlier gunboats, the Navy decided that the double-enders' machinery would be built exclusively by private contractors, again because its machine shops already had too much work on hand. The hulls, on the other hand, would be divided between public and private shipyards, nine assigned to the various Navy yards and three let out for contract. An advertisement for proposals appeared in early June. Preprinted contracts were signed later in the summer.[9]

These ships, although constructed using traditional techniques, obviously posed something of a challenge because of the double-ended requirement. For that reason, and because there was no standard hull design for this class, the Navy gave the three hull contractors more leeway than in contemporary non-ironclad contracts. The agreement contained one important stipulation: the draft of a fully loaded and armed gunboat could not exceed six feet nine inches. To achieve that goal, the contractors were allowed to increase both the size and displacement of the hull "at their discretion." If they exceeded the mandated draft, they would be penalized on a sliding scale, losing one thousand dollars per inch if the draft was seven feet or less, and forfeiting fifteen hundred dollars per inch if the draft were between seven feet and seven feet three inches. Otherwise, the contract contained the same standard clauses that appeared in the ninety-day gunboat and *Ossipee*-class sloop contracts. It followed the latter more closely first because the government could seize the vessel and its machinery if the contractor missed his delivery date, and second because the frequency of payments to the contractor was higher. In fact, the contract called for eight separate payments. They were not equal like the *Ossipee* payments, but they provided more money to the contractor earlier in the construction process.[10]

The Navy built two more classes of double-ended gunboats during the war, the *Sassacus* and *Mohongo* classes. Unlike the *Octorara* class, whose nine different hull designs stretched the concept of class to its limits, these were standardized ships. Their power plants, with one notable exception, were again Isherwood designs. The *Sassacus* gunboats were advertised for in the summer of 1862, with contracts let early that fall, while the *Mohongo* gunboats were contracted for in June and July 1863. Once again, the preprinted contracts produced by the Navy for these two classes drew heavily on past experience, with all the familiar tenets spelled out. In many ways, these two contracts reflect the Navy's confidence in the Union's shipbuilding infrastructure to produce the required vessels. The *Sassacus* was the largest class (again with the possible exception of the Jeffersonian gunboats) of warships built in the United States before World War I. The *Mohongo* gunboats were iron-hulled vessels, making them the first class of warships in the nation's history to be so. Clearly, the Navy thought its oversight mechanisms were working, for it could have easily justified the inclusion of a trial clause into the hull contract of either class.[11]

These final two classes did introduce one more significant contract modification, but it had nothing to do with the quantity of ships ordered or uniqueness of design. Earlier non-ironclad contracts held back a specified dollar amount pending a successful long-term trial of the hull or machinery in question. So, for example, an *Ossipee*-class machinery contract called for a reservation of twenty-two thousand dollars, and a *Sassacus*-class contract held back twenty thousand dollars. The idea was to leave the contractor with enough money to complete his obligation while withholding enough to guarantee a successful end product. The later contracts for the *Sassacus* and *Mohongo* class gunboats copied their reservation scheme from the first ironclad contracts. Rather than a specific dollar amount, their contracts required a 20 percent reserve to be withheld from the six equal payments made to the builder over the course of construction. When the Navy accepted the ship, the reserve would be released. Why the change was made

The U.S. Navy and the Origins of the Military-Industrial Complex

remains unclear, but it did give the Navy both flexibility and added leverage in a marketplace that was trying to cope with an 80 percent rate of inflation over the course of the war.[12]

At the same time that it began standardizing hull contracts, the Navy devised a similar instrument for engines. By the summer of 1862, the Navy developed a standard preprinted contract form for steam machinery and accessories that incorporated the lessons learned with earlier contracts. Like the hull contracts, it allowed the supervising Navy engineer to reject poor materials and workmanship, allotted a specific amount of time for the contractor to complete the contract, gave the Navy a lien on the machinery, and penalized the contractors for any delays beyond the stipulated delivery date. The incentives for early delivery found in the later double-ender hull contracts had not yet appeared.

The contract also defined a payment schedule that reserved a set percentage of the total contract price pending a successful trial, a first for machinery agreements. Like the hull contracts, the percentage withheld was 20 percent, perhaps recognizing that contractors needed more operating capital in an inflationary marketplace. The engines also had to perform without flaw for an additional three months. If repairs were necessary during that period, they would be made at the contractor's expense. Of course, the Navy took on some obligations during the trial period. It had thirty days from the time of delivery to prepare the vessel for sea and get the short trial under way. Any additional time wasted would be deducted from the three-month follow-up, after which time the contractor would receive the withheld funds.[13]

The Navy's recent experience with Cornelius Bushnell and the ill-fated *Galena* undoubtedly played some part in the incorporation of the new procedures into the 1862 contracts. The *Galena*'s original contract made only a generic reference to a trial trip and final inspection of the ironclad, saying that final payment would be made after the vessel was "tried and tested under this contract to the satisfaction of the party of the second part." This feature was slightly modified shortly thereafter "to mean three months for the test from and after the date the vessel is ready for sea," but the only condition that the Navy placed on Cornelius and Henry Bushnell was that "she shall have stability, speed, &c." The Navy's inability to conduct the required sea trials within three months after delivery cost the government, but even had the trials been carried out successfully, the vagueness of these terms, when linked to Bushnell's strong political connections in Washington, probably would have resulted in full payment for an obviously inferior vessel. The 1862 contract's specific conditions would avoid that problem.[14]

Inflationary pressures and material shortages introduced one final modification. The rapid increase in the number of hulls and engines put under contract in 1861 and early 1862 created all kinds of delays, with the Navy finding it harder and harder to get contracted items delivered within the time frame specified in the various agreements. Contractors who did not want to be penalized by the incentive-delay clauses generally blamed everyone but themselves when it came to explaining why a hull or power plant had not been delivered according to schedule. Two specific complaints surfaced time and time again in their correspondence with the Navy Department. First, they blamed unreliable subcontractors who had overextended themselves or were not able to fulfill their obligations in the first place for not delivering necessary components of an engine or hull on time. Second, they blamed those same subcontractors for delivering substandard products that had to be returned or discarded and replaced. Of course, the contractors themselves were rarely at fault.

The Navy addressed these issues in the 1862 engine agreements. Many contractors were simply overwhelmed by the war effort and had made optimistic claims that circumstances made almost impossible to carry out, as the forthcoming discussion of ironclad contracts makes clear. All earlier hull and machinery contracts held private firms to strict delivery timetables. Trying to give contractors the benefit of the doubt in an otherwise chaotic environment, some contracts contained a provision that required delivery by the due date "unless prevented by the act of the government, or by circumstances beyond [their] control." Many contractors tried to use this final clause to justify delays, no matter what the cause. The latest engine contracts defined things much more clearly, explaining

it being understood that by "circumstances beyond the control of the parties of the first part," is meant accidents by fire or water to the machinery on the premises of the parties of the first part, or while being erected in the vessel; but delays by persons furnishing the parties of the first part with stock or material, or caused by loss of castings or forgings condemned for any reason whatever, are not within the meaning of the phrase "circumstances beyond the control of the parties of the first part."

If nothing else, the new phrasing would force potential contractors to give serious consideration to their ability to carry out the terms of any agreement with the Navy.[15]

The new contract form represented more than just wishful thinking by the Navy Department. Historian and naval engineer Frank M. Bennett lists seventy-six ships contracted for by the Navy in 1862. The power plants for at least thirty-eight of those ships were built under the terms of the new preprinted contract. The process must have worked reasonably well, for the Navy used the new language again in the *Wampanoag*-class engine agreements, signed in late 1863.[16]

In general, contracts let for power plants and non-ironclad warships over the course of the war showed a clear evolutionary path, with the Navy continually refining its contract language based on practical experience. The process was not without its problems. Cost overruns and delays regularly strained relations between the government and its contractors. However, it did provide the Union with large numbers of the kinds of ships it so desperately needed to fight a coastal-riverine war. In retrospect, this part of the contract experience seems to have worked relatively well because it dealt with steam engines and traditional shipbuilding techniques, technologies whose problems had largely been worked out by the time of the war. There were new designs and concepts, especially in the case of the double-ended gunboats, but nothing that required radical readjustment.

That, unfortunately, was not the case with the Navy's entire contract experience. The major challenge facing the Navy Department, as the building of the first three ironclads so aptly demonstrated, was the construction of armored warships. The task was exacerbated by the need for significant numbers of these vessels, whose experimental nature and unorthodox construction methods created all kinds of new problems. When it was all said and done, the contract process did not fare nearly as well as it did with more traditional ships.

As the Union considered in 1861 what it would take to quell the rebellion, many concluded that victory might depend in part on the Navy's ability to reduce the coastal fortifications defending key Southern cities. To do so, the Navy needed heavily armored shallow-draft vessels capable of carrying a few large caliber weapons to within battering range of these forts. Secretary of the Navy Gideon Welles had been bombarded with designs for ironclads throughout the fall and winter of 1861. Although most were summarily rejected or set aside pending further examination, the Navy took a closer look at turreted ironclads, which seemed to meet the Union's needs. By the beginning of December, the department and certain members of Congress had become convinced that the Navy's future rested with turreted coastal ironclads.

As the discussions moved into the planning phase, the level of debate in Congress over ironclads steadily mounted. On 17 December, Congressman Charles B. Sedgewick, chairman of the House Committee on Naval Affairs, introduced a bill appropriating $10 million for the construction of twenty turreted ironclads based on a budget and plans drawn up by John Lenthall, chief of the Bureau of Construction and Repair, and Engineer in Chief Benjamin Isherwood. The bill passed the House on 19 December and moved to the Senate, where it encountered strong opposition, not passing until 7 February.[17]

The reason for the delay between the passage of the House and Senate bills rested with Lenthall and Isherwood's design. It called for ironclads using turrets based on the design of Capt. Cowper Phipps Coles of the Royal Navy, which had been published in 1860. Unlike John Ericsson's *Monitor,* this turret design relied on thicker armor placed in fewer layers and had a sloping armored glacis to protect the base of the turret from enemy shot. It also rested on a metal base ring and bearings instead of the spindle used in the *Monitor*-style plan. Ericsson and his partners viewed the introduction of this design with some trepidation, for it would mean both a blow to prestige and a loss of future contracts. Ericsson, the supreme egoist, was also convinced that his design was simply better, a point he made clear in an extended letter to Secretary Welles on 23 December.

Ericsson could do more than protest on technical grounds. He and his partners, including Cornelius Bushnell, John Winslow, John Griswold, and Erastus Corning, had formidable political connections in both the Lincoln administration and Congress. Calling on all the influence at their command, they forced a compromise. Their supporters used their authority in the Senate to stall passage of the bill until a deal could be worked out with Welles. In a letter dated 7 February to John Hale, chairman of the Senate Naval Affairs Committee, the secretary bowed to reality and said that the Navy would be open to a variety of designs, specifically mentioning Ericsson and his December proposal. Having received these assurances, which virtually guaranteed Ericsson and his partners future business with the Navy, Hale released the bill from committee, which passed the same day with a $10 million appropriation.[18]

Barely two weeks after the bill passed, the Navy advertised for its first class of ironclads. The "twenty gunboats" number that had been attached to this bill was something of a misnomer. As it turned out, the Navy Department contracted for only ten monitors, the *Passaic* class. Their contracts, signed in March and April 1862, reflected the Department's experience with the first three ironclads, which in the case of the *Galena* and *New Ironsides*, was still ongoing.[19]

Like the first ironclad contracts, the *Passaic* agreements called for an on-site inspector with the authority to reject poor workmanship and materials at any stage of the construction process. There was also a well-defined time frame for construction, although the amount of time allotted to individual ships within the class varied by contractor and was linked to the total contract price. Contractors opting for shorter construction times would be rewarded with a higher contract price if they succeeded. However, unlike the machinery and hull contracts signed by the Navy in 1861, there was no stated financial penalty for delays. The payment schedule closely followed that of the *Monitor*. The contractor submitted bills in increments of fifty thousand dollars. The Navy paid the bills, reserving 25 percent as a guarantee of a successful trial. Whereas the earlier contracts had accepted each ironclad after a "satisfactory" trial, the *Passaic* agreements required "every defect or breakage for one month after trial trip [to] be repaired at the expense of the [contractor]." The trial itself had to be conducted within sixty days of delivery to the Navy.[20]

There was another interesting new clause in these contracts that testified to the difficulties and uncertainties of ironclad construction at this point in the war. The original *Monitor* was so revolutionary that it was difficult to determine its exact strengths and weaknesses, even after the Battle of Hampton Roads. The Navy presumed it would receive continual feedback from the field that could be translated into design improvements for the *Passaic* class. Therefore, the *Passaic* contracts declared that "improvements of the form . . . suggested by either party, and agreed upon, shall be adopted as the work progresses." Unfortunately, the contract never made clear exactly how that was supposed to happen. In general, that was the problem with the *Passaic* contracts. They made clear stipulations but lacked the enforcement mechanism to carry them out. There were no penalty clauses for late delivery, no clear-cut way to assess the success of the trial and determine how much of the 25 percent reserve would be paid, and no negotiating mechanism for determining design changes made in the course of construction. Not only did the Navy not address these questions, but it also took advantage of the clause to make several changes to the *Passaics* during construction. The end result was significant delays in their delivery with the nine ships of the class built on the East Coast entering service between November 1862 and April 1863.[21]

Before these flaws became apparent, the Navy began letting additional contracts. Although *Monitor*-style gunboats are most often associated with coastal operations, they were not restricted to the Atlantic seaboard. As the *Passaic* class began construction, the Navy Department began letting contracts for turreted riverine warships, the *Milwaukee*-class ironclads. Two of the four ships were contracted to James B. Eads, a St. Louis engineer, in late May. Eads was no stranger to the government when it came to naval affairs. Not long after the fall of Fort Sumter, Eads had received an invitation from Edward Bates, Lincoln's attorney general, to come to Washington and discuss what kinds of warships were best suited to protect the Mississippi River. That summer and fall, he built the city-class casemated ironclads, which quickly made their mark on the western rivers. Although he personally built only two of the four *Milwaukee*-class ironclads, the design of all four was the product of his fertile mind.[22]

The hindsight of even two months made a significant difference in the contract terms Eads and his partners had to fulfill. First, the trials for acceptance of the ship and its machinery were expanded and the terms more explicitly defined. Rather than one generic trial for the entire weapons system, the contractors now had two trials to contend with, a short seventy-two-hour trial for the machinery and a longer two-month trial for the rest of the ship. This was new for ironclads but had been standard for machinery contracts since well before the war. Any flaws or defects revealed over the course of either trial would be corrected at the contractor's expense. The contract also introduced additional clauses from earlier wartime contracts. For example, in earlier ironclad contracts the Navy had maintained its right to liquidate an unfinished ship to recover costs. Now, as it had in

The U.S. Navy and the Origins of the Military-Industrial Complex

earlier contracts for more traditional ships, it attached a lien to the ironclads and their machinery, giving it a more solid legal claim if the contractor failed to live up to the terms of the agreement.

Finally, and perhaps most important, these preprinted forms introduced standard penalties for delayed delivery. To this point in the war, the *New Ironsides* had been the only ironclad whose contract contained such a clause. Interestingly enough, there was no incentive clause for early delivery. To make sure there was no confusion about the delivery date, the contract not only listed the number of months allotted for construction, but also recorded the exact date when the completed ironclad was due in the Navy's hands. There is no direct evidence to support such a link, but the Navy Department's ongoing frustration with the *Galena* might have played a role in the incorporation of some of the new contract language. The influence of these contracts certainly extended beyond the *Milwaukee* class. The same form was used for other riverine ironclads, including the *Chillicothe, Indianola, Marietta,* and *Sandusky.*[23]

It is also interesting to note what did *not* appear in the *Milwaukee*-class contracts. Unlike the first-generation ironclad contracts for the *Monitor, Galena,* and *New Ironsides,* the *Passaic*-class agreements allowed for design changes in midcourse, perhaps because so many alterations were made during construction to the earlier ships. By the time the Navy printed up contract forms for the riverine ironclads, it had modified its stance, at least on paper. The clause allowing "improvements [to] . . . be adopted as the work progresses" disappeared. In its place, the contractor was given the authority to increase, but not decrease, a ship's lineal dimensions to meet the contract's draft requirements. The Navy's specifications for the rest of the ironclad, especially the armor and ordnance, would be followed as written. The intent to avoid the delays and chaos associated with modifications made after the initial contract was a noble one, but reality made that impossible, as the Navy's next set of contracts so aptly demonstrated.[24]

Even as the *Milwaukee*-class contracts were taking shape, the Navy began revising its administrative structure to deal more effectively with private industry. The problem was that the parameters that had defined the government's relationship with individual companies were changing. Contracts devised in the 1840s and early 1850s had been for *individual* ships or power plants and met the limited needs of a particular situation. Things changed slightly in the mid-1850s, when a contract might be duplicated to cover all of the ships or machinery for a particular class, as in the case of the *Merrimack*-class frigates and 1857 and 1858 sloops. The complexity and uncertainty of the first wartime ironclads caused a regression back to individual contracts. However, by 1862 the Navy found itself almost overwhelmed by the sheer number of vessels required for the successful prosecution of the war effort. Drawing upon its past experience and incorporating the lessons it had learned from past mistakes, the Navy began using preprinted contracts on a larger scale, trying to retain control over as much of the shipbuilding process as possible.

In the case of the ironclads, the increasing number of contracts with firms located all along the eastern seaboard led to the creation of a separate office in New York City to oversee ship and machinery contracts with private companies. Although nominally headed by Rear Adm. Francis H. Gregory, Chief Engineer Alban C. Stimers ran this "monitor bureau," creating his own fiefdom in the process. It was through the oversight measures carried out by Stimers's office that the Navy tried to bring order to an otherwise chaotic process. In doing so, it forged solid and long-lasting relationships with the most prominent shipbuilding firms in the country. The Navy built these relationships around rules and regulations applied across the board to all contractors. Although the Navy maintained a close correspondence with each individual firm, it also began to deal with contractors as a collective group "to establish rules . . . explaining the course to be pursued in all cases," using circular letters to set policy and communicate uniform decisions. There was a similar office set up in St. Louis, but, as William Roberts points out, it "never reached the level of influence that the New York office would attain."[25]

Stimers's monitor bureau soon found itself very busy. Not only did the *Passaics* require attention, but the Navy was preparing to let contracts for another nine monitors. Those warships, the *Canonicus* class, were advertised for in August 1862. Their contracts were let that fall, before any of the *Passaics* had undergone their trials. These contracts, benefiting again from the Navy's aggregate experience, looked familiar but introduced additional refinements. Unlike the *Milwaukee* contracts, the *Canonicus* agreements did not call for a short machinery trial and a longer full trial of the entire vessel. Instead, they required only a long trial, just like the *Passaics*. This trial, however, was different in two important ways. First, the length of the trial was doubled to sixty days, just like the *Milwaukee* contracts. Second, the Navy inserted a new clause requiring "every defect or breakage [in the machinery] for one month after trial trip [to] be repaired at the expense of the [contractor]." This was different in that the *Passaic* contracts had called for no defects for a period after the trial trip, but did not stipulate that the contractor would pay for repairs. The Navy was closing potential loopholes. At the same time, it tried to encourage contractors by offering financial incentives for early completion while still reserving the right to penalize them for delays.[26]

Based on the Navy's advertisement, most contractors assumed that they were applying to build a minor variation of the *Passaics*. That was not the case. In fact, plans for the new class of ironclads were not complete when the contracts were signed. John Ericsson was supposed to design the new monitors. However, he was engrossed in building six of the *Passaics* and had not completed the necessary plans. Stimers compensated for this by setting up an office in New York near Ericsson's that would take his general drawings and translate them into specific plans. Despite the lack of specifics, contractors looked at the new contracts, saw that the new warships would be built "upon the general plan of vessels now building," and submitted bids based on the *Passaic* class.

At this point, the Navy's wartime needs clashed with its procurement process. The problem would get even more complicated because several of these contracts were let to companies that had never built ironclads for the Navy. Not only had they not built ironclads, but they were located well inland, west of the Allegheny mountains on the Ohio River. Their location, which made delivery of key components interesting, and lack of experience strained the Navy's contract procedures in ways it had not foreseen. However, the Navy (and the war effort) had reached a critical juncture where demand exceeded the ability of East Coast firms to supply the Navy's needs. There was no choice. Any chance these firms had to get a good start was dashed by the lack of plans. They fumed and pestered the Navy, afraid that they would be caught by the delayed delivery clause in the contract that stipulated a deduction of five hundred dollars for every day a ship was late. Even though Secretary Welles extended all contract dates by two weeks to appease them, it took yet another week before the general plans were sent out. Even then, the contractors suffered from repeated design changes, dictated by Stimers's office.

In the end the continued changes and lack of contractor experience seriously delayed all of the *Canonicus* ironclads. One year after their contracted completion dates, only the first four, all built on the East Coast, were close to being ready for launching. Of this class, only five would be commissioned by war's end. The other four, all built inland, would not see combat. As early as August 1863, the Navy had unofficially decided not to penalize the contractors. The contract provisions, when pushed to the limit, failed. Although it bothered the Navy, Welles and his subordinates were more concerned about getting the vessels into service. The immediate needs of wartime took priority.[27]

Even as the Navy realized that its contract mechanism was not working particularly well for ironclads, it forged ahead and applied yet another modification of the contract mechanism to a new class of ironclads, the *Casco* riverine monitors. Another Ericsson-inspired design, these six-foot-draft monitors were designed for service on inland rivers, and, like the *Canonicus* monitors, were built both on the East Coast and farther inland. As the contracts were being signed, the Navy was already encountering significant delays with the *Canonicus* monitors. The new contracts reflected these delays and attempted to compensate for them as much as possible.

The biggest problem confronting the Navy was the question of design changes. Because plans were drawn even as the ships were contracted, and because the Navy planned on incorporating improvements learned from experience in the field into these monitors as they were built, the contracts more explicitly defined how the design process would work. Firms that chose to deal with the Navy were promised only a set of "general plans and specifications" and were told to draw up their own working drawings for the actual construction. Those drawings, of course, had to meet with the "monitor bureau's" approval. The contract further explained that the Navy had the right to make "alterations and additions to the plans and specifications at any time during the progress of the work as they may deem necessary and proper." Because the Navy recognized that such changes had caused financial hardship in the past, the agreement allowed adjustments to be made to the total contract price as the result of any such modifications. It also acknowledged delays caused by design changes in the past, holding contractors to the specified delivery timetable "unless arrested by any contingency which human foresight could not avert." Still, it encouraged contractors to push ahead with all dispatch by promising the now customary five-hundred-dollar-per-day incentive for early delivery.

At the same time that the Navy tried to be more realistic about the realities of wartime construction by inserting these new clauses, it also took steps to protect itself and ensure that the final product met its needs. Earlier ironclad contracts had required "all machinery . . . to be built in a substantial manner, strong and durable in every detail" and required the contractor to pay for any repairs within one month after the trial trip. The *Casco* contracts took this one step further, requiring "the vessel and the machinery" to meet this same standard. Presumably, if the Navy were going to have the contractors devise their own working plans, it wanted to make sure that the physical manifestation of those plans performed as expected.[28]

These changes looked good on paper, but in actual practice could not compensate for the charged atmosphere of wartime design. In reality, the additional leeway expected by the contractors never materialized, primarily because the Navy took the modification clauses too much to heart. Although the concept of the *Casco* monitors came from John Ericsson, many of the general plans were drawn by Stimers's draftsmen. As Stimers later explained, "All the plans, both generally and in detail, as well as the materials and workmanship, had to be approved by me. When, therefore, plans were drawn in my office, instead of by Captain Ericsson himself, I took advantage of the opportunity to improve them, and to throw upon him the *onus* of proving that my amendments were not good." Even before the contracts were let, Stimers changed the design of the engines and boilers, moved the propellers, and added water tanks and pumps that could alter the vessels' draft on demand. Other changes followed after the contracts were awarded. Incensed by Stimers's redesign, Ericsson disassociated himself from the project.

The result of Stimers's "improvements" was an unnecessarily complicated morass of specifications issued during the construction process as a ninety-two-page Specification Book that one workman scornfully referred to as the "monitor prayer book." Contractors did not dare to deviate from these specifications, which ultimately required them to build much more complicated warships than they ever expected. Many of the contractors for these ships were also relatively new to the process; the Navy's preferred builders were generally busy on earlier projects. They were therefore less likely to question the directives coming out of Stimers's office.[29]

The first ships of the class were a disaster, barely floating above water in some cases. They were initially designed to have fifteen inches of freeboard when fully loaded, but that freeboard virtually disappeared with the incorporation of Stimers's changes. It was calculated that the *Chimo's* deck, for example, would be mostly underwater when the turret, ordnance, and miscellaneous equipment were added to the already low-floating hull. Five of the vessels had their turrets stripped and were converted to rather unsatisfactory torpedo boats. The rest of the class underwent another expensive modification and had their decks raised twenty-two inches. Of the twenty ships in this class, only eight were commissioned by the end of the war, and the Navy kept them out of combat, fearful of the potential results. When it was all said and done, the Navy received ironclads that did not meet expectations and cost substantially more than originally planned.

The fiasco provoked a congressional investigation and called the Navy's contract procedures into question. Critics charged that the ad hoc creation of the "monitor bureau" had subverted the traditional oversight mechanisms, especially the Bureau of Construction and Repair and the Bureau of Steam Engineering. Gideon Welles had to agree, writing in his diary that "Stimers and Fox, had, I think, connived that they could do this work independent of the proper officers . . . ; probably hope to acquire reputation." Even so, they shared the blame with others, especially Lenthall and Isherwood, whom Welles faulted for not informing the department about the irregularities in the hope that Stimers would fail. Despite the recriminations that swirled through the Navy Department, there were few tangible ramifications. Stimers was reassigned and everyone else went back to their jobs. With the end of the war clearly in sight and the Navy already scaling back its shipbuilding efforts, substantial change or reform seemed unnecessary.[30]

Contract language was not the only thing evolving over the course of the war. More important for the Navy's future, the sheer number of contracts let forced the Navy to develop working relationships with a number of important firms. As the war went on, the Navy dramatically expanded the number of companies with which it did business, with the *Army and Navy Journal* reporting as late as September 1864 that "the greatest difficulty in preparing the numerous vessels built within the last three years has been the want of the requisite number of machinists and machine shops." Government shipyards built 71 of the 192 hulls contracted for during the war, but the pressing need for warships resulted in fifty-six different private firms constructing the other 121 hulls. The Navy's manufacturing shortcomings were more apparent when it came to steam technology. Of the 199 steam power plants ordered over the course of the war, the Navy yards built only six. Sixty-four different companies provided the necessary facilities and technological expertise to build the rest. Although not flawless, the general contract formula worked well, and the government found itself amply supplied with enough vessels for successful prosecution of the war effort.[31]

The Navy certainly developed preferences when it came to contractors. East Coast firms, which tended to be technically more sophisticated and possess the greatest experience, were decided Department favorites. However, the Navy could not be as discriminating as it would have liked in an environment in which contractors were valuable commodities, no matter where they were located. Therefore, the longer the war continued, the more the Navy was forced to use smaller, less established companies to satisfy its construction needs, whether for engines, hulls, or ironclads. Assistant Secretary of the Navy Gustavus Fox certainly recognized this during discussions over the *Canonicus* contracts, telling Stimers in August 1862 that "every shop capable of doing the work, shall have [a contract], both here and on the western waters." Stimers had suggested to Fox that those contracts be let by invitation, but Fox, even though he sympathized with Stimers's wish to use trusted firms, told the general inspector he had to advertise the new contracts just as the law required. Although it worked with companies both on the East Coast and in the interior, the Navy's contact with companies along the Atlantic seaboard proved most valuable over time. Many of the companies the Navy worked with west of the Allegheny mountains did not survive much past 1865. Those that did got out of the warship business as soon as the war ended. Stimers's instincts were right, but the demands of war forced the Navy to experiment with other firms. If anything, that experimentation confirmed what many officers probably suspected: established firms were more reliable and would continue to be so in the future.[32]

Relationships are not always cordial, and that was certainly the case with the Navy and its contractors, especially considering the confusion over contract prices created by the later wartime contracts. At times, the relationship became adversarial. Modifications made after the signing of the contract and delays beyond the control of the builders, coupled with an inflationary economy and the Navy's strict adherence to its new guidelines whenever possible, created confusion over how much more money, if any, the government owed different contractors. The bitter wrangling that finally settled the issue took years, extending in some cases into the twentieth century. When the Navy proved recalcitrant, aggrieved contractors flexed what political muscle they had. Although not all were satisfied by the outcome, a postwar investigation by the Senate Committee on Naval Affairs recommended that several firms be at least partially compensated for lost revenue and inflationary costs "caused by the delay and action of the Government." Additional claims were awarded in subsequent decades.[33]

Clearly, the process needed further refinement. Nevertheless, important precedents had been set. Although flawed, the Navy's contract language had taken significant steps toward the kind of language and procedures needed to build modern warships incorporating the latest technical advances. As warship construction became so sophisticated that it was clearly beyond the Navy's capabilities to construct all components, the process by which the Navy dealt with outside contractors became increasingly important and would continue to be so in the postwar years. There was a corresponding precedent set in terms of relationships. Although the wartime experience had tried and rejected any number of contractors, the Navy still developed close ties with several major companies on the Atlantic coast. Those ties, although strained at times, would be drawn upon more in the future, when the Navy once again tackled complicated new technologies.

7   Applying the Lessons of the Past

To the New Steel Navy, 1865–1883

Between 1865 and the issuing of contracts for the new steel Navy in 1883, the United States Navy solidified its relationship with a host of private companies. Not surprisingly, when it needed work done in the postwar years, the Navy turned to its wartime partners, and in the process maintained a vitally important network of contractors who understood its basic needs and procedures. Contract clauses evolved yet again to meet peacetime needs, retaining many of the wartime adjustments while introducing new requirements and stipulations that reflected budgetary and political realities. Despite some controversy, the process worked well throughout the 1870s. Therefore, when the Navy confronted its greatest challenge of the postwar era, building steel warships in the early 1880s, it could comfortably fall back on tried contract procedures and a network of private contractors accustomed to the Navy's particular requirements and restrictions.

The immediate postwar years saw the U.S. Navy change from the world's premier coastal defense force to a second-rate naval power. Congress, eager to return both the Army and the Navy to their antebellum size and stature, began pressing for budget reductions almost immediately after the war's end. Secretary of the Navy Gideon Welles, who had overseen the Navy's dramatic wartime growth, fumed as the legislators began their assault. In early 1866, he railed in his diary against "demagogues of small pattern [who] exhibited their eminent incapacity and unfitness for legislation . . . by making no appropriations, or as few as possible for the Navy, regardless of what is essential." Welles stalled Congress as long as he could. Although he significantly pared back the Navy, it was, as late as December

1867, more than twice as big as it had been in 1860. That did not last. In 1868, Congress wielded its budget axe with a vengeance, dramatically cutting appropriations. Welles, who had initially asked for more than $47 million and then cut his request to $24 million, got barely $20 million out of Congress for the Navy.[1]

The lack of congressional funds and the popular perception both within and without the Navy that the service's primary mission was commerce protection meant there would be no construction programs in the immediate future matching even the scale of the antebellum frigate or sloop projects. For the next fifteen years, the Navy would not seriously contemplate building an entire class of warships. The problem only got worse when Welles left office in March 1869 and was replaced by Adolph Borie, a spineless political appointee who effectively turned control of the Navy Department over to Adm. David D. Porter. Borie himself resigned in July and was replaced by George Robeson, but he too gave Porter an almost free rein. Porter, who was convinced that the quality of the Navy and its seamen had been in decline since the introduction of steam, would not encourage the construction of modern warships. If anything, he caused the Navy to regress by insisting that captains use sail whenever possible and reprimanding those who fired up their boilers and resorted to steam, no matter what the circumstance.[2]

The rhetoric surrounding the budget cuts and Porter's pursuit of "efficiency" hid the real problem facing the Navy in the late 1860s and early 1870s: graft and corruption. Millions of dollars were appropriated to repair and maintain obsolete warships whose military effectiveness was minimal at best. Most of the repair and maintenance contracts, not surprisingly, went to politically connected contractors from influential districts. There were few naval contractors left in this period of retrenchment (seven by one count), but those still in business more than survived. In hindsight, the excesses are readily apparent. From 1869 to 1876, when "economy" was all the rage, the Bureau of Construction and Repair's annual appropriations were far higher than in the years 1884 to 1891, when the Navy undertook several major new construction programs. To make matters more interesting, significant amounts of money never made it to the shipyards, instead lining of pockets of politicians and contractors. Even in a relatively permissive environment, corruption and graft on this scale could only be tolerated for so long, and public outcry eventually prompted an investigation that led

The U.S. Navy and the Origins of the Military-Industrial Complex

to lots of finger pointing and a search for a suitable scapegoat. Still, that was all in the future at the beginning of this period.[3]

Future investigations aside, the Navy's postwar contract procedure remained essentially the same. The Navy entered into a limited number of individual contracts after the war, but those agreements followed the wartime guidelines developed for entire classes of ships with only minor modifications, even using similar standardized forms. The 1871 contract between the Navy and John Roach for the engines of the *Tennessee* serves as a typical example, reflecting the continued evolution of contract guidelines from the Civil War through the 1870s.

Originally built during the Civil War as the *Madawaska*, the *Tennessee* became the source of postwar controversy, earning a reputation as a financial sinkhole. After laying up the ship in ordinary in 1867, the Navy spent more than half a million dollars for repairs and modifications between 1869 and 1871. The vessel embarked on a three-month cruise and then returned for additional repairs that took another three years to complete. John Roach, a private contractor from New York City, was awarded the contract for general repairs and a set of new machinery. In return, not only would he receive monetary compensation but also the *Tennessee*'s old engines to sell for scrap. This arrangement, coming at a time when general corruption within the Grant administration was coming to light, provoked a congressional investigation. Roach became a convenient target because the Navy already had a set of unused duplicate engines at the Washington Navy Yard built for a sister ship, and the *Tennessee*'s original engines had never been condemned by a board of survey.[4]

The *Tennessee*'s machinery contract duplicated much of the preprinted wartime contracts, often incorporating entire paragraphs from the earlier documents. As it had with prior contracts, the Navy Department made both major and minor changes that reflected its past experience with the private sector. Although the circumstances surrounding the issuing of the *Tennessee* contract created much controversy, the contract itself represented another positive step in the evolving relationship between the government and private industry. Both parties incurred new obligations while benefiting from new safeguards at the same time.

Like the later wartime machinery contracts, the 1871 agreement with Roach required that the finished power plant conform to an attached list of specifications and include all necessary tools and spare parts. If, however, the Navy inadvertently left anything off the list, a new clause mandated that "the same shall be furnished by the said parties of the first part [the contractor] to the satisfaction of the said parties of the second part [the government] without extra compensation therefor." This clause would simplify negotiations during the construction process, making it clear that the government expected a fully functional and maintainable power plant. As it had with all its contracts during the previous two decades, the Navy demanded that "all the materials, workmanship, detail and finish shall be of the first class," and it reserved the right to appoint a superintendent to oversee construction at the contractor's premises. Like his predecessors, the superintendent had the authority to "inspect . . . and to peremptorily reject, in any stage of its progress, any materials or articles, or any piece or part which he may consider defective, either in quality of material or of workmanship, or in propriety of detail."[5]

The new contract also contained familiar clauses designed to protect the Navy from unscrupulous contractors and political influence. The contractor was required to furnish drawings "of every piece or part used in the construction" detailed enough to allow "the same again to be constructed." He also had to provide assurances that the United States would not be held liable for any patent fees, and agreed that "no member of Congress, officer of the Navy, or any person holding any office or appointment under the Navy Department, shall be admitted to any share or part of this contract or agreement, or to any benefit to arise therefrom." Nor could a partial interest in the contract be transferred to an outside party after the signing. Failure to comply with either of the last two clauses would result in a null and void contract.[6]

As the wartime ironclad programs so aptly demonstrated time and time again, one of the main points of contention during the Civil War was how much time a contractor had to complete his work and deliver a finished product to the Navy. The preprinted wartime contracts became increasingly detailed as the war went on, trying to rectify the confusion by spelling out the requirements in explicit terms, but the Navy still found itself arguing with contractors about the issue well after the end of the war. In fact, several cases were still pending as the Navy began negotiating with John Roach. Recognizing that the problem must be dealt with, the Navy made minor but important changes to the 1871 *Tennessee* contract based on its wartime experience.

Under the later wartime engine agreements, contractors were given a set period of time, usually two or three months after a hull had been delivered to them, to install all the necessary machinery, bunkers, spare parts, and miscellaneous equipment on board ship and have it "ready for continuous sea service . . . unless prevented by the act of the government, or by circumstances beyond the control of the [contractor]." This arrangement worked well when no substantial changes were made to the design of either the ship or its power plant. However, the constantly evolving technology that characterized the Civil War made major design changes a fact of life for most of these private firms. During the war, the government expected its contractors to make the necessary modifications to the hull to accommodate changes in the power plant. This expectation in turn led to serious delays and prompted the government to invoke penalty clauses with increasing regularity.

Perhaps because it ultimately repaid many of the assessed penalties after the war, the Navy inserted a new clause in the *Tennessee* contract acknowledging "that all changes in strengthening [the] hull for the more efficient erection of the engines, boilers, and their dependencies in this ship, or any modification rendered necessary in or about the hull for the more satisfactory fulfillment of this contract is to be made by the [Navy]." This modification protected both the government and private contractors by clearly defining each party's responsibilities. With this clause in effect, any penalty withheld by the government for failure to comply with the contract's terms was more likely to be upheld upon appeal because the contractor was more likely to be at fault. At the same time, the contractor would not be punished unnecessarily for delays caused by changes imposed by the government.[7]

The *Tennessee* contract contained the same procedures for the trial and acceptance of new machinery found in the earlier contracts. Again building on its wartime experience, the Navy transferred those procedures to the new contract almost verbatim. There were other transfers of effective wartime language as well. Early wartime machinery contracts had allowed contractors to "arrange and proportion the details of the said machinery in such manner as they shall deem best calculated to secure the most successful operation." Later wartime contracts removed that freedom, requiring firms to use standardized designs and to "rigorously [adhere] to . . . the general drawings furnished" by the Navy. The later requirement restricted the contractor's freedom of action while increasing the Navy's control over the project. It worked well enough in war that the Navy continued using it in peace. In part, this reflected a measure of technological stability. In the preceding decades, building steam engines had been a real craft, with several competing designs vying for attention. Each engine had its own idiosyncrasies and special requirements, which justified giving contractors a freer hand. By the early 1870s, the art of power plant construction had become more of a science, although still not perfect, especially with the move toward compound engines. As a result, the Navy had clearer expectations, making it easier to dictate terms and specifications to its contractors.[8]

The most significant difference between the wartime contracts and the *Tennessee* contract was the government's method of paying for work completed. Under the later wartime agreements, builders received a set number of equal payments, usually six or eight, over the course of the contract. Pending a successful trial of the completed vessel and machinery, 20 to 25 percent of each payment was withheld. Even though this was a vast improvement over early wartime payment schemes, it still proved less than satisfactory because it required contractors to have significant capital reserves to fund their work while awaiting payments from the government both during and after construction. The *Tennessee* contract took these difficulties into account, stipulating fifteen equal payments instead of six or eight and calling for a reservation of 16.66 percent instead of 20 or 25 percent.[9]

Despite the alleged improprieties surrounding John Roach and the *Tennessee*'s new engines, the 1871 contract itself represented the culmination of two decades of hard earned experience. The Navy now had a basic document that, with minor modifications, had stood the test of time and whose lessons would be applied to future contracts. More important, as it learned those lessons it also had developed a working relationship with a number of private companies that had become accustomed to handling government contracts for both hulls and engines. This network would be drawn upon extensively in the next decade as the Navy embarked on an ambitious rebuilding program.

With the end of the Civil War and the disappearance of surplus wartime funds in the years that followed, the Navy went from feast to famine. Americans lost interest in the fleet, asking only that it serve in its traditional roles of coastal defense and commerce protection. Because both missions could be served with stockpiled ironclads or traditional cruisers, the Navy exhibited little zeal for technological innovation. The United States quickly fell from one of the world's preeminent naval powers to a minor player on par with the larger South American republics and smaller European nations. Although the Navy more than adequately performed its designated missions, it suffered a series of embarrassments during the 1870s and early 1880s. The Navy's feeble reaction to the *Virginius* affair and its inability to protect American interests during the War of the Pacific showed just how far the fleet had deteriorated since the glory days of the Civil War.

The *Virginius* was an old Civil War blockade runner that was caught by the Spanish running guns to Cuban insurgents in 1873. The execution of forty-nine crewmen by the Spanish led to a brief war scare and the mobilization of the American fleet at Key West, Florida. The assembled fleet tried to carry out maneuvers, but its inability to do so quickly demonstrated the Navy's decrepit condition, a problem recognized at the highest levels of the Navy's officer corps. The War of the Pacific, which started in 1879 when Chile attacked Peru and Bolivia and quickly took the upper hand, made a similar point. The United States tried to bring an early end to the war, in part because of American financial interests in Peru. However, the American Pacific Squadron, containing only a few obsolete wooden vessels, was not taken seriously by the Chileans, who owned two new state-of-the-art British-built armored warships. Chile rather impolitely suggested that the United States mind its own business. The United States, unable to match Chilean naval power, backed down. Naturally, in light of these events, European observers no longer took the American fleet seriously, to the point of excluding it from published surveys of the world's navies.[10]

In this atmosphere of retrenchment and technological malaise came the first cursory efforts to provide the U.S. Navy with warships reflecting recent advances in naval engineering. The papers discussed in the early meetings of the United States Naval Institute (founded in 1873) were, on the whole, examinations of the prospects and implications of technological advances in warships. The House Naval Affairs Committee, especially members Benjamin W. Harris of Massachusetts and W. C. Whitthorne of Tennessee, made repeated proposals in the late 1870s for a complete reevaluation of naval policy. Reacting to the Navy's penchant for using funds earmarked for repairs to completely rebuild obsolescent warships, the committee wanted a systematic examination of shipbuilding policy.

However, its proposals repeatedly foundered in the Senate. Not until the Garfield administration were any serious steps taken toward rebuilding the Navy.[11]

Not long after assuming his post in early 1881, Secretary of the Navy William H. Hunt appointed an advisory board of fifteen naval officers to study the problem and make a recommendation. The board was chaired by Adm. John Rodgers, former captain of the ill-fated *Galena*, now in the twilight of his long and illustrious career. The Rodgers board (properly known as the First Advisory Board) spent the summer considering the future of the fleet. Reporting back to the secretary that fall, Rodgers and the panel recommended that the Navy immediately build sixty-eight ships, for a total cost of almost $30 million. Although desirable from a naval perspective, this request proved too much for the political tenor of the time, despite the approbation of Chester Arthur, who became president after Garfield was assassinated in July 1881. After much negotiating and wrangling, Congress authorized two steel ships in August of 1882, but did not appropriate any funds for their construction. Although congressional response looked disappointing, it was the catalyst for the creation of the Second Advisory Board in the fall of 1882 by a new secretary of the Navy, William Chandler. This board was chaired by Rear Adm. Robert Shufeldt. Taking a more realistic approach to the problem than its predecessor had, the Shufeldt board recommended only four steel ships. After some minor modifications to the proposal, Congress agreed and, on 3 March 1883, appropriated $1.3 million for the construction of three steel cruisers and a dispatch boat, the so-called (after the initials of their names) ABCD ships.[12]

These ships, although not quite as advanced as their European counterparts, provided the foundation of the new steel Navy that entered service in the coming decades. As such, their authorization and construction have been correctly described as a significant turning point in the history of the United States Navy. The years that followed, the remainder of the 1880s and 1890s, during which the problems of steel-production capacity and capability were worked out and the relationship between the Navy and the steel industry solidified, have been characterized as the formative years of the modern military-industrial complex. To a large extent, they were. However, failure to consider the Navy's earlier relationship with private industry ignores the true origins of this phenomenon.

One of the First Advisory Board's recommendations that found its way

The U.S. Navy and the Origins of the Military-Industrial Complex

into the March 1883 bill required that the vessels be built of *domestic* steel. Once again, the Navy confronted a technological challenge beyond its abilities. The government did not possess the necessary industrial capability, and there was some question about even the private sector's ability to provide the right kind of steel. Nonetheless, in some ways the Navy found itself on familiar ground: in reality, the problem was not how to build steel warships but how to introduce another new technology into the fleet. This was the kind of problem the Navy had tackled successfully in the 1850s with steam engines and in the 1860s with ironclad warships. Only the type of technology had changed. Although properly concerned with the mechanics of steel warship construction, the Navy knew where to start and how to go about the contract process. By late June, the Navy Department prepared a "list of firms to which blank proposals for construction of a steam cruiser of about 4500 tons displacement have been sent." Proposals had gone to Ward, Stanton and Company in Newburgh, New York; John Roach, who now owned the Morgan Iron Works in New York City; the Quintard Iron Works in New York City; the Pusey and Jones Company of Wilmington, Delaware; the Penn Works in Philadelphia; the William Cramp and Sons Ship and Engine Building Company in Philadelphia; Harrison Loring in Boston; the Harlan and Hollingsworth Company in Wilmington; the Union Iron Works in San Francisco; the Atlantic Works of East Boston; C. H. Delamater and Company of New York City; and H. A. Ramsay and Company of Baltimore.

The Navy Department chose most of these firms for the simple reason that it already knew something about them. Nine of the twelve companies had built either hulls or power plants for the Navy during the Civil War, and were therefore familiar with contract procedures and the kind of supervision the Navy demanded on its projects. A tenth company had built a set of engines for the service in 1858. Still, the prospect of building steel warships intimidated several of these firms. Some dropped out of contention almost immediately, to be replaced by other companies that responded to the government's public call for bids. Ultimately, only eight companies submitted bids. Even so, six of them had prior contract experience with the Navy. When the bids were opened, John Roach's Morgan Iron Works had submitted the lowest price for each of the four ships. Roach was duly awarded all four contracts.[13]

John Roach and the Morgan Iron Works brought a wealth of experience to these first contracts for steel warships. Although construction of the USS *Atlanta, Boston, Chicago,* and *Dolphin* was to be rife with controversy, with the three cruisers eventually forfeited and completed in the Navy's own yards, the firm was an excellent choice for making the transition to steel technology. Roach himself, at the Etna Iron Works during the Civil War, had been the primary contractor for the machinery of the *Peoria, Dunderberg, Neshaminy, Java, Ontario,* and *Keosauqua,* and a subcontractor for the machinery of the *Galatea, Glaucus, Neptune, Nereus, Pequot,* and *Somerset.* After the war, he built the power plants for not only the *Tennessee* but also the *Ranger,* as well as the hull and machinery of the rebuilt *Alert, Huron, Miantonomoh,* and *Puritan.* In addition, the Morgan Iron Works itself had constructed the machinery of the antebellum *Seminole* and the wartime *Chippewa, Katahdin, Kineo, Mahaska, Tioga, Wachusett, Ascutney, Chenango, Onondaga, Ammonoosuc,* and *Idaho.*[14]

The Navy's past association with John Roach and the Morgan Iron Works was significant for two reasons. First, both the contractor and his company were on the cutting edge of naval technology in the United States and had been so for years. Second, and more important, both the contractor and his company had established relationships with the Navy and were used to the constraints and conditions of the Navy's contract procedures. All of the ships listed above were built under what became standard contract guidelines during the 1850s, 1860s, and 1870s. When it came time to write up the contracts for the *Atlanta, Boston, Chicago,* and *Dolphin,* the Navy could rely on procedures dating back two decades and more. The technology for the ABCD ships was different, but Roach had some idea what he was getting into.

The contracts for all four ships showed their antecedents, sharing many common characteristics with earlier agreements. Like their predecessors, the ABCD contracts demanded that the steel warships "conform in all respects to and with the plans and specifications hereto annexed," provided by the Navy. The craftsmanship was to "be first-class and of the very best quality, and shall, from the beginning to the end of the work, be subject to the inspection of the Naval Advisory Board." Engine repairs required within four months of delivery would be made at the contractor's expense, and any patent fees incurred during the course of construction were his responsibility. The contractor also had a defined period of time to build each ship, during which time he would be paid in installments. When delivered, each vessel would undergo a trial trip. Successful completion of sea trials would lead to payment of a portion of the contract price held in reserve during construction. Roach would receive the final reserved amount after the vessel was completely fitted out for sea. Neither part of the reserve could be withheld for any delays beyond the contractor's control.

As had been the case from the 1850s through the 1870s, the ABCD contracts contained refinements based on past experience and present necessity. Before letting the contracts, the Navy conducted an inquiry into the kind of steel that would best suit its purposes and incorporated its findings into the agreement with Roach. In an effort to exert some control over Roach's implementation of the new technology, the contract clearly stated that "the steel to be used in the construction of the hull and boilers . . . shall conform to the 'tests of steel for cruisers' prescribed by the Naval Advisory Board." For the same reason, plans for any changes made to the agreement had to be drawn up by the contractor and "submitted to the Naval Advisory Board for approval before the material is ordered or the work commenced." These requirements limited Roach's freedom of action and ensured that the Navy knew at all times what it was buying.[15]

The service also took the opportunity to expand the clauses in the contract preserving the government's interests. For example, during the course of construction Roach was required to carry updated insurance "in the amount sufficient to cover all advance payments made under this contract, the loss, if any, to be stated in the policies as payable to the United States." Similarly, Roach built the power plants under strict weight guidelines. He was given a target weight for the engines of each ship. If he exceeded that weight by 5 percent, he paid a predetermined penalty. He would also pay a penalty "per ton for each ton of excess weight."[16]

Finally, the Navy inserted a protective clause that gave it enormous power over the entire shipbuilding process. This clause stipulated that "in case of the failure or omission of the contractors, at any stage of the work prior to final completion, from any cause other than the order of the Secretary of the Navy, to go forward with the work and make satisfactory progress toward its completion within the prescribed time, it shall be optional with the said Secretary to declare this contract forfeited." The contractor was then legally responsible for all payments made to date, with the completed work as collateral. The vendor could collect payment for as "much of the work as shall have been, at the time such forfeiture is declared, satisfactorily performed." Having paid this sum to the contractor, the Navy could—if it chose—finish the vessel itself. Even then, the government would not take on too much of a burden. The contractor was obligated to "surrender . . . all materials on hand, together with the use of the yard or 'plant,' and all machinery, tools, and appliances appertaining thereto and therefore used or necessarily to be used in and about the completion of the work."

This is exactly what happened with the *Atlanta, Boston,* and *Chicago.* Unfortunately for Roach, partisanship entered the contract process in a new and disturbing way in 1885. Because of the large dollar amounts associated with ship and engine contracts, the Navy had been very careful over the years to avoid any appearance of impropriety. Major congressional investigations in 1859 and 1872 pointed out some irregularities but generally cleared the Navy of any wrongdoing. However, the incoming Cleveland government, the first elected Democratic administration of the postwar era, raised politically charged questions about the contract and made it difficult for Roach to receive payment for work completed.

William C. Whitney, the new secretary of the Navy, was determined to root out what he saw as years of Republican corruption and influence in the larger operations of his department. Roach, because his *Tennessee* contract had been a prominent part of the 1872 investigation, became a convenient target of Whitney's ire. The secretary refused to accept the *Dolphin* pending a full review of the agreement, which prevented the contractor from receiving his final installment, money Roach needed to move forward on the *Atlanta, Boston,* and *Chicago* if he was to meet their contract deadlines. Roach's fate was placed in the hands of a board composed of two naval officers and a civilian engineer handpicked by Whitney. All were loyal Democrats with connections to the secretary. While waiting for the board's preordained result, Roach depleted his capital reserves, entered receivership, and forfeited the contracts for the three cruisers. The Navy finished them, in Roach's shipyard. In the end, partisan politics had interfered with the contract process, driving John Roach out of the shipbuilding business. Contractors who signed deals with the government in the wake of the Roach fiasco approached those contracts with some trepidation, demanding (and receiving) safeguards against such capricious action, but they continued working with the Navy.[17]

The introduction of steel warships into the fleet signaled the beginning of the United States Navy's slow return to respectability, and for this reason many historians use the ABCD ships as a clean break with the past, as a repudiation of the postwar "doldrums." Certainly, the building of these ships represented a significant turning point in the Navy's history, but both their contracts and contractor were firmly grounded in the past. These aspects can best be viewed as the culmination of an evolutionary process that traces its roots back to the reaction against faulty steam power plants in the 1850s.[18]

The Navy faced one continual question from the 1850s through the 1880s and beyond: how should new technology whose manufacture was clearly beyond the Navy's capabilities best be introduced into the fleet? This vital question remained constant even as the technology changed from steam engines to ironclads to steel warships. The answer, as the Navy quickly figured out, was to codify and regulate the process with contracts that drew upon the best expertise that American private industry had to offer while holding those same firms accountable and retaining enough flexibility to adapt to changing circumstances. During peacetime, things worked relatively well. At other times, especially during the Civil War when pressure to create the perfect design intervened, the process worked poorly or failed outright. Even so, the Navy kept experimenting out of necessity. As that happened, the Navy developed relationships with a select group of contractors who conducted a sizable portion of their business with the government and who became dependent, in part, on continuing those relationships. From those early relationships came the origins of the military-industrial complex.

Conclusion

The introduction of steam technology into the United States Navy presented special challenges to a service not noted for its administrative flexibility. Although most contemporary authorities agreed that the fleet of the future must contain steam warships, no one was quite sure how to incorporate the new technology. Steam technology differed from other innovations, such as modernized systems of ordnance or revised tactical doctrine, because it altered long-established administrative practice. It was new, not merely a redesigned variant of an existing technology. As such, it required new oversight mechanisms and procedures.

The Navy's first serious efforts to bring steam warships into the fleet in the 1840s and early 1850s resulted in a series of embarrassments that reflected poorly on its managerial capabilities. The spectacular failures of the *Allegheny, Princeton,* and *San Jacinto* demonstrated the Navy's incompetence on several fronts. To outside observers, the service seemed to be flailing wildly about with no sense of direction or timing. Although it would rather have made the issue of steam technology an internal problem, the constant state of flux on technical matters and the Navy's lack of facilities forced it to deal with private contractors. The inclusion of these contractors created new problems for the Navy's administrative apparatus because the disciplinary procedures that worked so well in the various Navy yards had little effect on civilian manufacturers.

Secretary of the Navy James C. Dobbin, who assumed office with the new Pierce administration in the spring of 1853, made adjustments to the administrative mechanism designed to compensate for the new realities of steam warship construction. Dedicated to the service's independence, he actively pushed for the construction of machine shops and engineering facilities at the large Navy yards along the Atlantic seaboard. However, Dobbin recognized that this was a long-term solution and that steps needed to be taken for the short term as well. His insistence on performance guarantees from private contractors, codified in the contracts for the new steam frigates in the summer of 1854, adequately addressed the problem and became standard practice shortly thereafter.

The construction of the *Merrimack* demonstrates the effectiveness of the performance guarantees. Although subject to the sporadic delays and complications associated with any major shipbuilding project of the period, the Navy's administrative apparatus performed admirably in regulating both its own work force at the Boston Navy Yard and the engine contractor, the West Point Foundry. The *Merrimack* entered service almost on schedule, the first of five ships in its class. More important, the engines performed as expected upon delivery. As it turned out, they would become a major problem later in the *Merrimack*'s career in both the United States and Confederate navies, but the power plants for this frigate and the rest of its class met every demand initially placed upon them by a wary Secretary Dobbin. The Navy had regained the upper hand and once again exercised its customary control over the construction process.[1]

Dobbin's peacetime adjustments to the administrative apparatus not only worked, but worked well. Therefore, when the Navy received funding for two different classes of sloops in the late 1850s, it followed a similar path. Because the sloops came so close on the heels of the *Merrimack* frigates, the Navy still did not have the capacity to build all of their power plants. Therefore, as it had just a few years earlier, the service contracted out the sloops' power plants. In doing so, it applied the same conditions, with some modification, to its agreements with private firms that it had with the frigates. Here again, with the notable exception of the *Pensacola*'s engines, the contract conditions gave the Navy the kind of product it wanted. The Navy used the *Brooklyn*, one of the *Hartford*-class sloops, to expand the contract process, signing an agreement with a New York shipbuilder for that vessel's hull. That contract closely followed the terms of the power plant agreements and worked just as well. The *Brooklyn* became one of longest serving ships of its class. From the Navy's perspective, it had a very practicable mechanism for working with private firms in place by the end of the 1850s. However,

Conclusion

that mechanism had been devised and tested only in the forgiving conditions of peacetime. War would be another matter.

The outbreak of war in the spring of 1861 found the Union woefully short of ships. With the Navy's limited shipbuilding capabilities quickly overwhelmed, the overtaxed bureaus turned to private industry for the construction of both steam power plants and entire warships out of necessity. In no case were private contractors more important than in the construction of the first ironclads, the *Monitor,* the *New Ironsides,* and the *Galena.* Once again, the Navy found itself confronted by a new technology whose manufacture was clearly beyond its limited capabilities. Already overwhelmed by the construction of traditional warships, the Navy did not have time to experiment with ironclad technology, so it decided right from the start that private firms would take up the challenge. This time, the challenges were even greater, for no American company had built anything like an ironclad warship before. Caught up in the chaos of wartime expansion but recognizing that it needed some way of monitoring private contractors, the Navy turned to the administrative mechanisms that had worked so well in peacetime.

Unfortunately, the Navy failed to realize the limitations of those mechanisms. Its peacetime procedures lacked the kind of flexibility required in the barely controlled confusion of war. On the surface, construction of the first ironclads differed little from the antebellum frigates and sloops. There were occasional delays, usually the result of design modifications or adverse weather. More often than not, especially in the early stages of construction, the officers supervising the process from Washington tolerated the temporary slowdowns. After all, when one considered the complexity of building a warship, such obstacles could almost be expected. However, as construction continued and pressure to launch an ironclad to confront the rebuilding *Merrimack* increased, the delays seemed to get longer. Commo. Joseph Smith, directly responsible for oversight of the ironclads' construction, came to the disheartening realization that civilian contractors could not be ordered or pressured like officers running a prewar Navy yard.

Used to dealing with a naval bureaucracy where rank and influence carried weight, Smith quickly learned that the recalcitrant contractors best understood the power of the purse. His only recourse lay with the performance guarantees written into the ironclad contracts, similar to those first used during the construction of the *Merrimack*-class frigates almost a decade earlier. Unfortunately for the Navy, it too had certain obligations under the terms of the contracts, obligations also written with prewar circumstances in mind. Certification of performance guarantees required formal testing of the contractor's work. The contracts stipulated that the Navy conduct trial trips to put each ship through its paces. The test had to take place within ninety days of the vessel's delivery to the Navy. However, in its zeal to use the new warships, the Navy sent them into combat as soon as possible. Only the *Monitor* got its trial; the *Galena* and *New Ironsides* were accepted by default. Unable to conduct trials in two of the three cases, the Navy found itself hampered by the very procedures and guidelines that worked so well before the war and had to pay the contractors the full contract price for what, in the *Galena*'s case, was an obviously inferior warship.

The prewar administrative mechanism used to give the Navy some measure of control over the building of the various frigate and sloop power plants by private contractors worked well because that was what the mechanism had been designed for. Although a major component of these warships whose complexity rivaled the hull itself, the power plant was only one part among many. Other components under the direct control of the various bureaus, such as the hull, stores, or rigging, were supervised by different mechanisms, usually through the chain of command. In peacetime, the Navy also had time on its side. Despite the occasional political pressure to get these vessels in service, the Navy could generally stall for time with no adverse effects.

The war changed everything. The Navy took an administrative mechanism designed for a particular purpose and applied it on a much broader scale because of its prewar success. In doing so, the Navy lost most of the day-to-day control it enjoyed in its own shipyards, pegging its hopes on a comprehensive examination of the finished product. Even though the government assigned on-site supervisors to the various projects, they had limited power over the contractors. The sheer magnitude, complexity, and speed of the ironclads' construction stressed the administrative mechanism to its limits, overwhelming it in some cases. The war itself destroyed any remaining flexibility because the Navy no longer had the luxury of extra time. There was constant pressure to get these ships into service as soon as possible; excessive delays might prove disastrous for the Union. As a result, the mechanism collapsed in on itself. Clearly, the early wartime experience demonstrated the weaknesses of the administrative effort.

Based on the problems that it encountered not only during construction of the first ironclads but also in subsequent programs, the Navy steadily revised its contract procedures over the course of the war. The sheer magnitude of wartime construction demanded a more formalized mechanism, so the Navy introduced preprinted contract forms for building entire classes of ships or large numbers of similar power plants. These forms, widely distributed to a number of private companies doing business with the government for the first time, conditioned both the Navy and these firms to the idea of working with each other. Revised at each iteration over the course of the war, they standardized changes in contract policy as the Navy struggled to find the right combination of incentives, penalties, and conditions for getting the best product possible from a variety of companies in wartime. The preprinted contracts brought order to an otherwise chaotic situation, and although they did not solve every problem, they made the massive wartime buildup possible.

These contracts had a mixed record during the war. They worked best when applied to traditional wooden hulls and steam power plants. Marine steam technology had made remarkable gains since the early 1850s, and although it was still temperamental at times, Benjamin Isherwood's standardized plans had eliminated much of the design guesswork. The contracts proved more problematic when used for ironclads. Ironclad technology was so new that there were no proven designs available. The Navy learned from experience, but gained that experience even as contracts were let for the second, third, and fourth generations of ironclads. In its effort to incorporate that experience as quickly as possible, the Navy introduced changes into ships already under construction. In the best cases, those changes caused significant delays. In the worst, they resulted in ships whose efficacy as ironclads was suspect at best. These negative effects were magnified because they were applied to entire classes of ships. Instead of one flawed ironclad (like the *Galena*) whose shortcomings were disturbing but easier to overlook, the Navy now had to explain why twenty ironclads (like the *Casco* light-draft monitors) would not perform as expected.

Despite the near catastrophes associated with some of these preprinted contracts, the Navy did not abandon their basic content after the war. Perhaps the Navy recognized, as one historian has suggested, that the problems in its wartime procurement policies stemmed more from organizational flaws than faulty contract language.[2] In any case, cooperation between the

Navy and private industry carried over into the postwar years, although on a necessarily reduced scale. Contractors now had a reasonable idea of what they might expect from a government contract. Based on their Civil War experience, they knew when to complain about things like the percentage of payments to be withheld pending successful trial of machinery, or how much supervision a Navy constructor might exercise over a given project. At the same time, the Navy built up a comfortable relationship with a number of private firms. As it contemplated the construction of steel warships, another new technology beyond the capabilities of its physical plant, it was able to draw up a list of potential builders based on past performance. The technology may have changed, but the experience could still be applied to the problem at hand.

The Navy's relationship with private contractors during the 1850s, 1860s, and 1870s and its effort to integrate them into the shipbuilding process foreshadowed the military-industrial complex that began taking shape during the construction of the new steel Navy in the 1880s and 1890s. Indeed, of the eight companies that submitted bids for the construction of three steel cruisers and one dispatch vessel in the summer of 1883, six had dealt with the Navy in one form or another before or during the Civil War. The winning bidder on all four contracts, John Roach of Chester, Pennsylvania, had successfully executed almost twenty wartime contracts and several postwar contracts. When the Navy awarded the contracts for the *Atlanta, Boston, Chicago,* and *Dolphin* in July of 1883, it was to a company with which it had dealt for twenty years. Just as important, the contract conditions were familiar to both Roach and the Navy. Although Roach was driven out of business because of these four contracts, it was not the contract language itself that did him in. Instead, he fell victim to political interference in the administration of the contract process, something the Navy had otherwise been relatively successful at avoiding over the years. His negative experience said more about flaws in Gilded Age politics than flaws in naval contract language.

The special relationship that developed between the government and the nation's larger steel companies did not suddenly materialize out of thin air. In determining how it would interact with Gilded Age industrial giants and private shipbuilders alike, the Navy drew upon its past, looking back to its earlier experiences with private contractors. That past showed clear evolutionary development from the steam engines of the 1850s through the ironclads of the 1860s to the revised engine and hull contracts of the 1870s. The officers and politicians responsible for forging the affiliations of the 1880s were products of their past and had evolved with the Navy's procedures. When it came time to build the steel Navy, that earlier era exerted its own subtle influence, for it was then that the antecedents of the military-industrial complex took shape.

Notes

Introduction

1. *Violation of Armor Contracts*, 53d Cong., 2d sess., 1894, H. Rept. 1468, 16, 645; "Schwab Defends Himself," 5; Cooling, *Gray Steel and Blue Water Navy*.
2. Eisenhower, "The Military-Industrial Complex," 339–41.
3. For an overview of the historiography, see Hackemer, "U.S. Navy and the Late Nineteenth-Century Steel Industry." The most complete account of the building of the first ships of the new steel Navy is found in Cooling, *Gray Steel and Blue Water Navy*.
4. Weir, *Building American Submarines*, 1. See also Weir, *Naval-Industrial Complex*, xv–xvi, 1, and *Building the Kaiser's Navy*.
5. McNeill, *Pursuit of Power*, 223–32; Smith, *Harpers Ferry Armory*, 18–19; Hounsell, *From the American System to Mass Production*, 15–65; Koistinen, *Beating Plowshares into Swords*, 79–81. McNeill quotation is from 232.
6. Cowburn, *Warship in History*, 211–12; Lambert, introduction to *Steam, Steel and Shellfire*, 12.
7. Vlahos, "Making of an American Style," 8–14; Ganzler, *Defense Industry*, 9–10.
8. For example, see Hagan, *This People's Navy*, 160; West, *Mr. Lincoln's Navy*, 29–31.
9. Nagle, *History of Government Contracting*, 181.
10. See Roberts, "'Irresistible Machines.'"
11. Koistinen, *Beating Plowshares into Swords*, 99–100, 172–77; Koistinen, *Mobilizing for Modern War*, 19–22. Koistinen's analysis is more sophisticated than that provided by other accounts. For example, Brandes's *Warhogs* makes much broader generalizations that draw only on the best-documented case studies, which practically excludes the Navy.

Chapter 1. The Navy Confronts New Technology, 1847–1854

1. Bauer, "Naval Shipbuilding Programs," 40.
2. For example, see Martin and Lender, *Respectable Army*; Kohn, *Eagle and Sword*; Crackel, *Mr. Jefferson's Army*; Symonds, *Navalists and Antinavalists*; Sharper, "Search for a Naval Policy," 27–45.
3. Schroeder, *Shaping a Maritime Empire*, 3–9, 63; White, *Jacksonians*, 213–14; Reynolds, *Command of the Sea* 2:364–66; Bauer, "Naval Shipbuilding Programs," 35–37.

4. Bauer, "Naval Shipbuilding Programs," 38–39; Smith, "Uncertain Passage," 101.

5. Merk, *Manifest Destiny and Mission in American History*, 31, 33.

6. Potter, *Impending Crisis*, 90–120, 199–224. For an example of the articles in the press, see Maury, "Commercial Prospects of the South," 686–98. Maury claimed the Amazon would rival or surpass the Mississippi Valley in productivity, especially in growing cotton. Of course, slavery would be a necessary component of any colonization of the region.

7. Urban, "Ideology of Southern Imperialism," 53–54; May, *Southern Dream of a Caribbean Empire*, 10–16.

8. McPherson, *Battle Cry of Freedom*, 107–9; May, *Southern Dream of a Caribbean Empire*, 3–10.

9. Curti, "Young America," 34–35.

10. "Young America!" 87.

11. Curti, "Young America," 35–45; Gara, *Presidency of Franklin Pierce*, 26–29, 35.

12. Richardson, *Compilation of the Messages and Papers of the Presidents*, 2731–32.

13. "Our Mission—Diplomacy and Navy," 35–37. For a similar point of view, see "Steam Navy," 3. This article wanted the U.S. Navy prepared to meet Europe on "equal terms." Background information on steam vessels in the United States between 1840 and 1850 is found in Merrill, "Decade of Transition," 1005–15.

14. "Our Mission—Diplomacy and Navy," 37.

15. Ibid., 41.

16. Woodhull, *Our Navy*, 1.

17. Ibid., 3–10.

18. For an acknowledgment of a naval officer's support for Young America, see Commo. Joseph Smith to Cdr. Andrew Hull Foote, 7 February 1854, Joseph Smith Papers.

19. Du Pont, *Report on the National Defences*, 21–22, 28; Merrill, *Du Pont*, 205–7. For an excellent discussion of British naval developments in the first half of the nineteenth century and the introduction of steam technology, see Lambert, *Battleships in Transition*.

20. Du Pont, *Report on the National Defences*, 23–24.

21. Stuart, *Naval and Mail Steamers of the United States*, 149–50.

22. Bennett, *Steam Navy of the United States*, 54–55, 74, 110–22; Senate, *Annual Report of the Secretary of the Navy, 1851*, 32d Cong., 1st sess., 1851, H. Exec. Doc. 2, 76–149; "United States Steamers," 186–87; Williams, "Secretary William A. Graham," 62–64; *Dictionary of American Biography* 2:402. For the power and influence of the Naval Affairs Committee on policy, see Albion, "Naval Affairs Committees," 1229. In 1860, the Navy officially recognized that patented improvements in machinery more than made up for the extra cost with increased efficiency. See Senate, *Annual Report of the Secretary of the Navy, 1860*, 36th Cong., 2d sess., 1860, S. Exec. Doc. 1, 9–10.

23. House, *Report of a Board of Engineers as to the Causes of Failure of Certain Steamers of the United States Navy*, 33d Cong., 1st sess., 1853, H. Misc. Doc. 2, 1–8. Despite Haswell's problems with the *San Jacinto*, his tenure as engineer in chief made technology more acceptable to an often skeptical Navy and improved the lot of the engineers, always considered second-class citizens by the naval establishment. See Dyson, "Charles H. Haswell and the Steam Navy," 225–30. This Board of Engineers, like the boards that appear later in this monograph, was temporary. Such boards were convened to consider particular problems. Once they issued their reports, they disbanded.

24. House, *Letters Explanatory of Estimates for the Naval Service*, 33d Cong., 1st sess., 1853, H. Misc. Doc. 4, 1–2. Dobbin may have collected some of his information from the figures on original cost and repairs given in House, *Information Respecting Navy Steamers Built Since 1835*, 32d Cong., 2d sess., 1853, H. Exec. Doc. 63. The House of Representatives asked for similar information on its own. See House, *Papers Giving Information in Reference to the Steam Navy of the United States*, 33d Cong., 1st sess., 1854, H. Exec. Doc. 65.

25. Hagan, *This People's Navy*, 138–41.

26. Langley, "James Cochrane Dobbin," 1:280, 286–87; *Dictionary of American Biography* 5:335–36. The tradition of receiving advice was understood by all parties involved. See Senate, *The Organization of the Naval Establishment of the United States, and the Navy Department*, 32d Cong., 2d sess., 1853, S. Rept. 365.

27. Senate, *Documents from the Navy Department*, 33d Cong., 1st sess., 1853, S. Exec. Doc. 1, 435. Smith had proposed a similar expansion to Dobbin's predecessor, John P. Kennedy. See his report in House, *Communications Addressed to the Committee of Ways and Means, on the Subject of Appropriations for the Naval Service*, 32d Cong., 2d sess., 1853, H. Misc. Doc. 7.

28. *Communications Addressed to the Committee of Ways and Means*, 545, 548.

29. Senate, *Annual Report of the Secretary of the Navy, 1853*, 33d Cong., 1st sess., 1853, S. Exec. Doc. 1, 307–8.

30. Ibid., 308–11.

31. Hagan, *This People's Navy*, 156; Schroeder, *Shaping a Maritime Empire*, 123–24; Jones, *Course of American Diplomacy*, 166–67; Richardson, *Compilation of the Messages and Papers of the Presidents*, 2748; Sprout and Sprout, *Rise of American Naval Power*, 141–43; *Congressional Globe*, vol. 28, pt. 1, 455, 465–66; ibid., vol. 28, pt. 2, 847, 856. For the speeches in support of the bill by Bocock and Lyon, see ibid., vol. 31, 422–25, 509–10.

32. "An Act to Authorize the Construction of Six First Class Steam Frigates, and for Other Purposes," 6 April 1854, Subject File, U.S. Navy 1775–1910, AC-Construction, Box 21, RG 45, National Archives.

33. Senate, *Report of the Committee on Naval Affairs*, 33d Cong., 1st sess., 1854, S. Rept. 271.

34. Dobbin to Charles Morris, Joseph Smith, and John Lenthall, 17 April 1854, Entry 13, RG 45. Martin came under Lenthall's authority, and therefore did

not receive an individual letter from Dobbin. For information on Lenthall, see "John Lenthall," Subject File, U.S. Navy 1775–1910, ZB-Biography, RG 45, Operational Archives, Naval Historical Center, Washington, D.C. See also the unpublished manuscript biography of Lenthall in the Thomas Hornsby Collection; Paullin, *Paullin's History of Naval Administration*, 213; Chapelle, *History of the American Sailing Navy*, 354.

35. Dobbin to Lenthall, 10 June 1854, Entry 13, RG 45. The famous tug of war conducted by the Royal Navy between HMS *Rattler* and HMS *Alecto* in 1844 proved the superiority of the screw over the paddle wheel. Not only was a screw steamer more efficient and faster, but its machinery could be placed entirely below the water line, out of an enemy's line of fire. See Penn, *"Up Funnel, Down Screw!"* 58–59. For an example of contemporary American opinion on the subject, see "Proceedings of an Adjourned Meeting," 275–80. For the definitive discussion of screw propellers in this period, see Taggart, "Early Development of the Screw Propeller," 259–76. For background on French and British naval experimentation with steam and propellers to this point, see Robertson, *Evolution of Naval Armament*, 230–45; Lambert, "Introduction of Steam," 14–29; Lambert, "Screw Propeller Warship," 30–46; Cowburn, *Warship in History*, 185–99.

36. Dobbin to Lenthall, 10 June 1854, Entry 13, RG 45; Preble, *History of the Boston Navy Yard*, 324. The original manuscript, completed in June 1875 and used in this monograph because it contains Preble's corrections and margin notes, is found in M118, RG 71. The National Archives published its own version of Preble's manuscript in 1955.

37. Canney, *Old Steam Navy* 1:46. The five frigates were the *Roanoke, Colorado, Minnesota, Wabash,* and *Merrimack*.

38. Ibid. 1:52–56. For a contemporary appraisal of George Steer's abilities, see Murphy, *American Ships and Ship-Builders*, 5–6.

39. Bernardo and Bacon, *American Military Policy*, 180; Bennett, *Steam Navy of the United States*, 141; Canney, *Old Steam Navy* 1:46–47.

Chapter 2. The Merrimack-Class Frigates: Learning to Manage New Technology, 1854–1856

1. Johnston, "Navy Yards and Dry Docks," 55–57. The commandant's responsibilities are found in House, *Rules and Regulations for the Government of the Navy of the United States*, 27th Cong., 3d sess., 1842, H. Doc. 148.

2. Smith to Gregory, 16 June 1854, Entry 31, RG 181; Preble, *History of the Boston Navy Yard*, M118, RG 71, 325.

3. Lenthall to Gregory, 9 May 1854, Entry 17, RG 181; Lenthall to Gregory, 9 June 1854, Entry 52, RG 181.

4. "John Lenthall," Subject File, U.S. Navy 1775–1910, ZB-Biography, RG 45, Naval Historical Center; Senate, *Annual Report of the Secretary of the Navy,*

1854, 33d Cong., 2d sess., 1854, S. Exec. Doc. 1, 390–93; House, *Letter from Secretary of Navy . . . Explanatory of the Recommendation Contained in his Annual Report, for the Increase of the Navy,* 33d Cong., 2d sess., 1855, H. Misc. Doc. 10.

5. For an example of the naval constructors' adaptability, see Lenthall to Gregory, 23 June 1854, Entry 17, RG 181. Secretary of the Navy James C. Dobbin to S. P. Houston, Chairman of the Committee of Ways and Means, 18 December 1854, Entry 32, RG 45. For an estimate of the cost of completing the necessary facilities at the various Navy yards, see Joseph Smith, Chief of the Bureau of Yards and Docks, to Dobbin, 24 November 1854, Entry 32, RG 45. For a more comprehensive analysis, see also House, *Estimates, Additional, from Bureau of Yards and Docks,* 33d Cong., 2d sess., 1855, H. Misc. Doc. 19. Dobbin eventually got the facilities he wanted, but the process took time. For example, at the Boston Navy Yard, $46,689.88 was spent on improvements to the yard for the year ending 30 June 1854, about the time the *Merrimack* started building. Spending jumped to $84,962.14 the next year, rose to $171,007.88 for the year ending 30 June 1856 and $211,923.89 for the following year, and peaked at $394,236.87 for the year ending 30 June 1858. Figures taken from Preble, *History of the Boston Navy Yard,* 429.

6. "Steam Machinery for United States Steam Frigates," 4.

7. Ibid.

8. James C. Dobbin to John Lenthall, Daniel B. Martin, William W. W. Wood, Henry Hunt, William H. Everett, and Charles W. Copeland, 6 September 1854, Entry 13, RG 45. This kind of advisory work was a normal part of the wide-ranging duties engineering officers encountered during the early years of the steam Navy. See Senate, *Memorial of Engineers of Navy for Reorganization of Corps,* 32d Cong., 1st sess., 1852, S. Misc. Doc. 45.

9. James C. Dobbin to John Lenthall, Daniel B. Martin, William W. W. Wood, Henry Hunt, William H. Everett, and Charles W. Copeland, 6 September 1854, Entry 13, RG 45.

10. John Lenthall, Daniel B. Martin, W. W. W. Wood, Henry Hunt, W. H. Everett, and C. W. Copeland to James C. Dobbin, 20 September 1854, Entry 278, RG 45; Thurston, *History of the Growth of the Steam-Engine,* 389–90; Canney, *Old Steam Navy* 1:48; "Steam Navy of the United States," 126–28; Church, *Life of John Ericsson* 1:133–34; Eskew, *Our Navy's Ships and Their Builders,* 361–62. The mechanical attributes of these boilers are found in Merrick, "On the Evaporative Efficiency of Martin's Vertical Tubular Boilers," 388–89. For good general contemporary commentaries on marine steam engines, see Murray, *Rudimentary Treatise on Marine Engines and Steam Vessels;* Main and Brown, *Marine-Steam Engine.*

11. John Lenthall, Daniel B. Martin, W. W. W. Wood, Henry Hunt, W. H. Everett, and C. W. Copeland to James C. Dobbin, 22 September 1854, Entry 278, RG 45. The lack of standardization in engine design is illustrated in Smith, *Short History of Naval and Marine Engineering,* 142–59.

12. Tomblin, "From Sail to Steam," 203–5.

13. Eskew, *Our Navy's Ships and Their Builders*, 363–64; Bennett, *Steam Navy of the United States*, 145–51.

14. *Merrimack* Contract, Entry 143, RG 45. Contracts for the other steam frigates are also found in this entry. They have the same conditions attached. Copies of the contracts should also be found in Entry 33, RG 19. However, this entry is missing from inventory and is presumed destroyed.

15. Dobbin to Commodore Gregory, 3 October 1854, Entry 11, RG 181; Gregory to Benjamin F. Delano, 16 December 1854, Entry 3, RG 181; Lenthall to Gregory, 29 November 1854, Entry 17, RG 181.

16. Engineer in Chief Daniel B. Martin to Dobbin, 13 December 1854, Entry 278, RG 45; Martin to Dobbin, 1 December 1854, ibid.; Martin to Dobbin, 19 December 1854, ibid.

17. Parrott to Dobbin, 17 January 1855, Entry 11, RG 181; Gregory to Lenthall, 22 March 1855, Entry 16, RG 181; Dobbin to C. Swackhamer, Navy Agent, 17 February 1855, Entry 6, RG 45; Dobbin to Swackhamer, 16 April 1855, Entry 6, RG 45.

18. Lenthall to Gregory, 29 May 1855, Entry 17, RG 181.

19. Gregory to Dobbin, 14 June 1855, Entry 34, RG 45; *Boston Daily Advertiser* cited in Benham and Hall, *Ships of the United States Navy and Their Sponsors*, 107; "Launching of U.S. Steam Frigate *Merrimac*"; Gregory to Dobbin, 15 June 1855, Entry 34, RG 45; unnamed weekly magazine quoted in Snow, "Metamorphosis of the *Merrimac*" 1519.

20. Gregory to Lenthall, 25 May 1855, Entry 16, RG 181.

21. Gregory to Lenthall, 14 July 1855; Gregory to Lenthall, 20 July 1855; Gregory to Lenthall, 8 August 1855; Gregory to Lenthall, 16 August 1855, ibid.

22. *Merrimack* Contract, Entry 143, RG 45; Gregory to Lenthall, 5 October 1855, Entry 16, RG 181.

23. For the relationship between line officers and engineers, see Karsten, *Naval Aristocracy*, 65–66; Cooling, "United States," 12–14.

24. "Steam Machinery for United States Steam Frigates," 4.

25. Lenthall to Dobbin, 7 May 1856, Entry 49, RG 19.

26. Stringham to Lenthall, 28 December 1855, Entry 16, RG 181; Stringham to Dobbin, 31 December 1855, Entry 34, RG 45; Stringham to Lenthall, 18 December 1855, Entry 16, RG 181; Delano to Stringham, 21 December 1855, Entry 35, RG 181.

27. Stringham to Lenthall, 23 January 1856, Entry 16, RG 181; Stringham to Morris, 21 January 1856, Entry 22, RG 181; Stringham to Dobbin, 23 January 1856, Entry 34, RG 45; Commo. Joseph Smith to Stringham, 31 January 1856, Entry 23, RG 181; Delano to Stringham, 29 January 1856, Entry 35, RG 181; Stringham to Lenthall, 29 January 1856, Entry 16, RG 181; 3d Asst. Engineer Henry B. Nones Jr. and 3d Asst. Engineer Richard M. Bartleman to Shock,

4 February 1856, Entry 33, RG 181; Shock to Stringham, 4 February 1856, Entry 33, RG 181; Stringham to Lenthall, 4 February 1856, Entry 16, RG 181; Stringham to Lenthall, 11 February 1856, Entry 16, RG 181; Stringham to Dobbin, 21 February 1856, Entry 34, RG 45; entries for 20 February 1856, 21 February 1856, 24 February 1856, Log, USS *Merrimack*, RG 24. Stringham to Lenthall, 25 February 1856, Entry 16, RG 181; "Sailing of the New Steam Frigate Merrimac"; "Steam Frigate Merrimac."

28. "Trial Trip of the United States Steamer Merrimac," 276; "Screw Steamers of the Navy," 9; Dobbin to Navy Agent C. Swackhamer, 6 March 1856, Entry 6, RG 45.

29. Canney, *Old Steam Navy* 1:48–50.

30. Isherwood, *Experimental Researches in Steam Engineering* 1:213, 214–15. For general background on Isherwood's motivations and methodology, see Dyson, "Benjamin Franklin Isherwood," 1141–42.

31. "Screw Steamers of the Navy," 65. The United States also considered subsidizing mail steamers, but questions over the ability of such vessels to carry an adequate armament killed the project. See "Ocean Mail Steamers," "Increase of the Navy," "Our Naval Affairs," and "Turning Merchant Ships into Men-of-War."

32. Bennett, *Steam Navy of the United States*, 146; Canney, *Old Steam Navy* 1:50; "Screw Steamers of the Navy," 60–61.

33. Dobbin to Swackhamer, 19 March 1856, Entry 6, RG 45; Dobbin to Swackhamer, 15 May 1856, ibid; Dobbin to Swackhamer, 22 August 1856, ibid.; Dobbin to Swackhamer, 15 November 1856, ibid.

34. Senate, *Report of the Secretary of the Navy, Upon Various Subjects Pertaining to the Naval Establishment*, 36th Cong., 2d sess., 1861, S. Exec. Doc. 4, 59.

35. Busk, *Navies of the World*, 105; Canney, *Old Steam Navy* 1:50; Smith, "Her Majesty's Frigate *Diadem*," 166; *London Times* quoted in Snow, "Metamorphosis of the *Merrimac*," 1519; Bathe, *Ship of Destiny*, 8; Davis, "History of the U.S. Steamer *Merrimack*," 245–48; Senate, *Information as to the Time at Which Each of the Vessels of the Navy were Built, the Original Cost Thereof, the Cost of Repairs, and Their Present Condition*, 35th Cong., 1st sess., 1858, S. Exec. Doc. 70. For data on the engines' performance, see Geoffroy, *Facts Connected with the Cruise*. For a more complete account of the Confederate capture and conversion of the *Merrimack*, see Bathe, *Ship of Destiny*, 8–13; Flanders, *Merrimac*; Davis, *Duel Between the First Ironclads*, 6–13, 26–41.

Chapter 3. Expanding the Fleet: The Shallow-Draft Sloops, 1857–1860

1. For Maury's views on the region's economic potential, see Williams, *Matthew Fontaine Maury*, 197–201.

2. Maury, "Progress of the Republic," 523.

3. Ibid. For an example of Maury's influence, see "Maury on South America and Amazonia," 412–49.

4. Du Pont, *Report on the National Defenses*, 20.

5. Senate, *Annual Report of the Secretary of the Navy, 1853*, 308.

6. Senate, *Annual Report of the Secretary of the Navy, 1854*, 392–93.

7. Richardson, *Compilation of the Messages and Papers of the Presidents*, 2821.

8. House, *Letter from Secretary of Navy . . . Explanatory of the Recommendation Contained in his Annual Report, for the Increase of the Navy*.

9. Senate, *Annual Report of the Secretary of the Navy, 1855*, 34th Cong., 1st sess., 1855, S. Exec. Doc. 1, 14.

10. Senate, *Annual Report of the Secretary of the Navy, 1856*, 34th Cong., 3d sess., 1856, S. Exec. Doc. 5, 415; Lenthall to Dobbin, 18 March 1856, Entry 49, RG 19; *U.S. Statutes at Large* 11:246–47.

11. Schroeder, *Shaping a Maritime Empire*, 94, 124–29; Bourne, *Britain and the Balance of Power in North America*, 178–87; Senate, *Report of the Committee on Naval Affairs, on the Construction of Naval Vessels*, 35th Cong., 2d sess., 1859, S. Rept. 363, 2.

12. Stampp, *America in 1857*, 219–29; Jones, *Disrupted Decades*, 127–28; Holt, *Political Crisis of the 1850s*, 199–200.

13. *U.S. Statutes at Large* 11:247; Bennett, *Steam Navy of the United States*, 154.

14. "Steam War Sloops," 355.

15. Tomblin, "From Sail to Steam," 228–30; House, *Naval Contracts and Expenditures*, 35th Cong., 2d sess., 1859, H. Rept. 184, report, 36–37, testimony and documents, 98, appendix, 237–51.

16. *Merrimack* Contract; "Contract for Machinery &c of the *Lancaster*, Sloop of War," Entry 143, RG 45.

17. "Contract for Machinery &c of the *Lancaster*, Sloop of War"; Isherwood, *Experimental Researches in Steam Engineering* 1:214–15.

18. *Merrimack* Contract.

19. Robert P. Parrott to Silas H. Stringham, 25 January 1856, Entry 5, RG 181.

20. "Contract for Machinery &c of the *Lancaster*," Entry 143, RG 45; Tomblin, "From Sail to Steam," 233–35.

21. Hull Contract for *Brooklyn*, Entry 143, RG 45.

22. Canney, *Old Steam Navy* 1:65–66.

23. Senate, *Annual Report of the Secretary of the Navy, 1857*, 35th Cong., 1st sess., 1858, S. Exec. Doc. 11, 585, 802.

24. Bourne, *Britain and the Balance of Power in North America*, 186–205; Schoultz, *Beneath the United States*, 66–71.

25. Historians disagree over exactly how much influence Buchanan had on the Ostend Manifesto and whether or not he played a role in watering down the rhetoric, but he never took a strong stand against annexation at any point of the process. See Klein, *President James Buchanan*, 234–41; Smith, *Presidency*

of *James Buchanan*, 15. For Toucey's perspective, see Toucey, *Speech of the Hon. Isaac Toucey.* For a similar viewpoint expressed in the Southern press, see "State of the Country. The President's Message and the Reports and Documents of the Departments," 82, 102.

26. Sprout and Sprout, *Rise of American Naval Power*, 146–47; Tomblin, "From Sail to Steam," 238.

27. Koistinen, *Beating Plowshares into Swords*, 99.

28. *U.S. Statutes at Large* 11:319; Canney, *Old Steam Navy* 1:71; Senate, *Annual Report of the Secretary of the Navy, 1857*, 35th Cong., 1st sess., 1858, S. Exec. Doc. 11, 618–19; "New War Steamers," 301–3, 307.

29. House, *Naval Contracts and Expenditures*, appendix, 252–54.

30. Ibid., 264–65, 284.

31. Senate, *Report of the Secretary of the Navy, Upon Various Subjects Pertaining to the Naval Establishment*, 58–59.

32. All of the 1858 sloop contracts are found in Entry 143, RG 45.

33. Bennett, *Steam Navy of the United States*, 161.

34. Ibid., 161–64; Canney, *Old Steam Navy* 1:67–69; "Contract for Engines, Boilers, Screw & Shafting &c U.S. Sloop of War *Pensacola*," Entry 143, RG 45. Donald Canney cites Senate, *Failure of Engines of Pensacola*, 37th Cong., 2d sess., 1863, S. Misc. Doc. 70, as a source on this matter, but the document does not appear to exist. For the Navy's protracted battle with Dickerson, which extended well into the Civil War, see Sloan, *Benjamin Franklin Isherwood*, 106–7.

35. House, *Naval Contracts and Expenditures*, report, 47, 52, 89, appendix, 325; Sherman, *John Sherman's Recollections*, 128–31.

36. Isherwood, *Experimental Researches in Steam Engineering* 1:230; Busk, *Navies of the World*, 116; Canney, *Old Steam Navy* 1:83.

Chapter 4. The Union and Ironclad Warships, 1861

1. Allard, "Naval Technology During the American Civil War," 114–22. For a general introduction to European naval advances, see Baxter, *Introduction of the Ironclad Warship*, 1–210; Padfield, *Guns at Sea*, 168–70. For an example of the contemporary debate within British naval circles, see Russell, *Fleet of the Future.*

2. Baxter, *Introduction of the Ironclad Warship*, 41–52; Senate, *Annual Report of the Secretary of the Navy, 1841*, 27th Cong., 2d sess., 1841, S. Doc. 1, 382. The three ships were the USS *Michigan*, USS *Allegheny*, and USS *Water Witch*. See also Albion, *Makers of Naval Policy*, 191–92; Senate, *Letter of the Secretary of the Navy, in Answer to a Resolution of the Senate of the 18th Instant, in Relation to the Contracts Made with Robert L. Stevens for the Construction of a Steam Floating Battery*, 37th Cong., 2d sess., S. Doc. 34, 1862. For further cost overruns see

House, *Annual Report of the Secretary of the Navy, 1857*, 35th Cong., 1st sess., 1857, H. Exec. Doc. 2, 582. For an overview of the history of the Stevens Battery, see Orth, "Stevens Battery," 92–99.

3. Senate, *Report of the Committee on Naval Affairs, on the Construction of Naval Vessels*, 1–2. These wooden steam ships were equal to or better than similar vessels in the navies of other nations and would be outclassed only in a battle with the French or British fleets.

4. For Lincoln's proclamations, see "Proclamation Calling Militia and Convening Congress," 15 April 1861; "Proclamation of a Blockade," 19 April 1861; "Proclamation of a Blockade," 27 April 1861, in Lincoln, *Collected Works of Abraham Lincoln* 4:331–32, 338–39, 346–47. For Davis's proclamation, see U.S. Navy Department, *Official Records of the Union and Confederate Navies in the War of the Rebellion*, ser. 2, 3:96–97 (hereafter cited as *ORN*; series 2 unless otherwise noted). The Confederate Congress did not formally authorize letters of marque until 6 May, but Lincoln's response was based on Davis's public proclamation. For the Confederate Congress' authorization, see *ORN* 1:335–40. The numbers of vessels, harbors, and miles of coastline are from West, *Mr. Lincoln's Navy*, 44–45.

5. West, *Mr. Lincoln's Navy*, 46–54; Albion, *Makers of Naval Policy*, 195; Soley, "Union and Confederate Navies," 614–16, 623. Lenthall cited in Baxter, *Introduction of the Ironclad Warship*, 242.

6. West, *Mr. Lincoln's Navy*, 29–31; Senate, *Report of the Committee on Naval Affairs, on the Construction of Naval Vessels*, 16–17.

7. McPherson, *Battle Cry of Freedom*, 279; West, *Mr. Lincoln's Navy*, 35–38.

8. Welles, *Diary* 1:41. Unfortunately, Welles's diary does not begin detailed entries until the summer of 1862. The introduction, written several years after the war, remains useful for describing his impressions of the first year of the war. See also West, *Mr. Lincoln's Navy*, 36–43; Long, "Gosport Affair," 155–72; West, *Gideon Welles*, 108–10.

9. Davis, *Duel Between the First Ironclads*, 7–8; Trexler, *Confederate Ironclad "Virginia" ("Merrimac")*, 1–9. A statement from Commissioner William H. Peters to Governor John Letcher of Virginia describing the condition of the Norfolk Navy Yard after the Federal evacuation can be found in *ORN* 2:107–12. By February 1862, Mallory could report to President Davis that "the construction of vessels and their equipments of gun carriages, ordnance and ordnance stores, the manufactures of steam engines and of shot and shell are all progressing satisfactorily" at Norfolk. Mallory to Davis, 27 February 1862, *ORN* 2:153–54.

10. For a summary of Mallory's career, see Melvin, "Stephen Russell Mallory," 137–60; Durkin, *Stephen R. Mallory*; Mallory to Conrad, 10 May 1861, *ORN* 2:69

11. Davis, *Duel Between the First Ironclads*, 9–13; for Brooke's testimony of events, see *ORN* 1:783–88; for Mallory's version, see ibid. 2:174–76; see also Mallory's letter of 18 July 1861 to Jefferson Davis in ibid. 2:76–79 describing the condi-

tion of the Norfolk yard and the status of the *Merrimack*. See also Flanders, *Merrimac*.

12. Bennett, *Steam Navy of the United States*, 262–63.

13. "From the Report of the Secretary of the Navy, July 4, 1861. Iron-Clad Steamers or Floating Batteries," in Secretary of the Navy, *Report of the Secretary of the Navy in Relation to Armored Vessels*, 1; Bennett, *Steam Navy of the United States*, 263; Albion, *Makers of Naval Policy*, 195.

14. Christley, "Mystic River Builds an Ironclad," 130; Wells, *Original United States Warship "Monitor,"* 7–8; deKay, *Monitor*, 71–73.

15. Salter, *Life of James W. Grimes*, 145–46, cited in Albion, *Makers of Naval Policy*, 196; Baxter, *Introduction of the Ironclad Warship*, 246.

16. *Congressional Globe*, 25 July 1861; 30 July 1861; 1 August 1861; "Act of Congress Authorizing the Construction of Iron-Clad Vessels," in Secretary of the Navy, *Report of the Secretary of the Navy in Relation to Armored Vessels*, 1. See also Bennett, *Steam Navy of the United States*, 263.

17. "Copy of Advertisement Calling for Plans and Specifications. Iron-Clad Steam Vessels," in Secretary of the Navy, *Report of the Secretary of the Navy in Relation to Armored Vessels*, 2.

18. Albion, *Makers of Naval Policy*, 196. For general reaction to ironclads among naval officers and constructors, see Boynton, *History of the Navy During the Rebellion*, 156–57. Gideon Welles to Joseph Smith, 8 August 1861, Entry 13, RG 45. The original manuscript copy of the orders has Dahlgren's name on it with Davis's name pencilled in. For Davis's appointment, see Welles to Smith, 20 August 1861, Entry 13, RG 45.

19. "Report on Iron Clad Vessels," in Senate, *Annual Report of the Secretary of the Navy, 1861*, 37th Cong., 2d sess., 1861, S. Doc. 1, 152; Smith to Welles, 2 September 1861, Entry 32, RG 45.

20. "Report on Iron Clad Vessels," 152.

21. Ibid.

22. Ibid., 154.

23. Ibid.

24. "From the Report of the Secretary of the Navy, December 2, 1861. Armored Ships," in Secretary of the Navy, *Report of the Secretary of the Navy in Relation to Armored Vessels*, 8. For a contemporary discussion of the special problems associated with the construction of ironclads, see Russell, "On the Professional Problem Presented," 17–91.

25. "Report of Board to Examine Plans of Iron-Clad Vessels, Under Act of August 3, 1861," in Secretary of the Navy, *Report of the Secretary of the Navy in Relation to Armored Vessels*, 5–7; "Report on Iron Clad Vessels," 154–55.

26. "Report on Iron Clad Vessels," 154–55; West, *Mr. Lincoln's Navy*, 104–5.

27. "Report on Iron Clad Vessels," 156; Contracts and Bonds 1861, Entry 42, 249, RG 71.

28. Hunter, "Heavy Industries Before 1860," 211–13.

29. Ibid., 214–16; Paskoff, *Industrial Evolution*, 109–10. Porter and Livesay, *Merchants and Manufacturers*, 72–74; Fisher, *Epic of Steel*, 99.

30. Williamson, *Growth of the American Economy*, 214; Paskoff, *Industrial Evolution*, 73–75; Still, "Monitor Builders," 26.

31. Williamson, *Growth of the American Economy*, 217–18.

32. Ibid., 218–19. For a more extended discussion of the role of steamboats, see Kent T. Healy, "American Transportation Before the War Between the States," in Williamson, *Growth of the American Economy*, 172–88.

33. "Manufacture of Armor Plates," 229.

34. Roberts, "Neglected Ironclad," 110, 119; Holley, "Iron-Clad Ships and Heavy Ordnance," 85–86. For a more detailed explanation, see Holley, *Treatise on Ordnance and Armor*. For much of the war, there were still too few mills capable of rolling the thicker plates, causing Secretary Welles to broach the subject to the chairman of the Senate Naval Committee and ask what alternatives the nation might consider. See Senate, *Letter of the Secretary of the Navy to the Chairman of the Committee on Naval Affairs of the Senate of the United States, in Relation to the Construction of Iron-Clad Steamers, &c*, 37th Cong., 2d sess., 1862, S. Exec. Doc. 4; House, *Annual Report of the Secretary of the Navy, 1862*, 37th Cong., 3d sess., 1862, H. Exec. Doc. 1, 35–37.

Chapter 5. Confronting Reality: The Problems of Wartime Construction, 1861–1862

1. Agreement between C. S. Bushnell and Company, John F. Winslow, John A. Griswold, and W. L Barnes, agent, 16 August 1861, Cornelius Scranton Bushnell Papers.

2. Contracts and Bonds 1861, Entry 42, 249–50, RG 71; Commo. Joseph Smith to C. S. Bushnell and Company, 14 November 1861, Subject File, U.S. Navy 1775–1910, AD-Design and General Characteristics 1860–1910, Box 51, RG 45 (hereafter cited as Correspondence Relative to Ironclads).

3. Contracts and Bonds 1861, 249–50; Smith to Bushnell, 30 September 1861, Correspondence Relative to Ironclads.

4. Contracts and Bonds 1861, 251.

5. deKay, *Monitor*, 97. deKay later points out that Bushnell said after the war that these terms were "standard provisions in government contracts of the period" (104), but dismisses the remark, perhaps because it gets in the way of the story he wants to tell.

6. Welles, "First Ironclad Monitor," 17–31.

7. Cornelius S. Bushnell to Gideon Welles, 1877, in Johnson and Buel, *Battles and Leaders of the Civil War* 1:748; Milligan, *Gunboats Down the Mississippi*, 12–15; Milligan, "From Theory to Application," 126–27; "Samuel Hartt Pook," *National Cyclopaedia of American Biography* 4:532. The city class iron-

clads were the *St. Louis, Carondelet, Louisville, Pittsburg, Mound City, Cincinnati,* and *Cairo.*

8. "Mystic River Builds an Ironclad," 132; Niven, *Gideon Welles,* 366–69; "Negotiations for the Building of the *Monitor,*" in Johnson and Buel, *Battles and Leaders of the Civil War* 1:748–50; Wheeler, *John F. Winslow,* 26–30; John Ericsson to Cornelius Bushnell, 11 September 1861, Cornelius Scranton Bushnell Papers. Undated agreement between John F. Winslow, John A. Griswold, and C. S. Bushnell and Company, Cornelius Scranton Bushnell Papers. A copy of this undated agreement also exists in Box 3, Folder 56, John A. Griswold Papers.

9. deKay, *Monitor,* 91–93; Roberts, "Neglected Ironclad," 111, 114; Davis, *Duel Between the First Ironclads,* 42–44.

10. Smith to Pook, 21 October 1861; Smith to Pook, 22 October 1861; Smith to C. S. Bushnell, 2 November 1861; Smith to Pook, 2 November 1861; Smith to Pook, 4 November 1861; Smith to Bushnell, 7 November 1861; Smith to Pook, 8 November 1861, Correspondence Relative to Ironclads.

11. Smith to Bushnell, 2 November 1861; Smith to Bushnell, 7 November 1861; Smith to Pook, 11 November 1861, Correspondence Relative to Ironclads.

12. Smith to Bushnell, 13 November 1861; Smith to Pook, 13 November 1861; Smith to Bushnell, 14 November 1861; Smith to Martin, 14 November 1861; Smith to Bushnell, 18 November 1861; Smith to Bushnell, 18 November 1861; Smith to Martin, 19 November 1861; Smith to Martin, 19 November 1861; Smith to Griswold, 19 November 1861; Smith to Bushnell, 21 November 1861; Smith to Martin, 21 November 1861; Smith to John A. Griswold, 21 November 1861; Smith to Martin, 22 November 1861; Smith to Bushnell, 3 December 1861; John F. Winslow to Smith, 6 March 1862; Smith to Pook, 8 March 1862; Smith to Winslow, 8 March 1862; Smith to C. S. Bushnell and Company, 10 March 1862, Correspondence Relative to Ironclads; Pook to Bushnell, 13 March 1862, Cornelius Scranton Bushnell Papers.

13. Smith to Bushnell, 7 November 1861; Smith to Pook, 4 November 1861, Correspondence Relative to Ironclads. For direct threats to collect "large forfeitures for every day the vessel is short of delivery," see Smith to Bushnell, 5 December 1861; Smith to Winslow, 5 December 1861, ibid.

14. Minthorne to Smith, 16 January 1862; Pook to Smith, 21 January 1862; Pook to Smith, 8 February 1862, Correspondence Relative to Ironclads.

15. Pook to Smith, 8 February 1862; Pook to Smith, 10 February 1862; Smith to Pook, 12 February 1862; Pook to Smith, 10 February 1862; Smith to Pook, 15 February 1862, Correspondence Relative to Ironclads; Contract Ledger for Ironclads 1861–1862, Entry 48, 317, RG 71.

16. Davis, *Duel Between the First Ironclads,* 47, 53; Roberts, "Neglected Ironclad," 114.

17. Adm. Louis M. Goldsborough to Assistant Secretary of the Navy Gustavus

Vasa Fox, 23 February 1862, in Fox, *Confidential Correspondence of Gustavus Vasa Fox* 1:244.

18. Davis, *Duel Between the First Ironclads*, 76–137; Goldsborough to Fox, 16 March 1862, in Fox, *Confidential Correspondence of Gustavus Vasa Fox* 1:249.

19. Smith to Bushnell, 16 April 1862, Correspondence Relative to Ironclads. For the Navy's perspective on the situation on the Peninsula, see Gideon Welles to Flag Officer Louis M. Goldsborough, 17 April 1862, Louis Malesherbes Goldsborough Papers.

20. Smith to Chief Engineer Joseph Farron, 17 April 1862, Correspondence Relative to Ironclads; Gen. George Brinton McClellan to Asst. Secretary of the Navy Gustavus V. Fox, 20 April 1862, in Department of War, *War of the Rebellion: Official Records of the Union and Confederate Armies* (Washington, D.C.: GPO, 1880–1901) (hereafter cited as *OR*), ser. 1, vol. 11, pt. 3, 115; entry for 21 April 1862, Log, USS *Galena*, RG 24; Fox to McClellan, 22 April 1862, Department of War, *OR*, ser. 1, vol. 11, pt. 1, 119; Davis, *Duel Between the First Ironclads*, 153–55.

21. Griswold to Bushnell, 24 April 1862, Cornelius Scranton Bushnell Papers; Bushnell to Griswold, 21 April 1862; Bushnell to Griswold, 28 April 1862; Bushnell to Griswold, 1 May 1862, Box 3, Folder 56, John A. Griswold Papers; Smith to Bushnell, 17 May 1862, Correspondence Relative to Ironclads.

22. Report of Lieutenant Newman, U.S. Navy, Executive Officer of USS *Galena*, 16 May 1862; Additional Report of Lieutenant Newman, U.S. Navy, Executive Officer of USS *Galena*, 16 May 1862; Additional Report of Lieutenant Newman, U.S. Navy, Executive Officer of USS *Galena*, 18 May 1862, *ORN*, ser. 1, vol. 7, 359–62.

23. For a more detailed argument on this point, see Hackemer, "Other Union Ironclad," 243–46.

24. Smith to Rodgers, 21 May 1862; Smith to Bushnell, 22 May 1862, Correspondence Relative to Ironclads.

25. Contracts and Bonds 1861, 249; Smith to Bushnell, 2 June 1862; Smith to Goldsborough, 6 June 1862, Correspondence Relative to Ironclads.

26. Commo. Charles Wilkes to Welles, 16 July 1862, *ORN* 7:576; Smith to Bushnell, 1 August 1862, Correspondence Relative to Ironclads; Waldo Abbott (Bushnell's private secretary) to Griswold, 6 August 1862, Box 3, Folder 56, John A. Griswold Papers; Contract Ledger for Ironclads 1861–1862, 317. The Delamater Iron Works claimed the Navy owed it $306.21 for additional work on the *Galena*'s engines, but it is not certain if they ever collected that amount. See Cornelius H. Delamater to John Lenthall, Chief of the Bureau of Construction, Equipment and Repairs, 14 August 1862; Delamater to Lenthall, 11 September 1862, Entry 71, RG 19.

27. Roberts, "Neglected Ironclad," 119.

28. Stuart Farrar Smith Papers; *Galena* Log, RG 24. For an eyewitness account of the Battle of Mobile Bay from the *Oneida*, including a description of the

Galena's role, see Edward N. Kellogg Papers; U.S., Naval History Division, *Dictionary of American Naval Fighting Ships* 3:6–7. Frank Bennett points out that the Navy used the *Galena* to build a ship of the same name in the late 1870s, during the Navy's lean years. According to this scenario, the Navy submitted requests to Congress for repairs to existing ships, but broke up those ships and used the money to finance new vessels. A second *Galena* was in fact launched in 1880, but this deception cannot be documented. See Bennett, *Steam Navy of the United States*, 272.

Chapter 6. Refining the Naval-Industrial Relationship: The Civil War Years

1. Bennett, *Steam Navy of the United States*, 218.
2. Laing, *American Ships*, 319–24; Canney, *Old Steam Navy* 1:91–94.
3. *Aroostook* hull contract, Entry 235, RG 19; *Huron* machinery contract, Entry 39, RG 19.
4. Canney, *Old Steam Navy* 1:94; Allard, "Benjamin Franklin Isherwood," 306; *Huron* machinery contract; Laing, *American Ships*, 333.
5. Samuel Francis Du Pont to Gideon Welles, 18 September 1861, *ORN*, ser. 1, vol. 12, 209.
6. *Aroostook* hull contract; *Huron* machinery contract; Laing, *American Ships*, 325–27; Tomblin, "From Sail to Steam," 263–64.
7. Canney, *Old Steam Navy* 1:94–95; Gideon Welles to John Lenthall, 5 June 1861, Entry 13, RG 45; Welles to Lenthall, 6 June 1861, Entry 13, RG 45.
8. *Juniata* machinery contract, Entry 232, RG 217.
9. There is some confusion over the construction timetable for these gunboats. Frank Bennett claims they were "begun during the summer and fall of 1861," whereas Donald Canney says the Navy Department did not place advertisements calling for proposals until August. Bennett is probably right. Writing to John Lenthall at the end of June about the first double-enders, Gideon Welles refers to an advertisement appearing on 4 June. Bennett, *Steam Navy of the United States*, 221; Canney, *Old Steam Navy* 1:109; Welles to Lenthall, 25 June 1862, Entry 13.
10. *Cimarron* contract, Entry 235, RG 19.
11. The "notable exception" was the *Algonquin*. Edward Dickerson, not chastened by the failure of the *Pensacola* before the war, used his political connections to get his engine placed on the gunboat so it might directly compete with an Isherwood power plant on a ship from the same class. Not only did Dickerson again deliver his engine late, but his machinery was thoroughly trounced by Isherwood's in a series of trials. Canney, *Old Steam Navy* 1:113–20; Allard, "Benjamin Franklin Isherwood," 310–11.
12. McPherson, *Battle Cry of Freedom*, 447.
13. Blank contract in Entry 155, RG 45.

14. Contracts and Bonds 1861, 249–50; Commo. Joseph Smith to C. S. Bushnell and Company, 30 September 1861, Subject File, U.S. Navy 1775–1910, AD-Design and General Characteristics 1860–1910, Box 51, RG 45.

15. Blank contract, Entry 155, RG 45.

16. Bennett, *Steam Navy of the United States*, Appendix B. The thirty-eight contracts are found in Entry 155, RG 45. The actual number of contracts may be higher, but these are the only ones extant. *Pompanoosuc* machinery contract, in Senate, *Contracts for Steam Machinery and Settlements Thereunder*, 41st Cong., 2d sess., 1870, S. Rept. 256, 136–38.

17. Baxter, *Introduction of the Ironclad Warship*, 269–77.

18. Ibid., 277–81. Ericsson's proposal is reprinted on pages 358–60. For the Coles-Ericsson controversy, see Sandler, "Emergence of the Modern Capital Ship," 578–79; Padfield, *Guns at Sea*, 181–82. An excellent discussion of the machinations surrounding the authorization of these ironclads is found in Roberts, "Irresistible Machines," 37–45.

19. 20 February 1862 Advertisement in Entry 405, RG 19; *Passaic*-class contract, Subject File AC-Construction, Box 22, RG 45. Nine of the ten *Passaics* used this contract. The tenth, the *Camanche*, was destined for service on the West Coast, which called for special provisions in its contract. Therefore, that contract, although still based on the preprinted form, was handwritten to include those details. See Entry 42, vol. 19, RG 71.

20. *Passaic*-class contract, AC-Construction, Box 22, RG 45; Roberts, "Irresistible Machines," 81. The payment schedule differed slightly from that of the *Galena*, whose contract called for the contractor to submit bills of $20,000 *or more*. However, the same 25 percent reserve was used.

21. *Passaic*-class contract; Roberts, "Irresistible Machines," 85–95; U.S. Navy Department, *Monitors of the U.S. Navy, 1861–1937*, 10.

22. Eskew, *Our Navy's Ships and Their Builders*, 432. Milligan, *Gunboats Down the Mississippi*, 12–15; Milligan, "From Theory to Application," 126–27; Bennett, *Steam Navy of the United States*, 347–48. The city-class ironclads were the *St. Louis, Carondelet, Louisville, Pittsburg, Mound City, Cincinnati*, and *Cairo*.

23. *Chickasaw* contract, Entry 235, RG 19; Roberts, "Neglected Ironclad," 111.

24. Copies of the *Monitor, Galena*, and *New Ironsides* contracts are found in Entry 48, RG 71.

25. The most complete description of the "monitor bureau" is found in Roberts, "Irresistible Machines," especially chapters 4, 7, and 10. See also Paullin, *Paullin's History of Naval Administration*, 265; Sloan, *Benjamin Franklin Isherwood, Naval Engineer*, 66–67. The circular letters are found in Entry 1254, RG 19. Stimers's quoted phrase comes from a circular letter sent by Stimers on 31 August 1863. Roberts's phrase is from "Irresistible Machines," 72.

26. "Iron Vessels for River and Harbor Defense," 14 August 1862, Entry 405, RG 19; *Canonicus* contract, Entry 235, RG 19.

27. *Canonicus* contract; Roberts, "Irresistible Machines," 97–104, 135–38, 226–27,

277–78; Canney, *Old Steam Navy* 2:84–85; *Monitors of the U.S. Navy,* 20–23. For the Navy's difficulty finding enough East Coast firms with the capacity to take on additional work, see Tomblin, "From Sail to Steam," 303–6. For examples of the kinds of detailed changes required by Stimers's office, see Senate, *Relief for Additional Cost and Expense Beyond the Contract Price for the Construction of Naval Vessels and Machinery,* 38th Cong., 2d sess., 1865, S. Rept. 130. Not surprisingly, Ericsson's partisan biographer, William Conant Church, fails to mention anything about Ericsson's brief association with the *Canonicus* monitors in his *Life of John Ericsson.*

28. *Casco* contract, Entry 235, RG 19.

29. "Light Draught Monitors," in U.S. Congress, *Report of the Joint Committee on the Conduct of the War,* 94, 31; Tomblin, "From Sail to Steam," 326–30; Church, *Life of John Ericsson* 2:23–28.

30. Canney, *Old Steam Navy* 2:120–24; Roberts, "Irresistible Machines," 229–32; *Monitors of the U.S. Navy,* 24; Welles, *Diary* 2:349–51.

31. Church, "Various Naval Matters," 77. These numbers are extracted from Bennett, *Steam Navy of the United States,* Appendix B.

32. Tomblin, "From Sail to Steam," 353–56; Canney, *Lincoln's Navy,* 31; Fox to Stimers, 13 August 1862, quoted in Roberts, "Irresistible Machines," 99. The western shipbuilding companies simply found ironclad construction too unprofitable. If they survived the war, they turned to other pursuits. Roberts, "Irresistible Machines," 362–68.

33. For the postwar compensation issue, see Roberts, "Irresistible Machines," 368–75; Welles, *Diary* 2:201, 207; Senate, *Relief for Additional Cost and Expense Beyond the Contract Price for the Construction of Naval Vessels and Machinery; Record of a Board of Navy Officers Appointed to Inquire into and Determine How Much the Vessels-of-War and Steam Machinery Contracted for by the Department in the Years 1862 and 1863 Cost the Contractors Over and Above the Contract Price and Allowance for Extra Work,* 39th Cong., 1st sess., 1866, S. Exec. Doc. 18; *Investigation of the Navy Department,* 42d Cong., 2d sess., 1872, H. Rpt. 80, 19–20.

Chapter 7. Applying the Lessons of the Past: To the New Steel Navy, 1865–1883

1. 10 February 1866, Welles, *Diary* 2:430; Buhl, "Maintaining 'An American Navy,'" 146–47; House, *Revised Estimates—Navy Department,* 40th Cong., 2d sess., 1868, H. Exec. Doc. 111, 1–2.

2. House, *Annual Report of the Secretary of the Navy, 1870,* 41st Cong., 3d sess., 1870, H. Exec. Doc. 1/5, 156–57; Sprout and Sprout, *Rise of American Naval Power,* 177–79; Nagle, *History of Government Contracting,* 230; Apt, "Mahan's Forbears," 89–91.

3. Sandler, "Navy in Decay," 141.

4. Bennett, *Steam Navy of the United States,* 544–55. For a more detailed

explanation of the *Tennessee* controversy, see Swann, *John Roach,* 125–38. See also Canney, *Old Steam Navy* 1:133–44.

5. House, *Charges Against the Navy Department,* 42d Cong., 2d sess., 1872, H. Misc. Doc. 201, 104.

6. Ibid., 104–5, 108.

7. Ibid., 105.

8. Blank contract in Entry 155, RG 45; Canney, *Old Steam Navy* 1:149–53; Rippon, *Evolution of Engineering in the Royal Navy* 1:58–59. For a contemporary example of the move toward standardized engine designs, see Charles Cramp's description of his visit to British shipyards in 1871 in Buell, *Memoirs of Charles H. Cramp,* 111–17. Of course, not all contemporaries were so enamored of compound engines. See "Compound Engine in War Ships," 791–92. Even as late as the summer of 1877, a spirited discussion raged through the pages of the *Army and Navy Journal* over the merits and flaws of these engines.

9. The earlier wartime contracts are found in Entry 155, RG 45, and Senate, *Contracts for Steam Machinery and Settlements Thereunder.* For examples of the kinds of payment problems faced by contractors during the war, see House, *Relief of Certain Naval Contractors,* 43d Cong., 1st sess., 1874, H. Rept. 269.

10. Abrahamson, *America Arms for a New Century,* 9–15; Howarth, *To Shining Sea,* 215–23; Apt, "Mahan's Forbears," 91. For an example of just how severely the Navy's budget was slashed following the war, see House, *Letter from the Secretary of the Navy Transmitting Revised Estimates of Appropriations for That Department for the Ensuing Fiscal Year,* 40th Cong., 2d sess., 1868, H. Exec. Doc. 111.

11. For an example of contemporary reaction to the *Virginius* affair and the call for rebuilding the Navy, see Church, "Work for the Navy," 232. For the Navy's attempts to define the future of the fleet, see Apt, "Mahan's Forbears," 94–104.

12. The term "ABCD ships" refers to the cruisers *Atlanta, Boston,* and *Chicago* and the dispatch boat *Dolphin.* Paullin, *Paullin's History of Naval Administration,* 387–93; Cooling, *Gray Steel and Blue Water Navy,* 27–28; Johnson, *Rear Admiral John Rodgers,* 366–76; Johnson, "John Rodgers," 269–70. For the majority report of the First Advisory Board, see House, *Construction of Vessels of War for the Navy,* 47th Cong., 1st sess., 1881, H. Rept. 653. For the minority report, see House, *Condition of the Navy,* 47th Cong., 1st sess., 1881, H. Exec. Doc. 30. For the report of the Second Advisory Board, see Senate, *Report of the Naval Advisory Board,* 47th Cong., 2d sess., 1883, S. Exec. Doc 74.

13. Entry 200, RG 45; Cooling, *Gray Steel and Blue Water Navy,* 37–39. The number of firms with prior naval contract experience is based on information extracted from Bennett, *Steam Navy of the United States,* Appendix B. Of the twelve companies listed, prior contract experience could not be verified for Ward, Stanton and Company and H. A. Ramsay and Company. Of the

eight companies who bid on the ABCD contracts, prior contract experience could not be verified for Theodore Allen and Anthony Blaisdell of St. Louis and H. A. Ramsay and Company.

14. Bennett, *Steam Navy of the United States*, Appendix B; Swann, *John Roach*, 19–21.

15. Senate, *Letter from the Secretary of the Navy, Transmitting, in Response to Senate Resolution of March 5, 1886, Information Relative to the* Chicago, Boston, Atlanta, *and* Dolphin, 49th Cong., 1st sess., 1886, S. Exec. Doc. 153, 21–22. This document contains the text of all four contracts.

16. Ibid., 22.

17. Ibid., 23; Swann, *John Roach*, 209–34; Cooling, *Gray Steel and Blue Water Navy*, 71–84.

18. Howarth, *To Shining Sea*, 231–32; Knox, *History of the United States Navy*, 319–21; Sprout and Sprout, *Rise of American Naval Power*, 183–86; Beach, *United States Navy*, 320–22; Hagan, *This People's Navy*, 185–87; Potter, *Sea Power*, 159–60; Love, *History of the U.S. Navy*, 345–53. Although his essay focuses more on strategy than technology, an exception to this view is Lance Buhl, who sees the ABCD ships as the natural result of the Navy's historic commerce protection role, and therefore not a break with the past. See Buhl, "Maintaining 'An American Navy,'" 145–73.

Conclusion

1. Vital statistics for the five steam frigates (data is taken from Canney, *Old Steam Navy* 1:168):

Frigate	Launched	Commissioned	Cost of Building
Merrimack	15 June 1855	20 February 1856	$879,126.67
Wabash	27 October 1855	18 August 1856	$894,777.68
Minnesota	1 December 1855	21 May 1857	$894,152.96
Roanoke	13 December 1855	4 May 1857	$833,892.23
Colorado	10 June 1856	13 March 1858	$830,832.15

Accounts for the *Roanoke* and *Colorado* were not fully settled at the time this information was reported to Congress. Senate, *Information as to the Time at Which Each of the Vessels of the Navy were Built, the Original Cost Thereof, the Cost of Repairs, and Their Present Condition*, 10. On the surface, the commissioning dates given in the table suggest that the administrative apparatus and the performance guarantees codified by these contracts were not entirely successful. The *Merrimack*, however, was launched and commissioned ahead of schedule. The *Wabash, Minnesota*, and *Roanoke* are closer to the original target dates set shortly after the authorization of the frigates. The *Colorado* fell behind schedule because its engines were built by Anderson, Dulaney, and Company, the same company building the *Roanoke*'s machinery. The

Panic of 1857 and the earlier drop in the prices of stocks and bonds in late 1856 may have had some impact on the pace of construction of the later frigates as the Treasury felt the strain of the scarcity of specie and Congress tightened the purse strings. There was also a shortage of seamen at this time, which meant that the Navy had difficulty manning its vessels. As a result of these factors, the urgency that drove the original authorization and early construction of the frigates lessened considerably. Commissioning dates are a deceptive measure of the success of the administrative apparatus. Although the new procedures established some measure of quality control over certain aspects of the shipbuilding process, they could not compensate for the dissociated factors outlined above and keep construction on schedule. See Sprout and Sprout, *Rise of American Naval Power,* 147; Bennett, *Steam Navy of the United States,* 148–49; McPherson, *Battle Cry of Freedom,* 189–90.

2. Canney, *Lincoln's Navy,* 174–75.

Bibliography

Primary Sources

MANUSCRIPT COLLECTIONS

Bushnell, Cornelius Scranton. Papers. New York Historical Society, New York, N.Y.

Goldsborough, Louis Malesherbes. Papers. Manuscript Division. Library of Congress, Washington, D.C.

Griswold, John A. Papers. Manuscripts and Special Collections. New York State Library, Albany, N.Y.

Hornsby, Thomas. Collection. Philadelphia Maritime Museum, Philadelphia, Pa.

Kellogg, Edward N. Papers. Kellogg Collection. Manuscript Division. Library of Congress, Washington, D.C.

Smith, Joseph. Papers. Naval Historical Center. Navy Department Library, Washington, D.C.

Smith, Stuart Farrar. Papers. Manuscript Division. Library of Congress, Washington, D.C.

ARCHIVAL MATERIALS

National Archives New England Region, Waltham, Mass.

Records of Naval Districts and Shore Establishments. Office of the Commandant. Correspondence, 1823–1908. RG 181.

Entry 3. Press Copies of Miscellaneous Letters Sent. 1834–1908.

Entry 5. Miscellaneous Letters Received. 1823–1908.

Entry 9. Press Copies of Letters, Endorsements, and Telegrams Sent to the Secretary of the Navy. 1846–1908. This entry contains documents also found in RG 45, Entry 34, and has not been cited in the text.

Entry 11. Letters and Telegrams Received from the Secretary of the Navy. 1827–1908.

Entry 16. Press Copies of Letters and Endorsements Sent to the Bureau of Construction and Repair. 1846–1908.

Entry 17. Letters Received from the Bureau of Construction and Repair. 1842–1908.

Entry 22. Press Copies of Letters, Telegrams, and Endorsements Sent to the Bureau of Ordnance. 1846–1908.

Entry 23. Letters, Telegrams, and Circulars Received from the Bureau of Ordnance and Hydrography. 1842–63.

Entry 31. Letters and Telegrams Received from the Bureau of Yards and Docks. 1842–1908.

Entry 33. Letters Received from Yard Officials and Heads of Departments. 1855–1908.

Entry 35. Letters Received from Naval Storekeepers and Naval Constructors. 1855–67.

Entry 52. Circulars of the Bureau of Construction and Repair. 1843–92.

National Archives, Washington, D.C.

Naval Records Collection of the Office of Naval Records and Library. RG 45.

Entry 6. Letters to Commandants and Navy Agents. January 1808–December 1865. M441.

Entry 13. Letters to Bureaus of the Navy Department. September 1842–November 1886. M480.

Entry 32. Letters from Bureaus of the Navy Department. September 1842–December 1885. M518.

Entry 34. Letters from Commandants of Navy Yards and Shore Stations. January 1848–December 1886.

Entry 143. Contracts for Transportation of Mail and for Manufacture of Parts of Ships. April 1847–October 1860.

Entry 155. Contracts for Manufacture of Machinery for Vessels. August–December 1862.

Entry 200. Correspondence Concerning Construction of New Vessels ("Memoranda Concerning Construction of New Vessels"). April 1882–January 1888.

Entry 278. Reports of the Engineer in Chief. October 1844–November 1850, October 1853–April 1856.

Records of the Bureau of Navigation and the Bureau of Naval Personnel. RG 24.

Log. USS *Galena.* 3 vols. 21 April 1862 to 9 May 1863; 15 February 1864 to 22 November 1864; 29 March 1865 to 17 June 1865.

Log. USS *Merrimack.* 20 February 1856 to 22 April 1857.

Records of the Bureau of Ships. Records Relating to Supplies and Accounts. RG 19.

Entry 33. Contracts and Specifications for Steam Machinery. September 1853–May 1862. These records are not available and are listed as missing from inventory.

Entry 39. Contracts and Specifications for a Screw Gunboat, 1861.

Entry 49. Letters Sent to the Secretary of the Navy. August 1850–September 1867.

Entry 71. Letters Received. January 1862–December 1867.

Entry 235. Contracts for Construction of Naval Vessels, 1861–1864.

Entry 405. Proposals and Advertisements of Sales.

Entry 1254. Records of the Office of General Superintendence of Ironclads. Circular Letters Sent to Contractors. June 1863–July 1864, March–June 1865.

Records of the Bureau of Yards and Docks. RG 71.

Entry 42. Contracts and Bonds, 1861.

Entry 48. Contract Ledger for Iron Clads, 1861–1862.

History of the Boston Navy Yard, 1797–1874. M118.

Records of U.S. General Accounting Office, Records of the Accounting Officers of the Department of the Treasury. RG 217.

Entry 232. Naval Contracts. May 1795–October 1893.

Subject File, U.S. Navy 1775–1910. RG 45.

AC-Construction. Boxes 21–22.

AD-Design and General Characteristics 1860–1910, Ironclads, Correspondence Relative to, Between Commodore Joseph Smith & Various Designers and Builders. 1861 to 1863. Box 51.

Naval Historical Center, Washington, D.C.

Operational Archives. Subject File, U.S. Navy 1775–1910, ZB-Biography. RG 45.

GOVERNMENT DOCUMENTS

United States. *An Act Making Appropriations for the Naval Service for the Year Ending the Thirtieth of June, Eighteen Hundred and Fifty-eight. U.S. Statutes at Large* 11 (1857).

———. *An Act Making Appropriations for the Naval Service for the Year Ending the Thirtieth of June, Eighteen Hundred and Fifty-nine. U.S. Statutes at Large* 11 (1858).

U.S. Congress. *Report of the Joint Committee on the Conduct of the War.* Washington, D.C.: GPO, 1865.

U.S. Congress. House. *Annual Report of the Secretary of the Navy, 1851.* 32d Cong., 1st sess., 1851. H. Exec. Doc. 2. Serial 637.

———. *Annual Report of the Secretary of the Navy, 1857.* 35th Cong., 1st sess., 1857. H. Exec. Doc. 2. Serial 944.

———. *Annual Report of the Secretary of the Navy, 1862.* 37th Cong., 3d sess., 1862. H. Exec. Doc. 1. Serial 1158.

———. *Annual Report of the Secretary of the Navy, 1870.* 41st Cong., 3d sess., 1870. H. Exec. Doc. 1/5. Serial 1448.

———. *Charges Against the Navy Department.* 42d Cong., 2d sess., 1872. H. Misc. Doc. 201. Serial 1527.

————. *Communications Addressed to the Committee of Ways and Means, on the Subject of Appropriations for the Naval Service*. 32d Cong., 2d sess., 1853. H. Misc. Doc. 7. Serial 685.

————. *Condition of the Navy*. 47th Cong., 1st sess., 1881. H. Exec. Doc. 30. Serial 2027.

————. *Construction of Vessels of War for the Navy*. 47th Cong., 1st sess., 1881. H.R. 653. Serial 2066.

————. *Estimates, Additional, from Bureau of Yards and Docks*. 33d Cong., 2d sess., 1855. H. Misc. Doc. 19. Serial 807.

————. *Information Respecting Navy Steamers Built Since 1835*. 32d Cong., 2d sess., 1853. H. Exec. Doc. 63. Serial 679.

————. *Investigation of the Navy Department*. 42d Cong., 2d sess., 1872. H.R. 80. Serial 1542.

————. *Letter from Secretary of Navy . . . Explanatory of the Recommendation Contained in His Annual Report, for the Increase of the Navy*. 33d Cong., 2d sess., 1855. H. Misc. Doc. 10. Serial 807.

————. *Letter from the Secretary of the Navy Transmitting Revised Estimates of Appropriations for That Department for the Ensuing Fiscal Year*. 40th Cong., 2d sess., 1868. H. Exec. Doc. 111. Serial 1337.

————. *Letters Explanatory of Estimates for the Naval Service*. 33d Cong., 1st sess., 1853. H. Misc. Doc. 4. Serial 741.

————. *Naval Contracts and Expenditures*. 35th Cong., 2d sess., 1859. H. Rept. 184. Serial 1019.

————. *Papers Giving Information in Reference to the Steam Navy of the United States*. 33d Cong., 1st sess., 1854. H. Exec. Doc. 65. Serial 721.

————. *Relief of Certain Naval Contractors*. 43d Cong., 1st sess., 1874. H.R. 269. Serial 1624.

————. *Report of a Board of Engineers as to the Causes of Failure of Certain Steamers of the United States Navy*. 33d Cong., 1st sess., 1853. H. Misc. Doc. 2. Serial 741.

————. *Revised Estimates—Navy Department*. 40th Cong., 2d sess., 1868. H. Exec. Doc. 111. Serial 1337.

————. *Rules and Regulations for the Government of the Navy of the United States*. 27th Cong., 3d sess., 1842. H. Doc. 148. Serial 421.

————. *Violation of Armor Contracts*. 53d Cong., 2d sess., 1894. H.R. 1468. Serial 3273.

U.S. Congress. Senate. *Annual Report of the Secretary of the Navy, 1841*. 27th Cong., 2d sess., 1841. S. Doc. 1. Serial 395.

————. *Annual Report of the Secretary of the Navy, 1853*. 33d Cong., 1st sess., 1853. S. Exec. Doc. 1. Serial 692.

————. *Annual Report of the Secretary of the Navy, 1854*. 33d Cong., 2d sess., 1854. S. Exec. Doc. 1. Serial 747.

———. *Annual Report of the Secretary of the Navy, 1855.* 34th Cong., 1st sess., 1855. S. Exec. Doc. 1. Serial 812.

———. *Annual Report of the Secretary of the Navy, 1856.* 34th Cong., 3d sess., 1856. S. Exec. Doc. 5. Serial 876.

———. *Annual Report of the Secretary of the Navy, 1857.* 35th Cong., 1st sess., 1858. S. Exec. Doc. 11. Serial 921.

———. *Annual Report of the Secretary of the Navy, 1860.* 36th Cong., 2d sess., 1860. S. Exec. Doc. 1. Serial 1080.

———. *Annual Report of the Secretary of the Navy, 1861.* 37th Cong., 2d sess., 1861. S. Doc. 1. Serial 1119.

———. *Contracts for Steam Machinery and Settlements Thereunder.* 41st Cong., 2d sess., 1870. S.R. 256. Serial 1409.

———. *Documents from the Navy Department.* 33d Cong., 1st sess., 1853. S. Exec. Doc. 1. Serial 692.

———. *Failure of Engines of Pensacola.* 37th Cong., 2d sess., 1863. S. Misc. Doc. 70. Serial volume unknown.

———. *Information as to the Time at Which Each of the Vessels of the Navy Were Built, the Original Cost Thereof, the Cost of Repairs, and Their Present Condition.* 35th Cong., 1st sess., 1858. S. Exec. Doc. 70. Serial 930.

———. *Letter from the Secretary of the Navy, Transmitting, in Response to Senate Resolution of March 5, 1886, Information Relative to the* Chicago, Boston, Atlanta, *and* Dolphin. 49th Cong., 1st sess., 1886. S. Exec. Doc. 153. Serial 2340.

———. *Letter of the Secretary of the Navy to the Chairman of the Committee on Naval Affairs of the Senate of the United States, in Relation to the Construction of Iron-Clad Steamers, &c.* 37th Cong., 2d sess., 1862. S. Exec. Doc. 4. Serial 1082.

———. *Letter of the Secretary of the Navy, in Answer to a Resolution of the Senate of the 18th Instant, in Relation to the Contracts Made with Robert L. Stevens for the Construction of a Steam Floating Battery.* 37th Cong., 2d sess., 1862. S. Doc. 34. Serial 1122.

———. *Memorial of Engineers of Navy for Reorganization of Corps.* 32d Cong., 1st sess., 1852. S. Misc. Doc. 45. Serial 629.

———. *The Organization of the Naval Establishment of the United States, and the Navy Department.* 32d Cong., 2d sess., 1853. S.R. 365. Serial 671.

———. *Record of a Board of Navy Officers Appointed to Inquire into and Determine How Much the Vessels-of-War and Steam Machinery Contracted for by the Department in the Years 1862 and 1863 Cost the Contractors Over and Above the Contract Price and Allowance for Extra Work.* 39th Cong., 1st sess., 1866. S. Exec. Doc. 18. Serial 1237.

———. *Relief for Additional Cost and Expense Beyond the Contract Price for the Construction of Naval Vessels and Machinery.* 38th Cong., 2d sess., 1865. S.R. 130. Serial 1211.

———. *Report of the Committee on Naval Affairs.* 33d Cong., 1st sess., 1854. S.R. 271. Serial 707.

———. *Report of the Naval Advisory Board.* 47th Cong., 2d sess., 1883. S. Exec. Doc 74. Serial 2076.

———. *Report of the Secretary of the Navy, Upon Various Subjects Pertaining to the Naval Establishment.* 36th Cong., 2d sess., 1861. S. Exec. Doc. 4. Serial 1082.

———. Committee on Naval Affairs. *Report of the Committee on Naval Affairs, on the Construction of Naval Vessels.* 35th Cong., 2d sess., 1859. S.R. 363. Serial 994.

U.S. Department of the Navy. *Official Records of the Union and Confederate Navies in the War of the Rebellion.* 30 vols. Washington, D.C.: GPO, 1894–1922.

———. Naval History Division. *Monitors of the U.S. Navy, 1861–1937.* Washington, D.C.: GPO, 1969.

U.S. Department of War. *War of the Rebellion: Official Records of the Union and Confederate Armies.* 128 parts in 70 vols. Washington, D.C.: GPO, 1880–1901.

U.S. Secretary of the Navy. *Report of the Secretary of the Navy in Relation to Armored Vessels.* Washington, D.C.: GPO, 1864.

BOOKS

The Annals of the War Written by Leading Participants North and South. Edited by the editors of the *Philadelphia Weekly Times.* Philadelphia: Times Publishing, 1879.

Busk, Hans. *The Navies of the World: Their Present State and Future Capabilities.* London: Routledge, Warnes, and Routledge, 1859.

Du Pont, Samuel Francis. *Report on the National Defences.* Washington, D.C.: Gideon, 1852.

Fox, Gustavus Vasa. *Confidential Correspondence of Gustavus Vasa Fox, Assistant Secretary of the Navy, 1861–1865.* Edited by Robert Means Thompson and Richard Wainwright. 2 vols. New York: De Vinne Press, 1918–19.

Geoffroy, William. *Facts Connected with the Cruise of the United States Steam Frigate* Merrimac. Baltimore: Kelley, Hedian & Piet, 1860.

Holley, Alexander Lyman. *A Treatise on Ordnance and Armor: Embracing Descriptions, Discussions, and Professional Opinions Concerning the Material, Fabrication, Requirements, Capabilities, and Endurance of European and American Guns for Naval, Sea-Coast, and Iron-Clad Warfare. And Their Rifling, Projectiles, and Breech-Loading. Also, Results of Experiments Against Armor, from Official Records with an Appendix, Referring to Gun-Cotton, Hooped Guns, Etc., Etc.* New York: D. Van Nostrand, 1865.

Isherwood, Benjamin Franklin. *Experimental Researches in Steam Engineering.* Philadelphia: William Hamilton, 1863.

Johnson, Robert U., and C. C. Buel, eds. *Battles and Leaders of the Civil War.* 4 vols. New York: Century, 1887–88; Secaucus, N.J.: Castle, 1956.

Lincoln, Abraham. *The Collected Works of Abraham Lincoln.* Edited by Roy P. Basler. 9 vols. New Brunswick, N.J.: Rutgers University Press, 1953.

Main, Thomas J., and Thomas Brown. *The Marine-Steam Engine.* Philadelphia: H. C. Baird, 1865.

Murphy, John McLeod. *American Ships and Ship-Builders.* New York: Charles W. Baker, 1860.

Murray, Robert. *Rudimentary Treatise on Marine Engines and Steam Vessels, Together with Practical Remarks on the Screw and Propelling Power, as Used in the Royal and Merchant Navy.* 2d ed. London: John Weale Architectural Library, 1852.

Richardson, James D., comp. *Compilation of the Messages and Papers of the Presidents.* New York: Bureau of National Literature, 1897–1922.

Russell, John Scott. *Fleet of the Future: Iron or Wood?* London: Longman, Green, Longman, & Roberts, 1861.

Sherman, John. *John Sherman's Recollections of Forty Years in the House, Senate and Cabinet: An Autobiography.* Chicago: Werner, 1895.

Soley, James Russell. "The Union and Confederate Navies." In Johnson and Buel, *Battles and Leaders of the Civil War* 1:611–31.

Stuart, Charles B. *The Naval and Mail Steamers of the United States.* New York: Charles B. Norton, 1853.

Toucey, Isaac. *Speech of the Hon. Isaac Toucey, of Connecticut, Delivered in the United States Senate, March 3, 1854, on the Bill to Organize the Territories of Nebraska and Kansas.* Washington, D.C.: Sentinal Office, 1854.

Welles, Gideon. *Diary.* Edited by Howard K. Beale, assisted by Alan W. Brownsword. 3 vols. New York: Norton, 1960.

Welles, Gideon. "The First Ironclad Monitor." In Editors of the Philadelphia Weekly Times, *Annals of the War,* 17–31.

Woodhull, Maxwell. *Our Navy: What It Was, Now Is, and What It Should Be.* Washington, D.C.: H. Polkinhorn, 1854.

PERIODICALS

Church, William Conant, ed. "Various Naval Matters." *Army and Navy Journal,* 24 September 1864.

———. "Work for the Navy." *Army and Navy Journal,* 22 November 1873.

"The Compound Engine in War Ships." *Army and Navy Journal,* 25 July 1874.

Congressional Globe. 1854–1861.

Ford, John. "Manufacture of Armor Plates." *Journal of the Franklin Institute,* 3d ser., 74 (July–December 1862): 38–41.

Holley, Alexander Lyman. "Iron-Clad Ships and Heavy Ordnance." *Atlantic Monthly* 11 (January 1863): 85–94.

"Increase of the Navy." *New York Times,* 15 January 1855.

"The Launching of U.S. Steam Frigate *Merrimac*." *Boston Daily Evening Transcript*, 14 June 1855.

"Manufacture of Armor Plates." *Scientific American*, new ser., 6 (12 April 1862): 229.

Maury, Matthew Fontaine. "The Commercial Prospects of the South." *Southern Literary Messenger* 17 (October–November 1851): 686–98.

———. "Progress of the Republic." *Commercial Review* 1, no. 4 (December 1849): 510–23.

"Maury on South America and Amazonia." *Southern Quarterly Review* 8 (October 1853): 412–49.

Merrick, J. Vaughan. "On the Evaporative Efficiency of Martin's Vertical Tubular Boilers." *Journal of the Franklin Institute* (May 1856): 388–89.

"The New War Steamers." *Monthly Nautical Magazine and Quarterly Review* 2 (July 1855): 301–7.

"Ocean Mail Steamers." *New York Times*, 17 March 1854.

"Our Mission—Diplomacy and Navy." *Democratic Review*, July 1852, 33–43.

"Our Naval Affairs." *New York Times*, 8 December 1858.

"Proceedings of an Adjourned Meeting, Held February 25, 1851." *Journal of the Franklin Institute* 51 (April 1851): 275–80.

Russell, John Scott. "On the Professional Problem Presented to Naval Architects in the Construction of Iron-Cased Vessels of War." *Transactions of the Institution of Naval Architects* 2 (1861): 17–91.

"Sailing of the New Steam Frigate *Merrimac*." *Boston Daily Evening Transcript*, 25 February 1856.

"Schwab Defends Himself." *New York Times*, 6 July 1894, p. 5.

"Screw Steamers of the Navy." *U.S. Nautical Magazine and Naval Journal* 6 (April 1857): 59–66.

Smith, W. "Her Majesty's Frigate *Diadem* and the United States' Frigate *Merrimac*." *Artizan Magazine*, 1 July 1857, 166.

"State of the Country. The President's Message and the Reports and Documents of the Departments." *De Bow's Review*, new ser., 4 (January 1858): 78–107.

"The Steam Frigate *Merrimac*." *Boston Daily Evening Transcript*, 26 February 1856.

"Steam Machinery for United States Steam Frigates." *National Daily Intelligencer*, 8 July 1854, p. 4.

"Steam Navy." *New York Times*, 17 December 1852, p. 3.

"Steam Navy of the United States." *Journal of the Franklin Institute* 59 (February 1855): 126–29.

"Steam War Sloops." *Journal of the Franklin Institute* 65 (1858): 355.

"Trial Trip of the United States Steamer *Merrimac*." *Journal of the Franklin Institute* 60 (April 1856): 274–78.

"Turning Merchant Ships into Men-of-War." *New York Times,* 25 December 1858.

"United States Steamers." *Journal of the Franklin Institute* 57 (March 1854): 186–87.

"Young America!" *Democratic Review,* July 1852, 86–87.

Secondary Sources

MONOGRAPHS

Abrahamson, James L. *America Arms for a New Century: The Making of a Great Military Power.* New York: Free Press, 1981.

Albion, Robert Greenhalgh. *Makers of Naval Policy, 1798–1947.* Annapolis: Naval Institute Press, 1980.

Allard, Dean C. "Benjamin Franklin Isherwood: Father of the Modern Steam Navy." In *Captains of the Old Steam Navy: Makers of the American Naval Tradition 1840–1880,* edited by James C. Bradford, 301–22. Annapolis: Naval Institute Press, 1986.

Bathe, Greville. *Ship of Destiny: A Record of the U.S. Steam Frigate* Merrimac *1855–1862. With an Appendix on the Development of U.S. Naval Cannon from 1812–1865.* St. Augustine, Fla.: Privately printed, 1951.

Baxter, James Phinney. *The Introduction of the Ironclad Warship.* Cambridge: Harvard University Press, 1933; Hamden, Conn.: Archon Books, 1968.

Beach, Edward L. *The United States Navy: 200 Years.* New York: Henry Holt, 1986.

Benham, Edith Wallace, and Anne Martin Hall, comps. *Ships of the United States Navy and Their Sponsors, 1797–1913.* Norwood, Mass.: Plimpton Press, 1913.

Bennett, Frank M. *The Steam Navy of the United States: A History of the Growth of the Steam Vessel of War in the U.S. Navy, and of the Naval Engineer Corps.* Pittsburgh: Warren, 1896; Westport, Conn.: Greenwood Press, 1972.

Bernardo, C. Joseph, and Eugene H Bacon. *American Military Policy: Its Development Since 1775.* Harrisburg, Pa.: Military Service Publishing, 1955.

Bourne, Kenneth. *Britain and the Balance of Power in North America, 1815–1908.* Berkeley: University of California Press, 1967.

Boynton, Charles B. *The History of the Navy During the Rebellion.* New York: D. Appleton, 1867.

Brandes, Stuart. *Warhogs: A History of War Profits in America.* Lexington: University Press of Kentucky, 1997.

Buell, Augustus C. *Memoirs of Charles H. Cramp.* Philadelphia: J. B. Lippincott, 1906.

Buhl, Lance C. "Maintaining 'An American Navy,' 1865–1889." In *In Peace and War: Interpretations of American Naval History,* edited by Kenneth J. Hagan, 145–73. 2d ed. Westport, Conn.: Greenwood Press, 1984.

Canney, Donald L. *Lincoln's Navy: The Ships, Men and Organization, 1861–65.* London: Conway Maritime Press, 1998.

————. *The Old Steam Navy.* Vol. 1, *Frigates, Sloops, and Gunboats, 1815–1885.* Annapolis: Naval Institute Press, 1990.

————. *The Old Steam Navy.* Vol. 2, *The Ironclads, 1842–1885.* Annapolis: Naval Institute Press, 1993.

Chapelle, Howard I. *The History of the American Sailing Navy: The Ships and Their Development.* New York: Norton, 1949; New York: Bonanza Books, 1949.

Church, William Conant. *The Life of John Ericsson.* 2 vols. New York: Charles Scribner's Sons, 1911.

Cooling, Benjamin Franklin. *Gray Steel and Blue Water Navy: The Formative Years of America's Military-Industrial Complex, 1881–1917.* Hamden, Conn.: Archon Books, 1979.

————. "The United States: The Formative Democratic Framework, 1881–1905." In *Naval Technology and Social Modernization in the Nineteenth Century,* edited by Kenneth J. Hagan, 7–31. Manhattan, Kans.: Military Affairs, 1976.

Cowburn, Philip. *The Warship in History.* New York: Macmillan, 1965.

Crackel, Theodore J. *Mr. Jefferson's Army: Political and Social Reform of the Military Establishment, 1801–1809.* New York: New York University Press, 1987.

Davis, William C. *Duel Between the First Ironclads.* New York: Doubleday, 1975; Baton Rouge: Louisiana State University Press, 1981.

deKay, James Tertius. *Monitor: The Story of the Legendary Civil War Ironclad and the Man Whose Invention Changed the Course of History.* Thorndike, Maine: G. K. Hall, 1997.

Dictionary of American Biography. 20 vols. New York: Charles Scribner's Sons, 1928–36.

Durkin, Joseph T. *Stephen R. Mallory: Confederate Navy Chief.* Chapel Hill: University of North Carolina Press, 1954.

Eisenhower, Dwight D. "The Military-Industrial Complex." In *In War and Peace: An American Military History Anthology,* edited by Edward K. Eckert, 339–42. Belmont, Calif.: Wadsworth, 1990.

Eskew, Garnett Laidlaw. *Our Navy's Ships and Their Builders, 1775–1961: The Epic Story of the Evolution, Design and Construction of the U.S. Fleet.* Washington, D.C.: Privately printed, 1962.

Fisher, Douglas Alan. *The Epic of Steel.* New York: Harper and Row, 1963.

Flanders, Alan B. *The Merrimac: The Story of the Conversion of the U.S.S. Merrimac into the Confederate Ironclad Warship, C.S.S. Virginia.* N.P.: Privately printed, 1982.

Ganzler, Jacques S. *The Defense Industry.* Cambridge, Mass.: MIT Press, 1980.

Gara, Larry. *The Presidency of Franklin Pierce.* Lawrence: University Press of Kansas, 1991.

Hagan, Kenneth J. *This People's Navy: The Making of American Sea Power.* New York: Free Press, 1991.

Healy, Kent T. "Development of a National System of Transportation." In Williamson, *Growth of the American Economy,* 521–53.

Holt, Michael F. *The Political Crisis of the 1850s.* New York: Wiley, 1978; New York: Norton, 1983.

Hounsell, David A. *From the American System to Mass Production, 1800–1932: The Development of Manufacturing Technology in the United States.* Baltimore: Johns Hopkins University Press, 1984.

Howarth, Stephen. *To Shining Sea: A History of the United States Navy, 1775–1991.* New York: Random House, 1991.

Hunter, Louis C. "Heavy Industries Before 1860." In Williamson, *Growth of the American Economy,* 210–28.

Johnson, Robert Erwin. "John Rodgers: The Quintessential Nineteenth Century Naval Officer." In *Captains of the Old Steam Navy: Makers of the American Naval Tradition, 1840–1880,* edited by James C. Bradford, 253–74. Annapolis: Naval Institute Press, 1986.

———. *Rear Admiral John Rodgers, 1812–1882.* Annapolis: Naval Institute Press, 1967.

Jones, Howard. *The Course of American Diplomacy: From the Revolution to the Present.* New York: Franklin Watts, 1985.

Jones, Robert H. *Disrupted Decades: The Civil War and Reconstruction Years.* New York: Charles Scribner's Sons, 1973.

Karsten, Peter. *The Naval Aristocracy: The Golden Age of Annapolis and the Emergence of Modern American Navalism.* New York: Free Press, 1972.

Klein, Philip Shriver. *President James Buchanan: A Biography.* University Park: Pennsylvania State University Press, 1962.

Knox, Dudley. *A History of the United States Navy.* New York: Putnam, 1936.

Kohn, Richard H. *Eagle and Sword: The Beginnings of the Military Establishment in America.* New York: Free Press, 1975.

Koistinen, Paul A. C. *Beating Plowshares into Swords: The Political Economy of American Warfare, 1606–1865.* Lawrence: University Press of Kansas, 1996.

———. *Mobilizing for Modern War: The Political Economy of American Warfare, 1865–1919.* Lawrence: University Press of Kansas, 1997.

Laing, Alexander. *American Ships.* New York: American Heritage Press, 1971.

Lambert, Andrew. *Battleships in Transition: The Creation of a Steam Battlefleet, 1815–1860.* Annapolis: Naval Institute Press, 1984.

———. "The Introduction of Steam." In *Steam, Steel and Shellfire: The Steam Warship, 1815–1905,* edited by Robert Gardiner, 14–29. Annapolis: Naval Institute Press, 1992.

———. Introduction to *Steam, Steel and Shellfire: The Steam Warship, 1815–1905,* edited by Robert Gardiner, 7–13. Annapolis: Naval Institute Press, 1992.

———. "The Screw Propeller Warship." In *Steam, Steel and Shellfire: The Steam Warship, 1815–1905,* edited by Robert Gardiner, 30–46. Annapolis: Naval Institute Press, 1992.

Langley, Harold D. "James Cochrane Dobbin." In *American Secretaries of the Navy*, edited by Paolo E. Coletta, 1:279–300. 2 vols. Annapolis: Naval Institute Press, 1980.

Love, Robert W., Jr. *History of the U.S. Navy, 1775–1941.* Harrisburg, Pa.: Stackpole Books, 1992.

Martin, James Kirby, and Mark Edward Lender. *A Respectable Army: The Military Origins of the Republic, 1763–1789.* Arlington Heights, Ill.: Harlan Davidson, 1982.

May, Robert E. *The Southern Dream of a Caribbean Empire, 1854–1861.* Baton Rouge: Louisiana State University Press, 1973.

McNeill, William H. *The Pursuit of Power: Technology, Armed Force, and Society Since A.D. 1000.* Chicago: University of Chicago Press, 1982.

McPherson, James M. *Battle Cry of Freedom: The Civil War Era.* New York: Oxford University Press, 1988.

Merk, Frederick. *Manifest Destiny and Mission in American History: A Reinterpretation.* New York: Knopf, 1963.

Merrill, James M. *Du Pont: The Making of an Admiral.* New York: Dodd, Mead, 1986.

Milligan, John D. *Gunboats Down the Mississippi.* Annapolis: U.S. Naval Institute, 1965.

Nagle, James F. *A History of Government Contracting.* Washington, D.C.: George Washington University, 1992.

The National Cyclopaedia of American Biography. 63 vols. New York: James T. White, 1891–1984.

Niven, John. *Gideon Welles: Lincoln's Secretary of the Navy.* New York: Oxford University Press, 1973.

Padfield, Peter. *Guns at Sea.* New York: St. Martin's Press, 1974.

Paskoff, Paul F. *Industrial Evolution: Organization, Structure, and Growth of the Pennsylvania Iron Industry, 1750–1860.* Baltimore: Johns Hopkins University Press, 1983.

Paullin, Charles Oscar. *Paullin's History of Naval Administration, 1775–1911.* Annapolis: Naval Institute Press, 1968.

Penn, Geoffrey. *"Up Funnel, Down Screw!" The Story of the Naval Engineer.* London: Hollis & Carter, 1955.

Porter, Glenn, and Harold C. Livesay. *Merchants and Manufacturers: Studies in the Changing Structure of Nineteenth-Century Marketing.* Baltimore: Johns Hopkins University Press, 1971.

Potter, David M. *The Impending Crisis, 1848–1861.* New York: Harper and Row, 1976.

Potter, E. B. *Sea Power: A Naval History.* 2d ed. Annapolis: Naval Institute Press, 1981.

Reynolds, Clark G. *Command of the Sea: The History and Strategy of Maritime Empires.* 2 vols. Malabar, Fla.: Robert E. Krieger Publishing, 1983.

Rippon, Peter M. *The Evolution of Engineering in the Royal Navy.* Vol. 1, *1827–1939.* Tunbridge Wells, Kent: Spellmount, 1988.

Robertson, Frederick L. *The Evolution of Naval Armament*. New York: E. P. Dutton, 1921.

Schoultz, Lars. *Beneath the United States: A History of U.S. Policy Toward Latin America*. Cambridge: Harvard University Press, 1998.

Schroeder, John H. *Shaping a Maritime Empire: The Commercial and Diplomatic Role of the American Navy, 1829–1861*. Westport, Conn.: Greenwood Press, 1985.

Sharper, G. Terry. "The Search for a Naval Policy." In *In Peace and War: Interpretations of American Naval History*, edited by Kenneth J. Hagan, 27–45. 2d ed. Westport, Conn.: Greenwood Press, 1984.

Sloan, Edward William. *Benjamin Franklin Isherwood, Naval Engineer: The Years as Engineer in Chief, 1861–1869*. Annapolis: Naval Institute Press, 1965.

Smith, Edgar C. *A Short History of Naval and Marine Engineering*. Cambridge: Cambridge University Press, 1938.

Smith, Elbert B. *The Presidency of James Buchanan*. Lawrence: University Press of Kansas, 1975.

Smith, Geoffrey S. "An Uncertain Passage: The Bureaus Run the Navy, 1842–1861." In *In Peace and War: Interpretations of American Naval History*, edited by Kenneth J. Hagan, 79–106. 2d ed. Westport, Conn.: Greenwood Press, 1984.

Smith, Merritt Roe. *Harpers Ferry Armory and the New Technology: The Challenge of Change*. Ithaca, N.Y.: Cornell University Press, 1977.

Sprout, Harold Hance, and Margaret Sprout. *The Rise of American Naval Power, 1776–1918*. Princeton, N.J.: Princeton University Press, 1939.

Stampp, Kenneth. *America in 1857: A Nation on the Brink*. New York: Oxford University Press, 1990.

Swann, Leonard Alexander, Jr. *John Roach, Maritime Entrepreneur: The Years as Naval Contractor, 1862–1886*. Annapolis: U.S. Naval Institute, 1965.

Symonds, Craig L. *Navalists and Antinavalists: The Naval Policy Debate in the United States, 1785–1827*. Newark: University of Delaware Press, 1980.

Thurston, Robert H. *A History of the Growth of the Steam-Engine*. London: K. Paul, Trench, 1883; Ithaca, N.Y.: Cornell University Press, 1939.

Trexler, Harrison A. *The Confederate Ironclad "Virginia" ("Merrimac")*. Chicago: University of Chicago Press, 1938.

U.S. Naval History Division. *Dictionary of American Naval Fighting Ships*. 8 vols. Washington, D.C.: GPO, 1959–81.

Vlahos, Michael E. "The Making of an American Style." In *Naval Engineering and American Seapower*, edited by Randolph W. King, 3–29. Baltimore: Nautical & Aviation Publishing Company of America, 1989.

Weir, Gary E. *Building American Submarines, 1914–1940*. Washington, D.C.: Naval Historical Center, 1991.

————. *Building the Kaiser's Navy: The Imperial Navy Office and German Industry in the von Tirpitz Era, 1890–1919*. Annapolis: Naval Institute Press, 1992.

————. *The Naval-Industrial Complex and American Submarine Construction, 1940–1961*. Washington, D.C.: Naval Historical Center, 1993.

Wells, William S. *The Original United States Warship "Monitor."* New Haven, Conn.: Cornelius S. Bushnell National Memorial Association, 1899.

West, Richard S., Jr. *Gideon Welles: Lincoln's Navy Department*. Indianapolis: Bobbs-Merrill, 1943.

————. *Mr. Lincoln's Navy*. New York: Longmans, Green, 1957.

Wheeler, Francis B. *John F. Winslow, LL.D. and the Monitor*. Poughkeepsie, N.Y.: Privately printed, 1893.

White, Leonard D. *The Jacksonians: A Study in Administrative History*. New York: Macmillan, 1954.

Williams, Frances L. *Matthew Fontaine Maury: Scientist of the Sea*. New Brunswick, N.J.: Rutgers University Press, 1963.

Williamson, Harold F., ed. *The Growth of the American Economy: An Introduction to the Economic History of the United States*. New York: Prentice-Hall, 1944.

PERIODICALS

Albion, Robert Greenhalgh. "The Naval Affairs Committees, 1816–1947." U.S. Naval Institute *Proceedings* 78 (November 1952): 1227–37.

Allard, Dean C. "Naval Technology During the American Civil War." *American Neptune* 49 (Spring 1989): 114–22.

Apt, Benjamin L. "Mahan's Forbears: The Debate Over Maritime Strategy, 1868–1883." *Naval War College Review* 50 (Summer 1997): 86–111.

Bauer, K. Jack. "Naval Shipbuilding Programs, 1794–1860." *Military Affairs* 29 (Spring 1965): 29–40.

Christley, James L. "Mystic River Builds an Ironclad." *Log of Mystic Seaport* 32 (Winter 1980): 129–38.

Curti, Merle E. "Young America." *American Historical Review* 32 (October 1926): 34–55.

Davis, Charles H. "History of the U.S. Steamer *Merrimack*." *New England Historical and Genealogical Record* (July 1874): 245–48.

Dyson, George W. "Benjamin Franklin Isherwood," U.S. Naval Institute *Proceedings* 67 (August 1941): 1139–46.

————. "Charles H. Haswell and the Steam Navy." U.S. Naval Institute *Proceedings* 65 (February 1939): 225–30.

Hackemer, Kurt H. "The Other Union Ironclad: The USS *Galena* and the Critical Summer of 1862." *Civil War History* 40 (September 1994): 226–47.

———. "The U.S. Navy and the Late Nineteenth-Century Steel Industry." *Historian* 57 (Summer 1995): 703–12.

Long, John S. "The Gosport Affair." *Journal of Southern History* 23 (May 1957): 155–72.

Melvin, Philip. "Stephen Russell Mallory, Southern Naval Statesman." *Journal of Southern History* 10 (May 1944): 137–60.

Merrill, R. T. "The Decade of Transition: Our Early Steam Navy and Merchant Marine." U.S. Naval Institute *Proceedings* 78 (September 1952): 1005–15.

Milligan, John D. "From Theory to Application: The Emergence of the American Ironclad War Vessel." *Military Affairs* 48 (July 1984): 126–32.

Orth, Michael. "The Stevens Battery." U.S. Naval Institute *Proceedings* 92, no. 6 (June 1966): 92–99.

Roberts, William H. "The Neglected Ironclad: A Design and Constructional Analysis of the USS *New Ironsides*." *Warship International* 26, no. 2 (1989): 109–34.

Sandler, Stanley. "The Emergence of the Modern Capital Ship." *Technology and Culture* 11 (October 1970): 576–95.

———. "A Navy in Decay: Some Strategic Technological Results of Disarmament, 1865–69 in the U.S. Navy" *Military Affairs* (December 1971): 138–42.

Snow, Elliot. "The Metamorphosis of the *Merrimac*." U.S. Naval Institute *Proceedings* 57 (November 1931): 1518–21.

Still, William N. "Monitor Builders: A Historical Study of the Principal Firms and Individuals Involved in the Construction of USS *Monitor*." *American Neptune* 48 (Spring 1988): 106–29.

Taggart, Robert. "The Early Development of the Screw Propeller." *American Society of Naval Engineers Journal* 71 (May 1959): 259–76.

Urban, C. Stanley. "The Ideology of Southern Imperialism: New Orleans and the Caribbean, 1845–1860." *Louisiana Historical Quarterly* 39 (January 1956): 48–73.

Williams, Max R. "Secretary William A. Graham, Naval Administrator, 1850–1852." *North Carolina Historical Review* 48 (Winter 1971): 53–72.

UNPUBLISHED WORKS

Johnston, Robert Carey. "Navy Yards and Dry Docks: A Study of the Bureau of Yards and Docks 1842–1871." Master's thesis, Stanford University, 1953.

Roberts, William H. "'Irresistible Machines': Industrial Mobilization for the Union Navy, 1861–1865." Ph.D. diss., Ohio State University, 1999.

Tomblin, Barbara B. "From Sail to Steam: The Development of Steam Technology in the United States Navy, 1838–1865." Ph.D. diss., Rutgers University, 1988.

Index

ABCD ships, 126, 128, 130–31. *See also*
  Atlanta, USS; *Boston*, USS; *Chicago*,
  USS; *Dolphin*, USS
Alert, 128
Allegheny, 18–19, 20, 21, 132
American Pacific Squadron, 125
Ammonoosuc, 128
Anderson and Dulaney of Richmond, Va.,
  34
Archbold, Samuel, 51, 60
Army and Navy Journal, 116
Arthur, Chester, 126
Ascutney, 128
Atlanta, USS, 8, 128, 137
Atlantic Works, East Boston, Mass., 127

Baker Wrecking Company, 72
Baltic, 93
banking system collapse (1857), 49–50
Bates, Edward, 110
Bauer, K. Jack, 10, 27
Bennett, Frank M., 27, 41, 50, 62, 107
Benton, Thomas Hart, 24
bids for ship construction, 32–33, 54–55,
  59–60, 74, 127
Black Warrior, 24, 49
Board of Engineers, 18, 19–20
Bocock, Thomas S., 18, 24, 47, 58
boilers, insurance for, 54
Borie, Adolph, 120
Boston, USS, 8, 128, 137
Boston Navy Yard, 34, 50
Brooke, John M., 72
Brooklyn: contract procedures for, 7; hull
  contract for, 133; lien on until delivery
  of, 55; life-expectancy for, 56; power
  plant contract for, 51; time con-
  straints on construction of, 55–56
Buchanan, James, 49, 57, 65
Bureau of Construction and Repair, 25,
  116, 120

Bureau of Construction, Equipment and
  Repairs, 21, 39
Bureau of Ordnance and Hydrography, 25
Bureau of Steam Engineering, 63, 116
Bureau of Yards and Docks, 21
bureau system, 28–29
Bushnell, Cornelius S., 73; Ericsson and,
  87–88; Ericsson's turreted coastal
  ironclads design and, 108–9; *Galena*
  design changes and, 89; ironclad proposal of, 78; partners of, 83–84; Smith
  on, 90
Bushnell, Henry L., 78
Bushnell, Nathan Townsend, 73
C. S. Bushnell and Company: contract on
  trials for, 105–6; delays by, 91; ironclad
  contract of, 84–85; ironclad proposal
  of, 78; payments for *Galena*, 91, 93, 94,
  95
Busk, Hans, 66

Canney, Donald, 26, 40, 66, 100
Canonicus-class monitors, 112, 113–14
Carnegie Steel Company, 1–2
Casco riverine monitors, 114–16
Chandler, William, 126
Chenango, 128
Chicago, USS, 8, 128, 137
Chile, War of the Pacific and, 125
Chillicothe, 111
Chimo, 116
Chippewa, 128
Civil War: British and French naval innova-
  tions and, 67–68; contracting process,
  7–8, 96–97, 135–36. *See also* Confeder-
  ate Navy; Union Navy
Clayton-Bulwer Treaty (1850), 49
coastal ironclads, 108–9
Coles, Cowper Phipps, 108
Colorado, 34
Commercial Review, 46

commercial shipping, 11, 46, 56–57
completion payment, 34–35; for *Merrimack*,
    40–41; reserved pending success,
    104–5; withheld for *Galena*, 91, 93, 94.
    See also performance guarantees
Compromise of 1850, 12
Confederate Navy, 69–70, 71–72. *See also*
    Virginia, CSS
conflict of interest, Martin's boiler, 33. *See*
    also contracting process
Congress: *Casco*-class investigation by, 116;
    post–Civil War budget reductions,
    119–20; *Tennessee* repairs and new
    machinery contract investigation, 121.
    See also Bocock, Thomas S.; House of
    Representatives; Senate Committee
    on Naval Affairs
Congress, 92
Congress-class frigates, frameworks from, 25
Conrad, Charles M., 71
contracting process: Civil War, 7–8, 96–97,
    135–36; deadlines, 34, 111; Dickerson
    and, 62–63; evolving designs and,
    39–40; for 1858 expansion, 59–60;
    Galena trials and, 94–95; inspections,
    54, 102; for ironclad vessels, 74–75,
    77–78, 78, 84–86; Navy's authority to
    condemn improper and bad work,
    52–53; for ninety-day gunboats,
    100–101; partisan politics and, 63–65,
    130; *Passaic*-class, 109–10; perform-
    ance guarantees (1854), 31–32, 42;
    post–Civil War, 8–9; specifications
    (1854), 34–35; specifications (1857–58),
    51–52, 55; specifications (1858), 61;
    technology difficulties (1854) and,
    38–39, 52; for *Tennessee*, 121–24; war-
    ships of 1858, 60–62. *See also* comple-
    tion payment; engine contracts; hull
    contracts; installment payments
contracts, preprinted, 7, 122, 136; expanded
    use of, 101–2, 103; for *Milwaukee*-class,
    111, 112; for ninety-day gunboats,
    99–101; prelude to, 51–54, 60–62; for
    steam machinery and accessories,
    105–7
Copeland, Charles W., 32
Corning, Erastus, 108–9
corruption, Grant administration, 120–21
Crimean War, 4
Cumberland, 92

Cummings, Amos, 1–2

Dahlgren, John A., 17, 59, 72, 75
Davis, Charles H., 75–77
Davis, Jefferson, 68
deadlines, 34, 111. *See also* completion pay-
    ment
defects, contractor responsibility for, 113
Delamater, Cornelius, 88
C. H. Delamater Company, New York, 127
Delamater Iron Works, New York City, 90
Delano, Benjamin F., 35
Delaware Iron Works, New York City, 90
delays: due to materials shortages, 106–7;
    in ironclad construction, 90–91; for
    Passaic-class ironclads, 110; penalties
    for, 100–101, 105, 111; for *Roanoke* and
    Colorado, 34; wartime needs and,
    113–14
Democratic Review, 13
Demologos, 45
design improvements and changes, 136;
    for *Galena*, 86, 88–89; for *Merrimack*,
    39–40; Stimers approval for, 115. *See*
    also modifications clauses
Dickerson, Edward N., 62
Dobbin, James C., 6, 132–33; advisors of,
    21–22; bids evaluation and, 32; Board
    of Engineers and, 18, 19–20; budget
    questions for, 20; expansive budget
    requests of, 46–47, 48–49; lobbying
    efforts of, 29–30; *Merrimack* launch
    importance to, 39; on Navy's needs,
    47–48; seeks private contractors,
    30–31
Dolphin, USS, 8, 128, 130, 137
double-ended gunboats, 102–4
Douglas, Stephen A., 13
Drewry's Bluff, Battle of, 93–94
Dunderberg, 128
Du Pont, Samuel Francis, 16–17, 46, 101

Eads, James B., 110
early delivery incentives, 114
Eisenhower, Dwight D., 2
engine contracts: civilian (1854), 7; hull
    modifications and, 123; Navy comple-
    tion at contractor's expense, 102; for
    ninety-day gunboats, 101; standardiza-
    tion of, 105–6
England. *See* Royal Navy

About the Author

Kurt Hackemer first became interested in naval history as an undergraduate at the University of Chicago. While he was cataloging books and answering questions at the Great Lakes Naval Training Center library, a patron's request led to a detailed search for information about the Civil War ironclad *Galena*. Finding little published material, Hackemer decided to pursue the subject further in graduate studies at Texas A&M University, where he received his doctorate in 1994.

Dr. Hackemer, who specializes in naval and military history, is currently a professor of nineteenth-century American history at the University of South Dakota. He is the author of numerous articles published in journals including *Naval War College Review, Military History of the West, Journal of Military and Political Sociology,* and *The Historian*. He lives in Vermillion, South Dakota.